Advances in Cyber Security and Intelligent Analytics

We live in a digital world, where we use digital tools and smart devices to communicate over the Internet. In turn, an enormous amount of data gets generated. The traditional computing architectures are inefficient in storing and managing this massive amount of data. Unfortunately, the data cannot be ignored as it helps businesses to make better decisions, solve problems, understand performance, improve processes, and understand customers. Therefore, we need modern systems capable of handling and managing data efficiently. In the past few decades, many distributed computing paradigms have emerged, and we have noticed a substantial growth in the applications based on such emerging paradigms. Some well-known emerging computing paradigms include cloud computing, fog computing, and edge computing, which have leveraged the increase in the volume of data being generated every second. However, the distributed computing paradigms face critical challenges, including network management and cyber security. We have witnessed the development of various networking models—IoT, SDN, and ICN—to support modern systems requirements. However, they are undergoing rapid changes and need special attention. The main issue faced by these paradigms is that traditional solutions cannot be directly applied to address the challenges. Therefore, there is a significant need to develop improved network management and cyber security solutions. To this end, this book highlights the challenges faced by emerging paradigms and presents the recent developments made to address the challenges. More specifically, it presents a detailed study on security issues in distributed computing environments and their possible solutions, followed by applications of medical IoT, deep learning, IoV, healthcare, etc.

Advances in Cyber Security and Intelligent Analytics

Edited by
Abhishek Verma, Jitendra Kumar,
Hari Mohan Gaur, Vrijendra Singh,
and Valentina Emilia Balas

CRC Press
Taylor & Francis Group
Boca Raton London New York

CRC Press is an imprint of the
Taylor & Francis Group, an **informa** business

First edition published 2023
by CRC Press
6000 Broken Sound Parkway NW, Suite 300, Boca Raton, FL 33487-2742

and by CRC Press
4 Park Square, Milton Park, Abingdon, Oxon, OX14 4RN

CRC Press is an imprint of Taylor & Francis Group, LLC

Library of Congress Cataloging-in-Publication Data

Names: Verma, Abhishek, editor.
Title: Advances in cyber security and intelligent analytics / editors, Abhishek Verma,
    Jitendra Kumar, Hari Mohan Gaur, Vrijendra Singh, and Valentina E. Balas.
Description: First edition. | Boca Raton : CRC Press, 2023. | Includes
    bibliographical references and index.
Identifiers: LCCN 2022033769 (print) | LCCN 2022033770 (ebook) | ISBN
    9781032216003 (hardback) | ISBN 9781032216010 (paperback) | ISBN
    9781003269144 (ebook)
Subjects: LCSH: Computer networks--Security measures. | Internet--Security
measures. | Electronic data processing--Distriuted processing. | Computer
    security--Technologial innovations.
Classification: LCC TK5105.59 .A38226 2023 (print) | LCC TK5105.59 (ebook) |
    DDC 005.8--dc23/eng/20221017
LC record available at https://lccn.loc.gov/2022033769
LC ebook record available at https://lccn.loc.gov/2022033770

ISBN: 978-1-032-21600-3 (hbk)
ISBN: 978-1-032-21601-0 (pbk)
ISBN: 978-1-003-26914-4 (ebk)

DOI: 10.1201/9781003269144

Typeset in Sabon
by KnowledgeWorks Global Ltd.

Contents

Acknowledgements

We express our heartfelt gratitude to CRC Press (Taylor & Francis Group) and the editorial team for their guidance and support during the completion of this book. We are sincerely grateful to reviewers for their suggestions and illuminating views for each book chapter presented here in *Advances in Cyber Security and Intelligent Analytics*.

Editors

Prof. Abhishek Verma is an Assistant Professor in the Department of Computer Science & Engineering at IIIT Jabalpur, India (an institution of national importance). He obtained a Ph.D degree (2020) on the Internet of Things security from the National Institute of Technology Kurukshetra, Haryana, India. He has more than seven years of experience in research and teaching. He has published several research articles in international SCI/SCIE/Scopus journals and conferences of high repute. He is an editorial board member of Research Reports on Computer Science (RRCS) and active review board member of various reputed journals, including IEEE, Springer, Wiley, and Elsevier. His current areas of interest include Information Security, Intrusion Detection, and the Internet of Things.

Dr. Jitendra Kumar is an Assistant Professor in the Department of Computer Applications, National Institute of Technology Tiruchirappalli, Tamil Nādu, India (an institution of national importance) since May 2020. He earned his doctorate in Machine Learning and Cloud Computing from the National Institute of Technology Kurukshetra, Haryana, India in 2019. His research interests include Time Series Forecasting, Machine Learning, Evolutionary Algorithms, Cloud Management, and Optimization. He has authored and published a significant number of research articles in peer-reviewed and indexed journals and conferences of high repute. He has also authored a book on Machine Learning for Cloud Management. He has received three awards including best paper awards in international conferences. He is a senior member of IEEE and a member of several other IEEE societies, including CIS, TCCLD, and SIGHT. He is also a member of ACM and MIR Labs. He is an active review board member of various journals and conferences of repute such as *IEEE Transactions on Parallel and Distributed Systems, IEEE Transactions on Computers, IEEE Systems Journal, IEEE Access, IJCNN, FUZZ-IEEE,* and *CEC.*

Dr. Hari Mohan Gaur is currently in the School of Computer Science Engineering and Technology, Bennett University, India. He obtained Ph.D. from National Institute of Technology Kurukshetra, India in the area of Reversible and Quantum Computing. Hari Mohan Gaur has more than 15 years of experience in academic and research where he has also served on roles of administrative capacities. He is a distinguished researcher, well known in Academic Fraternity for his interdisciplinary research in the areas of Quantum Computation, Fault Tolerant Digital Design, IOT and Data Security in Cloud Environment. Dr. Gaur holds the credit of contribution in several quality research journals of international repute. He has received three awards including best paper awards in a peer reviewed international conference. He is a member of IEEE and several other societies of IEEE.

Prof. Vrijendra Singh is presently working as Professor at the Department of Information Technology at Indian Institute of Information Technology, Allahabad. He has over 20-plus years of experience in academics (teaching/training), research & development, and consulting. He has also worked at Dept. of Electrical Engineering, IIT Kanpur; as Senior Project Associate, Ecole Polytechnique Federale de lausanne (EPFL), Switzerland; as Visiting Research Faculty; and consultant to Putera Sampoerna Foundation, Jakarta (2012) for Course curriculum development in IT and allied areas. He has authored over 85 publications in reputed international journals, conference proceedings/book chapters, and edited one book. Currently, he is serving as Chairman, IEEE Computational Intelligence Society, UP Section, India, Advisor to Network Power Solution Enterprise, New Delhi, India, collaborator to NavAjna Technologies Pvt. Ltd., Hyderabad, India, and Consultant to Pragmalytics Technologies, Kochi, India.

 **Prof. Valentina Emilia Balas** is currently a Full Professor in the Department of Automatics and Applied Software at the Faculty of Engineering, "Aurel Vlaicu" University of Arad, Romania. She holds a Ph.D. Cum Laude, in Applied Electronics and Telecommunications from Polytechnic University of Timisoara. Prof. Balas is an author of more than 350 research papers in refereed journals and International Conferences. Her research interests are in Intelligent Systems, Fuzzy Control, Soft Computing, Smart Sensors, Information Fusion, Modeling and Simulation. She is the Editor-in Chief to International Journal of Advanced Intelligence Paradigms (IJAIP) and to International Journal of Computational Systems Engineering (IJCSysE), member in Editorial Board member of several national and international journals and is evaluator expert for national, international projects and Ph.D. Thesis. Prof. Balas is the director of Intelligent Systems Research Centre in Aurel Vlaicu University of Arad and Director of the Department of International Relations, Programs and Projects in the same university. She served as General Chair of the International Workshop Soft Computing and Applications (SOFA) in nine editions organized in the interval 2005–2020 and held in Romania and Hungary. Prof. Balas participated in many international conferences as Organizer, Honorary Chair, Session Chair, member in Steering, Advisory or International Program Committees and Keynote Speaker. Now she is working in a national project with EU funding support: BioCell-NanoART – Novel Bioinspired Cellular Nano-Architectures – For Digital Integrated Circuits, 3M Euro from National Authority for Scientific Research and Innovation. She is a member of European Society for Fuzzy Logic and Technology (EUSFLAT), member of Society for Industrial and Applied Mathematics (SIAM) and a Senior Member IEEE, member in Technical Committee e Fuzzy Systems (IEEE Computational Intelligence Society), Chair of the Task Force 14 in Technical Committee e Emergent Technologies (IEEE CIS), member in Technical Committee c Soft Computing (IEEE SMCS). Prof. Balas was past Vice-president (responsible with Awards) of IFSA – International Fuzzy Systems Association Council (2013–2015), is a Joint Secretary of the Governing Council of Forum for Interdisciplinary Mathematics (FIM) – a Multidisciplinary Academic Body, India, and recipient of the "Tudor Tanasescu" Prize from the Romanian Academy for contributions in the field of soft computing methods (2019).

Contributors

T. C. Adityaa
Puducherry Technological University
Puducherry, India

Piyush Agarwal
Graphic Era (Deemed to be
    University)
Dehradun, Uttarakhand, India

Chandrashekhar Azad
National Institute of Technology
Jamshedpur, India

Sarishma Dangi
Graphic Era (Deemed to be
    University)
Dehradun, Uttarakhand, India

A. Devi
IFET College of Engineering
Villupuram, India

Anshu Devi
Kurukshetra University
Haryana, India

B. Dhanalakshmi
BSA Crescent Institute of Science
    and Technology
Chennai, India

P. Dharanyadevi
Puducherry Technological
    University
Puducherry, India

Hari Mohan Gaur
School of Computer Science
    Engineering and Technology
Bennett University
Greater Noida, India

Mezzour Ghita
National and High School of
    Electricity and Mechanic
    (ENSEM) HASSAN II University
Casablanca, Morocco

Ishu Gupta
National Sun Yat-Sen University
Kaohsiung, Taiwan

Griguer Hafid
Mohammed VI Polytechnic
    University (UM6P)
Innovation Lab for Operations (ILO)
Ben Guerir, Morocco

M. C. Helen Mary
RIT, Kottayam
Kerela, India

Medromi Hicham
National and High School of
    Electricity and Mechanic
    (ENSEM) HASSAN II
    University
Casablanca, Morocco

B. Janet
National Institute of Technology
    Tiruchirappalli
Tamil Nadu, India

Siju John
Lincoln University College
    Malaysia & LUC MRC
    Kuttikkanam (Autonomous)
Peermade, Kerala, India

M. Julie Therese
Sri Manakula Vinayagar
    Engineering College
Puducherry, India

Florian K. Kaiser
Karlsruhe Institute of Technology
    (KIT)
Karlsruhe, Germany

Ramesh Kait
Kurukshetra University
Haryana, India

Jyoti Kandpal
National Institute of Technology
Arunachal Pradesh, India

Divya Kumar
MNNIT Allahabad
Prayagraj, Uttar Pradesh, India

Jitendra Kumar
National Institute of Technology
    Tiruchirappalli
Tamil Nadu, India

P. Ravi Kumar
Universiti Teknologi Brunei
Brunei

S. N. Kumar
Amal Jyothi College of Engineering
Kottayam, Kerala, India

Ankur Maurya
MNNIT Allahabad
Prayagraj, Uttar Pradesh, India

Pankaj Kumar Mishra
GB Pant University of
    Agriculture and Technology
    Pantnagar
Uttrakhand, India

Reshma MU
National Institute of Technology
    Tiruchirappalli
Tamil Nadu, India

Sharad Nigam
MNNIT Allahabad
Prayagraj, Uttar Pradesh, India

Shivanshu Oliyhan
National Institute of Technology
Jamshedpur, India

Alok Nath Pandey
Graphic Era (Deemed to be
    University)
Dehradun, Uttarakhand, India

Manoj Kumar Patra
National Institute of Technology
Rourkela, India

Jyoti Pokhariya
GB Pant University of Agriculture
    and Technology Pantnagar
Uttrakhand, India

P. Herbert Raj
Kalaimahal College of Arts and
    Science
Virudhunagar, India

L. Sai Ramesh
Anna University
Chennai, India

Virender Ranga
Delhi Technological
    University
Delhi, India

Bibhudatta Sahoo
National Institute of Technology
Rourkela, India

D. Santhadevi
National Institute of Technology
    Tiruchirappalli
Tamil Nadu, India

Thulasi M. Santhi
National Institute of Technology
    Tiruchirappalli
Tamil Nadu, India

Frank Schultmann
Karlsruhe Institute of Technology
    (KIT)
Karlsruhe, Germany

K. Selvakumar
National Institute of Technology
Trichy, India

B. Senthilnayaki
Anna University
Chennai, India

Sachin Sharma
Graphic Era (Deemed to be
    University)
Dehradun, Uttarakhand, India

Benhadou Siham
National and High School of
    Electricity and Mechanic
    (ENSEM) HASSAN II University
Casablanca, Morocco

Ashutosh Kumar Singh
National Institute of Technology
Kurukshetra, India

Niharika Singh
Bennett University (Times of India
    Group)
Noida, India

R. Sri Saipriya
Puducherry Technological University
Puducherry, India

Sharul Tajuddin
Universiti Teknologi Brunei
Gadong, Brunei

Kavish Tomar
Sunder Deep Group of Institution
Ghaziabad, India

Ashok Kumar Turuk
National Institute of Technology
Rourkela, India

K. Venkatalakshmi
University College of Engineering
    Tindivanam
Tindivanam, India

Abhishek Verma
PDPM Indian Institute of
    Information Technology
Design and Manufacturing
Jabalpur, Madhya Pradesh, India

Marcus Wiens
TU Bergakademie Freiberg
Freiberg, Germany

Chapter 1

Edge computing-enabled secure information-centric networking

Privacy challenges, benefits, and future trends

Kavish Tomar, Sarishma Dangi, and Sachin Sharma

CONTENTS

1.1 INTRODUCTION

The internet was initially designed with the goal of establishing communication and allowing resource sharing between end-to-end trusted hosts. The objective of the internet was to primarily forward the data packets among a limited number of stationary hosts and it has evolved today to become a far more advanced requisite that has laid the foundation of numerous other advanced technologies such as cloud computing, mobile cloud computing (MCC), edge computing, and Internet of Things (IoT) [1–4]. Over time, due to advancements in these technologies, the scope of the internet has changed tremendously. Now, a massive amount of data is searched and uploaded over the internet, and as per Cisco Visual Networking Index,

DOI: 10.1201/9781003269144-1

1

about 90% of the internet traffic is multimedia content [5]. The current usage pattern, preferences, and demand on the internet also show that a significant portion of internet traffic is generated by various video streaming and over-the-top (OTT) platforms such as YouTube, Netflix, Amazon Prime, Hotstar, and Hubulu. Most of the time, a similar type of data is fetched by a group of users and since the traditional internet architecture is IP-based, all the users get the copy of the same data from the source, which increases response time and requires more bandwidth. The current architecture of the internet is facing problems like quality of service (QoS), latency, storage and mobility issues, and reliability and needs a shift in its host-centric model to a content-centric model [6, 7].

Information-centric networking (ICN) as an emerging technology has received a lot of attention from the research community over the past few years [8–10]. In the current architecture of internet, the communication is based on IP addresses, i.e., the content is exchanged among named hosts. Hosts are named using systems such as Domain Name System (DNS) resolution and through Uniform Resource Locator (URL). However, ICN has bought a paradigm shift by incorporating location-independent naming as a key attribute. ICN is an approach in which the content is fetched by using names from any location in the network rather than the name of the communication host, i.e., IP address. In ICN, the contents are assigned a location that is independent and persistent; unique name, and contents are decoupled from the host in the network and the concept of in-network caching is used that helps in multicasting; and the main focus of ICN is data and information rather than point-to-point communication. The main features of ICN are name-based content identification and retrieval, distributed in-network caching, content-based security, and connectionless user-driven communication models [7, 11]. The key advantages that are offered by ICN are efficient content distribution, unique naming, host multi-homing, mobility, scalability, disruption tolerance, and security. Hence, the current requirements of the internet like content distribution, low latency, mobility, scalability, security, and trust are fulfilled by ICN.

Cloud computing is a well-known model that shifts computation tasks on remote servers and provides on-demand services at low cost from a shared pool of resources elastically but due to its centralized cloud architecture, it suffers from latency and mobility issues. To overcome these, edge computing is emerged to deal with increasing mobile and heterogeneous computing tasks at edges in the network. Edge computing brings computation, storage resources and bandwidth closer to the end user, which provides lower latency and helps in reducing backbone network traffic [12]. It can work on both downstream and upstream data. Edge computing provides QoS, low latency, location awareness, scalability, reduction in network traffic, which helps in achieving the current requirements of the internet. Some of the real-time applications of edge computing are cognitive assistance, body area networks (BANs), hostile environments, smart cities and homes, smart grids, augmented reality, video auditing, and language processing.

A combination of edge computing and ICN results in better performance and many other benefits such as shorter response time, mobility, bandwidth reduction, and storage. Future internet architectures like 5G radio networks, augmented reality, autonomous driving, and IoT demand real-time data analysis and need quick responses [13]. These requirements can easily be tackled by integrating ICN and edge computing. Edge computing brings computation near to the user and ICN provides in-network caching that provides low latency and QoS. Highly requested data can be cached at specific edges and congestion in the network can be reduced and bandwidth utilization can also be optimized. This is because ICN uses content names to fetch content in the network and provides security to content rather than communication channel and instinctively upholds many privacy and security features, namely provenance and user's privacy. But, in ICN-based models, the content name can be exposed to the communicating entities in the network, which increases the risk of various privacy threats such as timing and monitoring attacks, decisional interference attacks, censorship and anonymity mitigation, invasion and privacy attacks, and naming and signature privacy.

In this work, edge computing-enabled ICN is reviewed from a security perspective. The key privacy challenges faced by edge computing-enabled ICN are analyzed. A detailed study on benefits and challenges is also provided. A secure edge computing-enabled ICN-based architecture is provided along with a discussion on future trends. The key contributions of this work are outlined as follows:

- A review of privacy challenges based on edge computing-enabled secure ICN is provided.
- A discussion on benefits as well as challenges faced while incorporating ICN with edge computing is provided.
- Proposing a secure edge computing-enabled ICN model for secure and enhanced service delivery.
- A detailed analysis of future trends is provided for edge computing and ICN-based solutions

The rest of this work is organized as follows: Section 1.2 provides a summary of the related work in the area. Section 1.3 provides the technical background required for understanding the rest of the work. Section 1.4 outlines the privacy attacks and challenges for edge computing-enabled ICN. Section 1.5 discusses the benefits as well as challenges for edge computing-enabled ICN. Section 1.6 proposes secure computing-enabled ICN model. Section 1.7 outlines the future trends in the area followed by the conclusion of the work.

1.2 RELATED WORK

In this section, we outline the work that has discussed the privacy attacks in ICN-based architectures. In [14], the author identifies two main privacy attacks: information leakage through caches and surveillance and censorship. In the first attack, a malicious entity can identify which user is interested in which content item by requesting a content item and then by observing and computing the response time. The number of users of a shared cache is limited; if the caches are vested at low aggregation level then this makes it much easier for any malicious entity to identify the original user who requested the cached item. Furthermore, surveillance and censorship attacks are more potential because content items are named uniquely in ICN that can leak more information about content and make it convenient for privileged malicious entities to either block users' direct access to certain items or monitor users that access certain items. But this work is based specifically on the NDN-ICN architectures and these attacks can also exist under different architectures. Finally, the author proposes countermeasures based on NDN-ICN architecture to mitigate these attacks and classifies them into two categories for information leakage through caches: detection and prevention; and selective caching and tunneling for censorship and surveillance attack. In [15], the author identifies the privacy attacks based on content privacy, cache privacy, signature privacy, and naming privacy. In cache privacy, the attacker can extract information about a specific content item exchanged by the user and about the user of a specific content item by monitoring the response time. The attackers in cache privacy are distinguished into two classes: immediate neighbor and distant neighbor depending on the distance between the attacker and the victim. If the attacker is an immediate neighbor, the risk of the privacy attack is higher. The countermeasures proposed for this attack are wait before a reply, collaborative caching, delay the first k requests, and probabilistic caching. In content privacy attacks, an attacker can monitor and censor the user easily because the content is cached, and the attacker has more time to monitor the data. Countermeasures provided for content privacy are broadcast encryption, symmetric/asymmetric encryption, cover files, and proxy re-encryption. Name-based privacy attacks arise because of the semantic correlation present between the content name and the content itself. Bloom filters can be used to identify the content to reduce the risk of these attacks. In signature privacy attacks, the attacker can identify the content publisher that has signed the content to provide content provenance and integrity. Confirmer signatures, group signatures, ring signatures, and the use of ephemeral identities are some solutions proposed to diminish the risk of signature privacy attacks. But this work is also limited to certain design choices based on NDN-ICN architectures. In [16], the authors discussed various design choices for content naming, secure forwarding, advertisement, and lookup; their privacy requirements; and the effect of privacy attacks on them and proposed a generic ICN architecture. The author grouped privacy attacks into monitoring, decisional interference, and invasion attacks. DREAD (Damage, Reproducibility, Exploitability, Affected Users, and Discoverability) model is used to rank these attacks based on their feasibility and impacts on designs. The author then briefly reviewed the various ongoing researches that concern privacy in ICN architectures and proposed solutions to mitigate the privacy issues. In [17], the author explored privacy, security, and access control challenges in ICN deeply and discussed the proposed mechanisms to reduce these issues. The author classifies privacy attacks as timing attacks, censorship and anonymity attacks, communication monitoring attacks, protocol attacks, and naming-signature privacy. The limitations of the proposed approaches for diminishing attacks and augmenting privacy are discussed and later the work is concluded by providing a future direction for research about which class of ICN architecture is best suited for privacy. Table 1.1 presents the summary of the related work.

Table 1.1 Summary of related work

Identified privacy threats	Design choices	Countermeasures proposed
i. Information leakage through caches	NDN/CCN [14, 18]	a. Detection [19] b. Prevention
ii. Censorship and surveillance		a. Selective caching b. Tunneling [20]
i. Cache privacy	CON/NDN [15]	a. Wait before a reply b. Delay the first k requests [21] c. Collaborative caching d. Probabilistic caching [22]
ii. Content privacy		a. Symmetric/asymmetric encryption b. Broadcast encryption [23, 24] c. Proxy re-encryption [25] d. Cover files [26]
iii. Naming privacy		Bloom filters [27]
iv. Signature Privacy		a. Confirmer signature [28] b. Group signature [29] c. Ring signature [30] d. Use of ephemeral identities
i. Monitoring attacks ii. Decisional interference attacks iii. Invasion attacks	Various design choices [16]	Comparative study of already proposed solutions [14, 21, 20, 26, 31, 15]
i. Timing attacks	Comparative study on various design choices [17]	a. Delay for first k interests [15, 21] b. Delay for the first interest from each client [32, 33]
ii. Censorship and anonymity attacks		a. Non-proxy based mechanism [26, 31, 34] b. Proxy-based mechanism [20, 35–37]
iii. Communication monitoring attacks		a. Selective caching [14, 18] b. Secure tunneling [15]
iv. Protocol attacks		Use of rate-limiting requests
v. Naming-signature privacy		a. Name obfuscation [15, 38, 39] b. Overlay network [40–42]

1.3 BACKGROUND

In this section, we provide the necessary background needed to understand the remaining work. Advanced readers can safely skip this section.

1.3.1 Edge computing

Cloud computing has had an emphatic effect on IT discourse in the past decade. The key features of the cloud are on-demand self-service, resource pooling, rapid elasticity, measured services, and broad network access, and key services provided are IaaS stands for infrastructure as a service, PaaS stands for platform as a service, and SaaS stands for software as a service. All these services are on-demand accessible by the network from a shared pool of various resources such as applications, networks, and storage, and these resources can be allocated and can be released rapidly. Regardless of all these benefits, cloud computing has some limitations; in this era, few applications require storing huge amounts of data and real-time data analytics, which needs quick responses; but due to centralized cloud architecture, cloud is unable to fulfill these requirements and suffers from larger latency, low mobility, and requires higher bandwidth [1, 43].

To overcome these limitations of cloud computing, edge computing is emerged as a promising paradigm of computing, in which computation is performed at the edge of the network. Edge computing is a computing norm that brings services close to end users for reducing latency and works on both downstream data and upstream data [3, 44]. The edge device can be any networking or computing device that resides between cloud data centers and data sources, and this edge device plays as both data consumer and producer and provides privacy and security. Edge computing uses distributed model of server distribution, hence supporting high mobility, reducing the load from devices to cloud edge, providing low latency, heterogeneity, requiring low bandwidth, and being location aware [3, 43, 44].

Cloudlets [45] are also known as "micro cloud" or "data-center in a box" and operate in a similar way to small cloud computing architectures derived from centralized cloud computing. The objectives of cloudlets are to support collaborative mobile applications having enormous demand for resources and to offer firm computation resources at low latency to mobile devices and are focused on helping time-sensitive applications under bandwidth-bound conditions. The Cloudlet is the mid layer of a 3-tier architecture of edge computing and is placed nearby the mobile devices generally at a distance of a single hop and operates as virtual machines. These are accessible through rapid wireless links such as Wi-Fi and can work even without the internet [45–47].

MEC was introduced by ETSI (European Telecommunications Standards Institutes) in 2014 to push computation powers into radio access networks to support virtualization at the radio edge. MEC is situated in the base station of mobile networks and can be occasionally known as MCC. Initially,

MEC was proposed for mobile networks only, but now they can accept both fixed and mobile networks, and hence known as "Multiple-access Edge Computing" now [48]. MEC permits access to local resources by empowering the network edge to work in an isolated way. Latency can be reduced by MEC and they can provide location awareness, reliability, energy efficiency, context-awareness, more privacy, and benefits of close range and ultra-low latency, and can be a promising approach toward 5G networks. But, due to the load on MEC servers since most of the computation is done on them, they can be congested, and non-functioning of them can result in an immense cost for operators [45, 47, 49].

Fog computing enables storage, applications, and services closer to mobile users and serves as a bridge between the cloud and users. According to the Openfog community, fog computing is a horizontal, system-level architecture that is capable of enabling distributed computing operations, network services, and storage services in close vicinity to the end user from the cloud. In fog computing, data is managed locally at the edge of the network rather than being sent to the cloud servers that help in the improvement of QoS. The main attributes of fog computing are heterogeneity, real-time interaction, support for mobility, widespread wireless access, low latency, cognition, and interoperability [45, 50].

1.3.2 Information-centric networking (ICN)

ICN emerged as a promising approach toward fetching data by its name from any location in the network rather than the name of the communicating host, i.e., IP address. In ICN, the concept of in-network caching is used and contents are decoupled from the host in the network and the key focus is data and information rather than point-to-point communication. Because of the evolution of online music and video streaming platforms like YouTube, Amazon Prime, and Netflix, major traffic on internet is caused by videos, these applications require high bandwidth and the current internet architecture endures various limitations, such as absence of data identity in the network, insufficiency of proper storage management, deficit in mobility, insecurity, lack of efficient congestion control, bandwidth wastage [51].

To overcome these limitations and to provide faster data delivery, and to surmount the high demand for cost-effective and scalable content distribution, ICN provides a content-centric architecture based on Named Data Objects (NDOs), e.g., webpages, documents, and videos, unlike the current architecture that uses the concept of IP addressing and where communication is based on named hosts, e.g., webservers, laptops, PCs, and tablets.

In 1999, ICN approach was inaugurated in TRIAD [52] project, at Stanford University, and DONA (Data-Oriented Network Architecture) [53] project was launched in 2006 at UC Berkeley. PSIRP (Public Subscribe Internet Routing Paradigm) [54] project and PURSUIT (Public-Subscribe Internet Technology) project both are sponsored by the EU Framework 7 program (FP7). SAIL (Scalable and Adaptive Internet Solution) [55] project is a development in NetInf (Network of Information) [56] project proposed by European FP7 4WARD. CCN (Content-Centric Networking) [57] project was launched in 2007 proposed at PARC and the research is currently going on to improve CCN architecture known as Named Data Networks (NDN) [58, 59].

The four main principles that ICN follows are name-based routing, distributed in-network caching, location independence, and content security. Name-based routing techniques are used to produce routing paths in ICN instead of addressable hosts. ICN makes the data security self-contained from the time of its creation by providing content-based security and embedding security in each data unit using public-key cryptography. Distributed in-network caching provides multipoint to multipoint communication and prevents retransmission of the same data, which helps in reducing traffic load and latency of data delivery, and can be a good solution to enhance the total energy efficiency of a network. Location-dependent IP addresses are not required for communication in ICN, the entire communication is rooted on the name of the requested data. Hence, ICN is location-independent content-centric networking.

1.4 ICN PRIVACY AND SECURITY: ATTACKS AND SOLUTIONS

The key features of ICN architecture that make it unique from other networking architectures and are common in all ICN architectures are information object, routing, naming, caching, security, and Application Programming Interface (API) [26, 60, 61]. The main focus of ICN is the information object, which is the content itself, inattentive to its physical representation and where it is located. Distinct representations and copies for every representation can be present for each content. The schemes through which names are given to content refer to naming. These schemes are divided into two categories: hierarchical naming and self-certifying. Name resolution and name-based routing approaches are used to carry out routing [8]. Content name is resolute into single IP address or a set of them in name resolution approach, and then the request is forwarded to any one IP address utilizing any topology rooted on shortest path routing algorithm such as Open Shortest Path First (OSPF). However, in name-based routing, the request is forwarded according to the name of the content, and information of its state is stored en route. Thus, the content can be self-delivered to the receiver by using the reverse path. In ICN, caching adheres to the three principles, namely, pervasive, democratic, and uniform. The pervasive principle refers to that caching policy is accessible by each network node. Democratic principle shows that it is functional to all contents regardless of its provider. The uniform principle alludes that caching can be employed in all content irrespective of its protocols. In ICN, API is required to request the content and to deliver it. Content is published by a source and is made available for other network users. The subscriber sends a subscription message for interested content. In these two, publish and subscribe operations content name is utilized as the main parameter. Security and privacy are the main concern in ICN architecture. Since in ICN network any of the accessible copies can be used by user, and the security cannot be bound to communication endpoints or the storage locations [51, 62].

Most of the privacy concerns apply to all models but few are related to some specific architectures. Privacy attacks can aim the router, cached content, content names and signatures, and users' privacy (personal preferences or interests). Privacy attacks are categorized into timing attacks, monitoring attacks, decisional interference attacks, anonymity and censorship mitigation, invasion attack, discovery and protocol attack, and naming signature attacks [16, 17].

- **Timing attack:** An attacker scrutinizes the cached content at the shared router in these types of attacks. To identify cached content, the attacker leverages precise time management to discriminate which content has been requested and which content has not been requested [17].
- **Monitoring attack:** In monitoring attacks, an attacker wants to learn the preferences and interests of the victim and to identify content's popularity. The attacker has access to the similar edge router from which the content is retrieved by victim. It can be achieved through surveillance (by collecting information about the victim) and interrogation attacks (by forcing the victim to give information to use service), the identification attack (by linking collected information to the victim), and confidentiality breaching and disclosure attacks (by revealing information about a victim via the third party or trusted party) [18].
- **Decisional interference attack:** In these attacks, an attacker aims to prevent the victim from accessing content, advertising, and forwarding content belonging to certain owners or having certain characteristics. These goals can be achieved through identification attack, insecurity attack (by manipulating data pool), or distortion attack (by manipulating or deleting information flow) [51].
- **Censorship and anonymity mitigation:** Similarly, like other networks, anonymity in communication is essential in ICN also. Information about the client and requested content can be revealed due to a lack of anonymity. Later, this could be used to enable censorship [34].
- **Invasion attack:** Privacy-related information of the victim is attacked in this type of attack to cause (not necessarily) privacy-related harassment. The main goal of the attacker is to lure the victim into requesting or forwarding specific content. It can be achieved by insecurity and distortion attacks, exclusion (by preventing the victim from

removing a record from the data pool), and secondary use attacks (by reusing the previously collected information) [63].

- **Protocol and discovery attack:** Protocol and discovery attacks are specific to two ICN architectures, namely, CCN and NDN. An attacker exploits the pitfalls (e.g., name based matching and interest packet scope field) of these design features [15].
- **User name and signature privacy:** Many ICN models demand the content to be specifically solicited by user name. User names can be human-readable or non-human readable. In ICN, the content and its user name and signature require direct or indirect binding to ensure the authenticity of the content. This binding raises many privacy concerns; the content name reveals information regarding the provider and the content [16].

Here are some solutions provided to mitigate these attacks

i. **Solutions based on entropy [63]:** In [26], the author proposed a procedure that does not demand any special architecture or to share any secret key between the publisher and subscriber/user but needs adequate storage infrastructure. Although this approach cannot provide ideal privacy to the users, it makes it difficult to know the users' preferences to the attacker. The main focus of this approach is of two types of attack, namely, name-watchlist attack and content analysis attack [51]. The publisher breaks the original content into blocks of equal length and uses a secret cover file that is a multiple of block length in size [17]. While publishing the content, the publisher specifically selects cover content to mix and mixes two or more data blocks to create a chunk. For all the combinations that consists the content blocks and cover, the publisher runs exclusive operation to create a resultant encoded chunk for publishing. The name of the content and cover blocks are enumerated by the cryptographic hash function. The name of the chunk that is encoded is computed by taking the hash of the corresponding content and cover blocks [26].

   To retrieve the content, the subscriber must have the metadata, like content's length in blocks, content hash, corresponding cover block, names, and algorithms used for name generation. The publisher sends this metadata using secure back channels to verified subscribers. Using this metadata, the subscriber can receive content by requesting corresponding blocks and chunks. However, all the chunks that are created and published are publicly available, but in the absence of metadata, the attacker cannot decode the content. And if the attacker aims to decode the content without having metadata, it will be expensive in terms of computation [17, 26].

ii. **Solution based on mix-networks [63]:** ANDaNA [20] is an adaption of the onion-routing protocol built upon the NDN and provides privacy and anonymity to consumers/users/subscribers which protect users against surveillance and distortion attacks [16] and works as an anti-censorship tool [17]. Multiple encrypted layers are used by ANDaNA for routing messages from subscribers by using a chain of minimum two distinct anonymizing routers (ARs), the entry router and the exit router. These routers should not be a member of the similar administrative domain and should not share the identical name prefix as well, or can be selected by the subscriber using some parameters. The entry router can only identify the subscriber's identity and the exit router is only aware of the requested content.

While requesting the content, the subscriber securely distributes two symmetric keys to the ARs for encrypting original content and transmits the request toward the entry router, and then the entry router forwards the request toward the exit router. Upon receiving the content packet, the exit router encrypts the content packet by using the first symmetric key given by the subscriber along with the original name and signature and sends the encrypted packet to the entry router. The entry router removes the name and signature given by the exit router and encrypts the received ciphertext utilizing the second symmetric given by the subscriber and forwards the response with its original name and a new signature to the subscriber. Lastly, the subscriber decrypts the response and discards the signature provided by the entry router [16, 20].

The author proposed two versions of the protocols in ANDaNA, asymmetric and session-based [17, 20]. In the asymmetric version, the subscriber chooses a pair of ARs and encrypts the interest using their public keys. While returning, the content is encrypted using two symmetric keys that are generated by the subscriber and shared with each AR. In the session-based version of the protocol, the subscriber shares a secret key with each elected AR, using a two-packet interest/content handshake. The main advantage of this version over asymmetric is the better performance, since it reduces the computational cost and ciphertext size by reducing the use of public-key encryption [20].

iii. **Solution based on homomorphic encryption [63]:** Fotiou et al. [31] provide a mechanism that preserves privacy of content lookup by hiding the subscribers' interests without hiding their identity or location [16, 17]. Its high-level architecture has three main components: content publisher, content subscriber, and a hierarchical brokering system, in which each node is a broker and edge is a link between two brokers. This mechanism is based on the Paillier cryptosystem [64], a homomorphic approach based on public key. The publisher publishes content identifier to the brokering system, and the subscriber submits its query to the brokering system for the content location. The encrypted query is transmitted to the root broker that divides the query, keeps the corresponding part, and forwards the remaining to its successor broker till the query approaches the leaf brokers that correspond to it. The leaf broker resolves the query without decryption, computes a response, and then lead it toward its parent broker. Each broker resolves its corresponding query and forwards it to its parent broker until the encrypted result reaches the root broker, which then forwards it to the subscriber. The subscriber then decrypts the location of the desired content [16, 17, 31].

Although this approach hides subscriber preferences from the publisher and the third parties (brokering system), the subscriber has to perform a large number of operations for decryption and the brokers also have to perform many exponentiations that make it computationally intensive, and when the content space is flat, it has communication overhead also [31, 63].

1.4.1 Name-based security

Content-related security is classified into four categories: confidentiality, integrity, availability, and provenance [63, 65]. Confidentiality means that secure information can be accessed by eligible entities only. Integrity ensures the content has not been modified. Availability indicates that the content published in the network has been available and accessible to authorized receivers. Provenance means that the content item comes from the appropriate source. Self-certifying names and identity-based encryption (IBE) are two countermeasures for achieving name-based security. IBE is based on public-key cryptography in which public identity (e.g., email address) or content name prefix works as the public key [17, 63, 66]. In this, the publisher encrypts the data by using the subscriber's identity and then publishes it. The published data is decrypted by the secret private key originated by using a private key generator (PKG) which is corresponding to the identity. IBE provides flexible data confidentiality protection since the publisher does not require a certificate of public key of the subscriber. The publisher can also publish content to the network securely by selecting a content name and can ensure that only certain subscribers can get the private key associated to it to decrypt the data.

There are two approaches to protect the confidentiality of data with IBE: content encryption with subscriber's identity or using a content name or by using its prefix. The data is encrypted by identities and then signed by the publisher using the identity-based signature (IBS) scheme. The subscriber decrypts the cleartext from the cyphered content. For encryption and decryption of large contents, the computing cost is too high; to minimize that cost, key encapsulation mechanism (KEM) is used. In KEM, initially, the content is encrypted using a data encryption key mechanism (DEM) and then it is encrypted with the identity [66]. Despite its advantages, key revocation is still an issue and the harness of content name prefix like a public key still needs further investigation.

1.4.2 Content provenance encryption

Content provenance verification is a process that verifies that the content item comes from the appropriate and reliable source. When a subscriber wants to receive content from its original publisher for preventing spam and phishing-type attacks, provenance verification is used [67]. In [67], a secret key that is originated by the content publisher and a challenge-response protocol are used to achieve provenance verification. In [68], the author proposes a content provenance and integrity verification mechanism "Canary" that uses the concept of the Merkle tree. Canary generates a Merkle tree using segments of content with root hash working as the first content packet and signed by the publisher. When a subscriber requests any content, initially a Canary manifest is received containing the signed root hash and a list of segments. Content provenance can be verified by validating a single signed root hash.

1.4.3 Content integrity protection

Integrity means that the data has not been modified. The content integrity is preserved by the digital signature generated by the content publisher [67]. In [69], Wong et al. presented a security plane for the publisher/subscriber paradigm for ensuring data integrity [17]. Merkle tree security mechanism is employed to provide signature amortization and for preventing fake publications. The security plane functions like a broker amidst authentication procedure and forwarding functionalities. Content descriptor containing authentication information about content called metadata is stored in the security plane for preserving the subscriber from retrieving forged content through the data plane. The metadata is signed by the content publisher to prevent unauthorized modifications. For inserting metadata into the security plane, the publisher should initially authenticate themselves in the security plane by using a challenge-response authentication.

In [67], the author uses IBE scheme to generate digital signatures by following steps

1. Initially, the content publisher calculates the content hash (h) by operating a secure hash function.
2. A secret key ($SK_{name/h}$) is generated by invoking the *Extract* algorithm corresponding with the content name associated to the hash.

This secret key works as the content's digital signature that is recognized by *name*.

The digital signature can be authenticated by the subscriber applying the following steps

1. Calculate h.
2. Select random integer r.

3. Encrypt r using the IBE *Encrypt* algorithm. This r is used as key and public parameters.
4. Verify the ciphertext generated in the previous step and decrypt it by operating signature as key and the IBE *Decrypt* algorithm.

This solution does not seek the binding of the secret key with content. Here, the secret key works as public information, since the signature can only be generated by publishers, which provides an unforgeable association manner between the content and the publisher, and hence provides content integrity. In [68], the author proposes a mechanism that uses a single sign operation no matter the content size to validate the integrity and provenance of the content. A Merkle tree is generated with a signed root hash node and segments of the content. All segments contain the information of each hash node and signed root node for self-verification. The subscriber can verify the content integrity by validating the root hash node.

1.4.4 Content authentication

Content authentication is a process of verifying that the content is trustworthy that means the received content is that which is asked by the subscriber [67]. In [70], the author proposed two IBE-based authentication protocols through which a subscriber can validate whether a network entity is authorized to store requested content or not. In the first protocol, IBE *Encrypt* algorithm [71] is used to encrypt a random number by giving a content identifier as input and the subscriber has to execute this protocol before requesting each content item if he wants to validate the authenticity of multiple requested content items. In the second protocol, the same content prefix is used for a set of content identifiers, and by encrypting the random number with content name prefix as an input using the IBE *Encrypt* algorithm [71], the subscriber does not need to repeat the authentication protocol but in this protocol, the publisher has to originate a secret key associated to the content identifier and content prefix and has to share it with authorized network entities. In [67], the author proposed a solution for content authentication by generating a digital signature using an IBE scheme, which is chosen cipher-text attack secure [71]. In this scheme, no authorized network entity that has the secret key can generate a signature; it can be generated by the publisher only. Hence, the subscriber can trust that authenticated content is received by him.

1.4.5 Identity-based encryption

IBE is based on public key cryptography in which public identity (e.g., email id and contact number) or content name prefix works as the public key. IBE comprises four randomized algorithms, namely *Setup, Extract, Encrypt,* and *Decrypt* [66, 67, 71].

1. **Setup:** It is executed once by PKG and security parameter is taken as input and returns master secret key (MSKey) and specific public parameters (PParms). The MSKey is kept secret by PKG and utilized only to abduce further secret keys, while PPrms is available publicly.
2. **Extract:** PKG executes this and it takes MSKey, PParms, and subscriber id (Id) as inputs and renders a secret key (SKey) associated with Id.
3. **Encrypt:** Publisher executes this algorithm and it takes in the user's identity (Id), a message (MSG), and PParms as inputs and then return a ciphertext CT of MSG.
4. **Decrypt:** This algorithm is executed by the subscriber and it takes CT associated with SKey as input and then a message MSG is returned as output.

In IBE, the publisher encrypts the data with the subscriber's identity using *Encrypt* algorithm and then publishes it. The published data is decrypted by the subscriber with the secret private key generated by PKG which is corresponding to the identity using the *Decrypt* algorithm. IBE provides flexible data confidentiality protection since the publisher does not require a public key certificate of the subscriber. The publisher can also publish content to the network securely without a pre-established secure channel, by selecting a content name, and can ensure that only certain subscribers can obtain the private key associated with it to decrypt the data, without knowing them [66].

Key revocation is an issue [63] since MSKey is the most important key in IBE, and any entity that knows MSKey can regenerate all the keys extracted by PKG. Key escrow is also a problem because PKG knows all the secret keys, hence a trusted PKG is required to implement IBE [67]. Besides these, content name prefixes are used as the public key which is a new strategy and requires further investigation [17].

1.4.6 Identity-based proxy re-encryption

Proxy re-encryption is a scheme in which content is re-encrypted by a semi-trusted party (proxy) without knowing the underlying pain text. Identity-based proxy re-encryption (IB-PRE) is an enhanced version of the IBE scheme [67, 70, 72]. In [72], the author provides two more algorithms (RKgen and REencrypt) as an extension with the IBE [71] algorithm discussed above in Section 1.4.5.

1. **RKgen:** A user with secret key executes this. It accepts PParams, Skey associated with identity (Id1), and identities (Id1, Id2) as input and returns a re-encryption key $RK_{Id1 \rightarrow Id2}$.
2. **REencrypt:** A proxy executes this. It accepts PParams, $RK_{Id1 \rightarrow Id2}$, and ciphertext (CT_{Id1}) associated with Id1 as input and returns a re-encrypted ciphertext (CT_{Id2}) associated with Id2.

Re-encryption keys are originated by RKgen that are provided to the proxy and by using REencrypt, the proxy re-encrypts the encrypted content from one identity to another. IB-PRE proposed in [72] uses a HIBE [73] stands for the hierarchical identity-based proxy re-encryption scheme as building blocks and is unidirectional ($RK_{Id1 \to Id2}$ is used to re-encrypt content from subscriber A to B but vice-versa is not allowed), non-interactive (subscriber B is not involved in generating re-encryption key), non-transitive (no new re-encryption keys can be generated from the available key), space-optimal, and multi-usable (proxy is allowed to re-encrypt the output of re-encryption many times) in nature. But it has two open problems, first is finding efficient architecture to multi-use CCA-secure IB-PRE scheme, and second is to discover efficient IB-PRE secure in the conventional model. In [70], the author proposes two architectures based on IB-PRE [72] for securing content-sharing and access control policies. The first architecture allows subscribers to manage their own PKG so that a subscriber can generate its own secret key, and in the second architecture, need for proxy is mitigated. Content publishers authenticate storage nodes that consist of shared content, access control policies, and a list of familiar subscribers. Storage nodes operate as content publishers and re-encrypts content for authorized subscribers. Both the architectures are compatible with each other, i.e., a publisher using the first architecture can distribute the content to a subscriber using the other architecture. These architectures do not have key escrow problems and need any pre-shared secret information.

1.5 BENEFITS AND CHALLENGES

Integration of edge computing in ICN will result in many benefits described in the following text. Faster content retrieval and distribution – combining edge computing with ICN will speed up the retrieval and distribution of the content [74].

- **5G radio networks:** Enabling edge computing in ICN will enhance the performance of communication by mitigating the mileage among the services and the consumers in 5G networks and also solve the problem of storage, low latency, and mobility [75].
- **Optimization:** By implementing forwarding strategies at the edge gateways, the direction of traffic can be identified, which can be used to make optimized decisions about in-network retransmission and to detect packet loss [74].
- **Augmented reality:** Transmission Control Protocol/Internet Protocol (TCP/IP) protocol is the building block of existing AR and they depend on cloud computation which limits their potential. Introducing ICN

with edge computing in AR could provide lower latency with user privacy and low signaling cost in content retrieval [47].

- **Autonomous driving:** In autonomous driving, a latency of less than 10 ms is required to exchange data bidirectional [76]. Edge computing with ICN will solve the problem of mobility and latency.
- **Improved user experience:** Through envisaging users at the edge node and then by fetching interested content earlier on the edge node can minimize the average user access time and enhance the user experience [77].
- **Security and privacy:** By shifting computing resources and content-aware filtering on the network edge from remote server will improve the security of ICN and privacy of the users [78]. Regardless of all the benefits of enabling edge computing in ICN, there are still some challenges that need to be resolved.
- **Interoperability:** Edge networks use the concept of IP addresses and ICN is information centric, which makes them both incompatible with each other. Hence, making them interoperable is still an issue for researchers [47].
- **Mobility:** In edge computing-based ICN, any mobile user can be the publisher for a local audience, hence addressing publisher mobility is also important [75].
- **Security and privacy:** The user has to trust a third-party edge device for retrieving content, but any edge can be malicious. If a malicious edge became the publisher, it will increase the chances of leakage of interest and raise security and privacy concerns.

1.6 EDGE COMPUTING-ENABLED SECURE ICN ARCHITECTURE

The basic edge architecture is depicted in Figure 1.1, which consists of three layers: cloud computing, edge computing, and edge device. The Cloud Computing Layer is made up of centralized cloud servers that handle higher-level authentication and authorization, computation, and integration of activities delegated to edge servers, as well as data centers that store massive amounts of data created by various edge devices and servers. The intermediary layer between cloud computing and the edge device layer is the Edge Computing Layer. This layer consists of decentralized data centers, servers, network gateways, and other components that provide cloud computing services. It is primarily responsible for authentication and authorization, basic data analytics, task offloading, data storage, processing, buffering, filtration, and other core computing operations. All low-level electronic devices, such as IoT devices, health monitoring devices, smart home devices, and smart mobile devices, that handle duties such as detecting, controlling, and monitoring in the real world are included in the edge device layer.

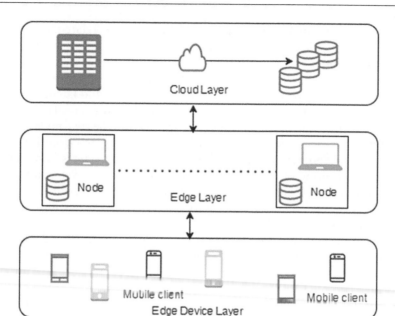

Figure 1.1 Edge computing architecture.

1.6.1 ICN interest forwarding

In ICN two kinds of packets are present: first is interest packet and second is content/data packet. The interest packet consists of the name of the content demanded by the consumer/subscriber and the content packet provides data in the response of matching interest. Three kinds of data structures are maintained by every node in ICN: Content Store (CS), Pending Interest Table (PIT), and Forwarding Information Base (FIB). CS caches data temporarily, PIT maintains a record of satisfied and pending interests, and FIB contains interfaces that are used to advance interest packet to immediate node toward data publisher FIB. Whenever a subscriber desires to access specific content or data, an interest packet is sent to the network by him. On receiving this interest packet, the node initially checks CS, if requested data is available or not. If the interest is available, the node responds with the data packet to the subscriber, else the node checks its PIT for matching entry. If the matching entry is present in the table, then PIT is updated by recording the incoming interface of the interest in the existing entry in PIT, and the interest packet is not forwarded further, else a new entry in PIT is created and the interest is forwarded through an interface(s) that are present in FIB. A simplified view of the processing of the interest packet is given in Figure 1.2.

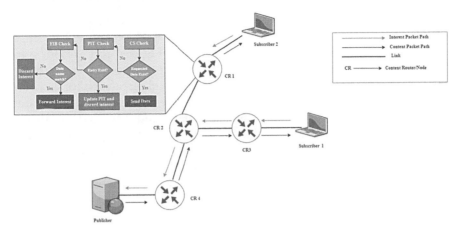

Figure 1.2 Simplified view of the processing of interest packet in ICN.

1.7 CONCLUSION AND FUTURE TRENDS

We have discussed the benefits and problems of ICN in terms of privacy and security. A safe ICN architecture based on edge computing is also demonstrated. We discussed future trends in safe ICN. We discussed the following future trends.

- **Compatibility issues:** Compatibility means two architectures or models that can exist simultaneously without any conflict. However, ICN and edge computing have two different architectures, ICN is content-based and edge computing is IP-based. Hence, this gives rise to the challenge of enabling edge computing and ICN coherently. The interoperability of both these paradigms is an open challenge that needs to be addressed.
- **Naming-related issues:** Naming is a challenge to be addressed in edge computing-enabled ICN architecture. Naming is a scheme used for name contents in ICN and is classified into two types mainly: hierarchical naming and self-certified or flat naming. The hierarchical naming scheme assigns human-readable names and the second one assigns names that are not human-readable but generated by using a cryptographic hash. But it is required to introduce naming schemes that can support mobility, scalability, and security in both edge networks and ICN. Content names are used to identify content in edge computing-enabled ICN architecture, and name-based routing is used as a routing mechanism that improves content retrieval and enhances security, but it may have issues in retrieval for real-time applications that include multimedia that is requested by millions of users on daily

basis. Potential solutions such as context-based naming can help in solving this issue. User mobility is instinctively supported by edge computing-enabled ICN architecture, but if a user acts as both subscriber and publisher, then there will be congestion in the network since naming-based routing schemes use flooding interest for recovering path. However, various works have been done in this regard but none of them supports mobility, scalability, and security altogether.

- **Caching-related issues:** Caching is a very important aspect to increase content availability and speed-up content retrieval. But to cache everything everywhere is not relevant since it will result in creating data redundancy in the network and wastage of cache resources. Integration of ICN with edge computing also raised a new caching challenge that is where to deploy caching, at the edge servers or ICN nodes or both.

- **Load balancing:** For efficient retrieval of content in edge computing-based ICN architectures, the network must support the use of multiple interfaces concurrently. Since ICN instinctively supports multi-interface communication, thus it is necessary to introduce load balancing strategies for edge computing-enabled ICN to minimize network congestion.

- **Mobility:** Subscriber mobility is supported by ICN, but edge computing-based ICN must provide publisher mobility as well, since the mobile user can also be a publisher to the subscribers of the locale and these mobile devices can move in the overall network. Hence, mechanisms are required to settle down the mobility issues of the publisher in edge computing-enabled ICN systems.

- **Security and privacy:** Instead of being a communication link, security and privacy protections are part of the information itself in ICN. The use of ICN to enable edge computing will pose security and privacy issues. Any interested user can obtain the data because of multicasting and in-network caching in ICN, and data is meant to stay inside untrusted nodes. Requesting customized services will generate privacy and security concerns. Various procedures have been proposed to handle security and privacy problems, but no such mechanism exists for mobile settings. As a result, further study is needed to develop solutions that can address security and privacy concerns in edge computing ICN networks.

In this paper, initially we talk about the limitations of current internet architecture and emergence of edge computing and ICN and then we explain the need of security and privacy. After that, a summary of previous work done in ICN privacy domain is presented with background of edge computing and ICN. Furthermore, we talked about the privacy attacks in ICN and their countermeasures and an edge computing-enabled secure ICN architecture is proposed with benefits and challenges. Finally, the work is concluded with some future trends.

REFERENCES

[1] G. Boss, P. Malladi, D. Quan, L. Legregni, and H. Hall, "Cloud Computing: IBM White Paper, Version 1.0," Available via DIALOG: http//www.ibm.com, 2007.

[2] H. Qi and A. Gani, "Research on mobile cloud computing: Review, trend and perspectives," in *2012 second international conference on digital information and communication technology and it's applications (DICTAP)*, 2012, pp. 195–202.

[3] W. Shi, J. Cao, Q. Zhang, Y. Li, and L. Xu, "Edge Computing: Vision and Challenges," *IEEE Internet Things J.*, vol. 3, no. 5, pp. 637–646, 2016, doi: 10.1109/JIOT.2016.2579198.

[4] L. Da Xu, W. He, and S. Li, "Internet of Things in Industries: A Survey," *IEEE Trans. Ind. Informatics*, vol. 10, no. 4, pp. 2233–2243, 2014.

[5] T. Cisco, "Cisco Visual Networking Index: Global Mobile Data Traffic Forecast Update, 2014–2019," *Growth Lakel.*, vol. 2011, no. 4, pp. 2010–2015, 2011.

[6] S. Sicari, A. Rizzardi, L. A. Grieco, and A. Coen-Porisini, "Security, Privacy and Trust in Internet of Things: The Road Ahead," *Comput. Networks*, vol. 76, pp. 146–164, 2015.

[7] S. Sicari, A. Rizzardi, L. A. Grieco, and A. Coen-porisini, "A Secure ICN-IoT Architecture," no. May, 2017, doi: 10.1109/ICCW.2017.7962667

[8] B. Ahlgren, C. Dannewitz, C. Imbrenda, and D. Kutscher, "A Survey of Information-Centric Networking," no. July, *IEEE Commun. Mag.*, pp. 26–36, 2012.

[9] L. A. Grieco, M. Ben Alaya, T. Monteil, and K. Drira, "Architecting information centric ETSI-M2M systems," in *2014 IEEE international conference on pervasive computing and communication workshops (PERCOM WORKSHOPS)*, 2014, pp. 211–214.

[10] M. Amadeo, O. Briante, C. Campolo, A. Molinaro, and G. Ruggeri, "Information-Centric Networking for M2M Communications: Design and Deployment," *Comput. Commun.*, vol. 89, pp. 105–116, 2016.

[11] J. Quevedo, D. Corujo, and R. Aguiar, "A case for ICN usage in IoT environments," in *2014 IEEE global communications conference, GLOBECOM 2014*, Feb. 2014, pp. 2770–2775, doi: 10.1109/GLOCOM.2014.7037227.

[12] Y. Xiao, Y. Jia, C. Liu, X. Cheng, J. Yu, and W. Lv, "Edge Computing Security: State of the Art and Challenges," *Proc. IEEE*, vol. 107, no. 8, 2019, doi: 10.1109/JPROC.2019.2918437.

[13] J. Wu, M. Dong, K. Ota, J. Li, and Z. Guan, "Big Data Analysis-Based Secure Cluster Management for Optimized Control Plane in Software-Defined Networks," *IEEE Trans. Netw. Serv. Manag.*, vol. 15, no. 1, pp. 27–38, 2018.

[14] T. Lauinger, N. Laoutaris, P. Rodriguez, T. Strufe, E. Biersack, and E. Kirda, "Privacy Risks in Named Data Networking: What is The Cost of Performance?," *ACM SIGCOMM Comput. Commun. Rev.*, vol. 42, no. 5, pp. 54–57, 2012.

[15] A. Chaabane, E. De Cristofaro, M. A. Kaafar, and E. Uzun, "Privacy in Content-Oriented Networking: Threats and Countermeasures," *ACM SIGCOMM Comput. Commun. Rev.*, vol. 43, no. 3, pp. 25–33, 2013.

[16] N. Fotiou, S. Arianfar, M. Särelä, and G. C. Polyzos, "A Framework for Privacy Analysis of ICN Architectures," in *Annual Privacy Forum*. Springer, Cham, 2014, pp. 117–132.

[17] R. Tourani, T. Mick, S. Misra, and G. Panwar, "Security, Privacy, and Access Control in Information-Centric Networking: A Survey," March 2016 [Online]. Available: http://arxiv.org/abs/1603.03409.

[18] T. Lauinger, N. Laoutaris, P. Rodriguez, T. Strufe, E. Biersack, and E. Kirda, "Privacy Implications of Ubiquitous Caching in Named Data Networking Architectures," *ACM Sigcomm*, vol. 42, no. 5, pp. 54–57, 2012.

[19] L. Deng, Y. Gao, Y. Chen, and A. Kuzmanovic, "Pollution Attacks and Defenses for Internet Caching Systems," *Comput. Networks*, vol. 52, no. 5, pp. 935–956, 2008.

[20] S. DiBenedetto, P. Gasti, G. Tsudik, and E. Uzun, "ANDaNA: Anonymous Named Data Networking Application," Dec. 2011 [Online]. Available: http://arxiv.org/abs/1112.2205.

[21] G. Acs, M. Conti, P. Gasti, C. Ghali, and G. Tsudik, "Cache privacy in named-data networking," in *2013 IEEE 33rd international conference on distributed computing systems*, 2013, pp. 41–51.

[22] I. Psaras, W. K. Chai, and G. Pavlou, "Probabilistic in-network caching for information-centric networks," in *Proceedings of the second edition of the ICN workshop on information-centric networking*, 2012, pp. 55–60.

[23] D. R. Stinson, "On some methods for unconditionally secure key distribution and broadcast encryption," in *Selected areas in cryptography*, 1997, pp. 3–31.

[24] D. Boneh, C. Gentry, and B. Waters, "Collusion resistant broadcast encryption with short ciphertexts and private keys," in *Annual international cryptology conference*, 2005, pp. 258–275.

[25] M. Blaze, G. Bleumer, and M. Strauss, "Divertible protocols and atomic proxy cryptography," in *International conference on the theory and applications of cryptographic techniques*, 1998, pp. 127–144.

[26] D. Kutscher, "ACM Special Interest Group on Data Communication," in *Proceedings of the ACM SIGCOMM workshop on Information-centric networking*, ACM, 2011.

[27] A. Broder and M. Mitzenmacher, "Network Applications of Bloom Filters: A Survey," *Internet Math.*, vol. 1, no. 4, pp. 485–509, 2004.

[28] D. Chaum, "Desinated-confirmer signature systems," Google Patents, Dec. 13, 1994.

[29] D. Chaum, "E. VanHeyst. Group Signatures," in *Advances in cryptology-EUROCRYPT*, 1991, vol. 91, pp. 257–265.

[30] R. L. Rivest, A. Shamir, and Y. Tauman, "How to leak a secret," in *Proc. international conference on the theory and application of cryptology and information security (ASIACRYPT)*, Springer Verlag, 2001.

[31] N. Fotiou, D. Trossen, G. F. Marias, A. Kostopoulos, and G. C. Polyzos, "Enhancing Information Lookup Privacy Through Homomorphic Encryption," *Secur. Commun. Networks*, vol. 7, no. 12, pp. 2804–2814, 2014, doi: 10.1002/sec.910.

[32] A. Mohaisen, X. Zhang, M. Schuchard, H. Xie, and Y. Kim, "Protecting access privacy of cached contents in information centric networks," in *Proceedings of the eighth ACM SIGSAC symposium on information, computer and communications security*, 2013, pp. 173–178.

[33] A. Mohaisen, H. Mekky, X. Zhang, H. Xie, and Y. Kim, "Timing Attacks on Access Privacy in Information Centric Networks and Countermeasures," *IEEE Trans. Dependable Secur. Comput.*, vol. 12, no. 6, pp. 675–687, 2014.

[34] A. Elabidi, G. Ben Ayed, S. Mettali Gammar, and F. Kamoun, "Towards hiding federated digital identity: Stop-dissemination mechanism in content-centric networking," in *Proceedings of the fourth international conference on security of information and networks*, 2011, pp. 239–242.

[35] S. C. Seo, T. Kim, and M. Jang, "A privacy-preserving approach in content centric," in *2014 IEEE 11th consumer communications and networking conference (CCNC)*, 2014, pp. 866–871.

[36] F. Tao, X. Fei, L. Ye, and F. J. Li, "Secure network coding-based named data network mutual anonymity communication protocol," in *Proceedings of international conference on electrical, computer engineering and electronics (ICECEE)*, 2015, pp. 1107–1114.

[37] R. Tourani, S. Misra, J. Kliewer, S. Ortegel, and T. Mick, "Catch me if you can: A practical framework to evade censorship in information-centric networks," in *Proceedings of the second ACM conference on information-centric networking*, 2015, pp. 167–176.

[38] M. Baugher, B. Davie, A. Narayanan, and D. Oran, "Self-verifying names for read-only named data," in *2012 proceedings IEEE INFOCOM workshops*, 2012, pp. 274–279.

[39] K. V Katsaros, L. Saino, I. Psaras, and G. Pavlou, "On information exposure through named content," in *10th international conference on heterogeneous networking for quality, reliability, security and robustness*, 2014, pp. 152–157.

[40] P. Martinez-Julia, A. F. Gomez-Skarmeta, J. Girao, and A. Sarma, "Protecting digital identities in future networks," in *2011 future network & mobile summit*, 2011, pp. 1–8.

[41] P. Martinez-Julia and A. F. Gomez-Skarmeta, "Using Identities to Achieve Enhanced Privacy in Future Content Delivery Networks," *Comput. Electr. Eng.*, vol. 38, no. 2, pp. 346–355, 2012.

[42] K. R. Sollins, "Pervasive persistent identification for information centric networking," in *Proceedings of the second edition of the ICN workshop on information-centric networking*, 2012, pp. 1–6.

[43] W. Z. Khan, E. Ahmed, S. Hakak, I. Yaqoob, and A. Ahmed, "Edge Computing: A Survey," *Futur. Gener. Comput. Syst.*, vol. 97, no. February, pp. 219–235, 2019, doi: 10.1016/j.future.2019.02.050.

[44] W. Shi, and S. Dustdar, S. "The Promise of Edge Computing," *Computer*, vol. 49, no. 5, pp.78–81, 2016.

[45] M. Talebkhah, A. Sali, M. Marjani, M. Gordan, S. J. Hashim, and F. Z. Rokhani, "Edge computing: Architecture, applications and future perspectives," *IEEE Int. Conf. Artif. Intell. Eng. Technol. IICAIET 2020*, 2020, doi: 10.1109/IICAIET49801.2020.9257824.

[46] F. Liu, G. Tang, Y. Li, Z. Cai, X. Zhang, and T. Zhou, "A Survey on Edge Computing Systems and Tools," *Proc. IEEE*, vol. 107, no. 8, 2019, doi: 10.1109/JPROC.2019.2920341.

[47] R. Ullah, S. H. Ahmed, and B. S. Kim, "Information-Centric Networking with Edge Computing for IoT: Research Challenges and Future Directions," *IEEE Access*, vol. 6, pp. 73465–73488, 2018, doi: 10.1109/ACCESS.2018.2884536.

[48] Y. Yu, "Mobile Edge Computing Towards 5G: Vision, Recent Progress, and Open Challenges," *China Commun.*, vol. 13, no. Supplement 2, pp. 89–99, 2016.

[49] "European Telecommunications Standards Institute Industry Specifica_tions Group, Mobile-Edge Computing—Service Scenarios. [Online]. Available: http://www.etsi.org/deliver/etsi_gs/MEC-IEG/001_099/004/01.01.01_60/gs_MEC-IEG004v010101p.pdf." [Online]. Available: https://www.etsi.org/deliver/etsi_gs/mec-ieg/001_099/004/01.01.01_60/gs_mec-ieg004v010101p.pdf, 2015.

[50] M. R. Rahimi, J. Ren, C. H. Liu, A. V Vasilakos, and N. Venkatasubramanian, "Mobile Cloud Computing: A Survey, State of Art and Future Directions," *Mob. Networks Appl.*, vol. 19, no. 2, pp. 133–143, 2014.

[51] N. Dutta, H. K. D. Sarma, R. Jadeja, K. Delvadia, and G. Ghinea, "Integrating Content Communication into Real-Life Applications. In *Information Centric Networks (ICN)*. Springer, Cham, 2021, pp. 169–194.

[52] D. R. Cheriton, "TRIAD: Translating Relaying Internetwork Architecture Integrating Active Directories," STANFORD UNIV CA DEPT OF COMPUTER SCIENCE, 2003.

[53] T. Koponen *et al.*, "A data-oriented (and beyond) network architecture," in *Proceedings of the 2007 conference on applications, technologies, architectures, and protocols for computer communications*, 2007, pp. 181–192.

[54] "FP7 PSIRP project (Online). Available: http://www.psirp.org/."

[55] "FP7 SAIL project. [Online]. Available: http://www.sail-project.eu/."

[56] C. Dannewitz, D. Kutscher, B. Ohlman, S. Farrell, B. Ahlgren, and H. Karl, "Network of Information (netinf)—An Information-Centric Networking Architecture," *Comput. Commun.*, vol. 36, no. 7, pp. 721–735, 2013.

[57] V. Jacobson, D. K. Smetters, J. D. Thornton, M. F. Plass, N. H. Briggs, and R. L. Braynard, "Networking named content," in *Proceedings of the fifth international conference on emerging networking experiments and technologies*, 2009, pp. 1–12.

[58] L. Zhang *et al.*, "Named Data Networking," *ACM SIGCOMM Comput. Commun. Rev.*, vol. 44, no. 3, pp. 66–73, 2014.

[59] M. A. Yaqub, S. H. Ahmed, Á. D. Á. Ccn, and Á. N. D. N. Á. Pub, "Information-Centric Networks (ICN)," pp. 19–34, 2017, doi: 10.1007/978-981-10-0066-9, 2017.

[60] M. Ion, J. Zhang, and E. M. Schooler, "Toward content-centric privacy in ICN: Attribute-based encryption and routing," *Proceedings of the 3rd ACM SIGCOMM workshop on Information-centric networking*, 2013, pp. 39–40.

[61] G. Xylomenos *et al.*, "A Survey of Information-Centric Networking Research," *IEEE Commun. Surv. Tutorials*, vol. 16, no. 2, pp. 1024–1049, 2014, doi: 10.1109/SURV.2013.070813.00063.

[62] E. G. Abdallah, H. S. Hassanein, and M. Zulkernine, "A Survey of Security Attacks in Information-Centric Networking," *IEEE Commun. Surv. Tutorials*, vol. 17, no. 3, pp. 1441–1454, 2015, doi: 10.1109/COMST.2015.2392629.

[63] N. Fotiou and G. C. Polyzos, "ICN Privacy and Name based Security," 2014.

[64] P. Paillier, "Public-key cryptosystems based on composite degree residuosity classes," in *International conference on the theory and applications of cryptographic techniques*, 1999, pp. 223–238.

[65] A. Ghodsi, T. Koponen, J. Rajahalme, P. Sarolahti, and S. Shenker, "Naming in content-oriented," in *ACM SIGCOMM Work. information-centric Netw.*, 2011, pp. 1–6.

[66] X. Zhang, K. Chang, H. Xiong, Y. Wen, G. Shi, and G. Wang, "Towards name-based trust and security for content-centric network," *Proc. – Int. Conf. Netw. Protoc. ICNP*, 2011, pp. 1–6, doi: 10.1109/ICNP.2011.6089053.

[67] N. Fotiou and G. C. Polyzos, "Name-Based Security for Information-Centric Networking Architectures," *Futur. Internet*, vol. 11, no. 11, 2019, doi: 10.3390/fi11110232.

[68] Y. Y. Shin, S. H. Park, Q. T. Thai, and S. H. Byun, "Canary: A scalable content integrity verifying protocol for ICN," *ICN 2019 – Proc. 2019 Conf. Information-Centric Netw.*, 2019, pp. 167–168, doi: 10.1145/3357150.3357418.

[69] W. Wong, F. Verdi, and M. F. Magalhães, "A security plane for publish/subscribe based content oriented networks," in *Proceedings of the 2008 ACM CoNEXT conference*, 2008, pp. 1–2.

[70] N. Fotiou and G. C. Polyzos, "Securing content sharing over ICN," in *ACM-ICN 2016 – Proc. 2016 third ACM Conf. information-centric Netw.*, 2016, pp. 176–185, doi: 10.1145/2984356.2984376.

[71] D. Boneh and M. Franklin, "Identity-based encryption from the Weil pairing," in *Annual international cryptology conference*, 2001, pp. 213–229.

[72] M. Green and G. Ateniese, "Identity-based proxy re-encryption," in *Proceedings of the ACNS*, 2007, pp. 288–306.

[73] C. Gentry and A. Silverberg, "Hierarchical ID-based cryptography," in *International conference on the theory and application of cryptology and information security*, 2002, pp. 548–566.

[74] S. Shi, J. Li, H. Wu, Y. Ren, and J. Zhi, "EFM: An edge-computing-oriented forwarding mechanism for information-centric networks," in *2020 third Int. Conf. Hot information-centric networking, HotICN 2020*, 2020, pp. 154–159, doi: 10.1109/HotICN50779.2020.9350827.

[75] R. Ullah, M. A. U. Rehman, M. A. Naeem, B. S. Kim, and S. Mastorakis, "ICN with Edge for 5G: Exploiting In-Network Caching in ICN-Based Edge Computing for 5G Networks," *Futur. Gener. Comput. Syst.*, vol. 111, pp. 159–174, 2020, doi: 10.1016/j.future.2020.04.033.

[76] E. Bastug, M. Bennis, and M. Debbah, "Living on The Edge: The Role of Proactive Caching in 5G Wireless Networks," *IEEE Commun. Mag.*, vol. 52, no. 8, pp. 82–89, 2014.

[77] Y. Tang, K. Guo, J. Ma, Y. Shen, and T. Chi, "A Smart Caching Mechanism for Mobile Multimedia in Information Centric Networking with Edge Computing," *Futur. Gener. Comput. Syst.*, vol. 91, pp. 590–600, 2019, doi: 10.1016/j.future.2018.08.019.

[78] J. Wu, M. Dong, K. Ota, J. Li, and Z. Guan, "FCSS: Fog-Computing-based Content-Aware Filtering for Security Services in Information-Centric Social Networks," *IEEE Trans. Emerg. Top. Comput.*, vol. 7, no. 4, pp. 553–564, 2019, doi: 10.1109/TETC.2017.2747158.

Chapter 2

Weighted attack graphs and behavioral cyber game theory for cyber risk quantification

Florian K. Kaiser, Marcus Wiens, and Frank Schultmann

CONTENTS

2.1 INTRODUCTION

Society is undergoing a comprehensive digital transformation. This can be seen in the increasing penetration of information and communication technology, which is also known as digitalization or digital transformation. Discussions on digitalization investments frequently are strongly focused on the benefits neglecting any risks that may come with digitalization. However, the increasing penetration of broad aspects of modern life with information and communication technology does not only introduce benefits bringing high levels of comfort, efficiency, and productivity but also novel risks making modern life more vulnerable to attacks. That is, cyber risks pose an increasing threat to modern life. Consistently, cyberattacks are observed to have tremendous impacts on worldwide economic performance leading to a necessity of managing these risks (World Economic Forum 2022). Hence, ensuring cyber security while leveraging on the benefits of digitalization is a key challenge of modern life and a necessary prerequisite for the successful and sustainable digitalization.

However, managing cyber risks is challenging for professionals as currently there is no profound and commonly accepted methodology for

DOI: 10.1201/9781003269144-2

quantitative cyber risk assessment. This is because established methods for quantitative risk assessment are oftentimes not suitable for the field of cyber risk. Hence, security experts rely on heuristics or qualitative risk assessment (e.g. expert judgments or guesswork). Besides neglecting strategic interactions between defenders and attackers, current approaches to quantitative cyber risk management oftentimes suffer from oversimplified attacker models considering attackers to be inherently and illicitly malicious. Yet, defending against illicitly malicious attackers can easily lead to a distorted and undifferentiated picture of the attack landscape. If we consider, that "everything out there is hackable with enough time, with enough tools, with enough expertise" (Stephanie Domas), there would not be a state of security given this attacker model. However, if attackers are not considered to be illicitly malicious but motivated by a more realistic and differentiated mix of motives like affiliation, achievement or power, it is possible to use defense strategies in a more targeted and thus resource-saving way. That is, attackers' motivations in conducting an attack should have a more prominent role in discussions on cyber security than they have currently. Thus, cognitive science and motivational foundations of attacker models can be considered as an important step ahead in cyber risk analysis (Veksler et al. 2020).

Yet, till now, the quantification of cyber risks seems to be an unsatisfactorily solved scientific problem. Zeller and Scherer (2021) state that there is no scientifically recognized methodology for quantifying cyber risks with high accuracy. Consistently, security professionals oftentimes need to trust on their gut feeling in risk management.

Within this work, we contribute to close this research gap by combining technical analyses of a system relying on cyber threat intelligence and cognitional, behavioral factors. In doing so, our work provides the first actionable approach for attacker quantification based on behavioral cyber game theory. Our contributions are the following:

- we introduce a behavioral attacker-defender game;
- operationalize the game based on cyber threat intelligence;
- encode the attacker-defender game in an attack graph;
- weight the attack graph relying on computational models of motivation taking into account different incentivizing factors; and
- solve the defender-attacker game by backward induction enabling an a priori quantification of attack probabilities:
  - in a single-player game and
  - in a two-player game.

The rest of the work is organized as follows. First, an introduction to the theoretical foundations and related work in cyber risk quantification is given. In Section 2.3, we introduce the proposed methodology for risk quantification. Afterward, we present the results of methodology, discuss the main insights and come to a brief conclusion.

2.2 LITERATURE OVERVIEW AND THEORETICAL FOUNDATIONS

2.2.1 Cyber risk quantification

Although academic research increasingly acknowledges the impact of cyber risks on economic performance, there is a lack of a systematic formal methodology for their quantification (Zeller and Scherer 2021). Setting up models for understanding and quantifying cyber risks is challenging as cyber risks are in many aspects far from being understood comprehensively (Woods and Böhme 2021). Common risk management practices, which are mainly based on statistical approaches, thereby seem not suitable or at least insufficient as defenders and attackers are considered to play "a dynamic cat and mouse game" (Elitzur et al. 2019). This reflects the adaptive behavior of perpetrators to the (defensive) actions taken by the defenders (e.g. security analysts or business managers) and highlights the importance of risk quantification approaches that allow to consider this processes of strategic adaption (e.g. game theory). Beyerer and Geisler (2016) highlight the importance of focusing on the strategic interactions for quantifying security and line out that these must not be ignored.

Since the counterparties on both sides (attacker and defender) make an adjustment to the strategy chosen by the other (strategic/intelligent adversaries), risk quantification must take into account this adaptive behavior and can learn from their experience. Consistently, Rass et al (2017) state that game theoretical models can be applied to the field of cyber risk quantification. Zarreh et al. (2019) demonstrate the possibility to predict attackers' behavior (probability of choosing a specific attack strategy) in the field of cyber risk by relying on game theoretical approaches and use this information to quantitatively assess cyber security. Durkota et al. (2019) propose a defender-attacker game focusing on security investments given limited security budgets. The space of possible actions that may be taken by attackers is represented by attack graphs.

According to the quantification method taken, there are different measures for cyber risk. Taking game theoretical methodology, practical security against rational attackers can be defined as the state where every attack is non-profitable for attackers (Buldas et al. 2006). Yet, other approaches (e.g. technical analyses) propose different measures (e.g. k-zero-day safety, Wang et al. 2013). Taking together, cyber risk quantification and cyber risk management, which needs to be based on these quantitative measures for cyber risk, seem to be "more art than science" (Woods and Böhme 2021) at the moment.

2.2.2 Behavioral cyber game theory

Recent research in cyber security mainly focuses on an operational level, presenting attack techniques for exploiting specific vulnerabilities or discussing the feasibility of specific defensive means against a specific attack

(Attiah et al. 2018). Research on the dynamic interaction between defenders and attackers and the interdependence of their actions are on the other hand rare (Attiah et al. 2018). Game theoretic models aim at providing insights into those dynamics between attackers and defenders (Veksler et al. 2020). Furthermore, game theory has proven to be a promising technique for solving many real-world problems not only in the field of cyber risk.

In general, game theory is a mathematical framework for analyzing interdependent decisions taken by strategically acting rational agents (Durkota et al. 2019, Do et al. 2017). Rationality is hereby not primarily limited to monetary pay-outs (which is often the standard case of game theory conceptualization) but may rather include further components such as monetary equivalent pay-outs, psychological payoffs or social motivations (often in the context of behavioral game theory). Actionable computational models for the motivational differentiation are inter alia presented by Merrick (2016). Game theoretical models can be descriptive but may also have normative power. Furthermore, each game can be depicted as a game graph.

A special case of these game graphs may be attack graphs. Attack graphs present a graphical representation of attack scenarios consisting of different layers representing an ontological model of an attack. Furthermore, attack trees are a special form of attack graphs where only one root is allowed (Ingoldsby 2010). "Attack tree analysis (ATA) is a prominent graphical model technique used for modelling attack scenarios (...) Quantitative attack tree analysis utilises data analytics to predict attack rates and probability of success" (Verma et al. 2019). These concepts are used for decomposing the complex interrelations in cyber security making them accessible for analysis (Nguyen et al. 2017). It is a helpful means for understanding the interaction of vulnerabilities, exploits, attack techniques, and patterns. For this purpose, attack graphs frequently consist of multiple ontologies that can help to describe the state of a system. In the same sense, attack graphs can encode every action an attacker can undertake and hence can be considered a tool for modeling network security with game theoretical means (Anwar and Kamhoua 2020). Kamdem et al. (2017) employ attack graphs and focus their analysis on the impact of vulnerabilities on the security on energy systems. Therefore, they craft a vulnerability multi-graph. Kamdem et al. (2017) analyze the vulnerability multi-graph based on a two-player defender-attacker zero-sum Markov game. Furthermore, Wang et al. (2008) employ a vulnerability-focused attack graph for giving a probabilistic security metric. Anwar et al. (2020) presents a network graph analyzed in terms of network security. They thereby focus on the effects of network diversity on security. The graph is analyzed in terms of a two-player non-zero-sum game. Anwar et al. (2020) focus within their work on the trade-off between costs for deploying a diversified network and reachable security. Gratifications or payoffs can be included in the game graph as instant or terminal gratifications. If gratifications are included in the game graph or probabilities for breaking a specific node (e.g. successfully taking a specific action), the graph frequently is called a weighted game graph.

Current game theoretical models in cyber risk management frequently consider attackers to be malicious utility maximizers, where attackers aim at maximizing the impact inflicted on the defenders' side. That is, attacker modeling nowadays oftentimes reflects oversimplified cognitive models together with extreme motivational assumptions (Kaiser et al. 2022). The inclusion of more differentiated cognitive models in attacker modeling, including individual attacker preferences, is considered to be able to provide "fairly high improvements over normative GT approaches in reducing the potential for successful attacks" (Veksler et al. 2020). That is, as such behavioral game theoretical models would give a more precise picture of the threat landscape. According to criminology and psychology, three incentive-based theories of motivation (achievement [ach], affiliation [aff], and power [pow]) form the basis of differentiating attackers. "Achievement motivation drives humans to strive for excellence by improving on personal and societal standards of performance" (Merrick 2016). Achievement motivation includes the striving for success, individual development, creativity, curiosity, and cognitive challenge. Power motivation describes the aim to reach a superior position among individuals, social groups, and nations, respectively, to gain influence over others. "Power-motivated individuals select high-incentive goals, as achieving these goals gives them significant control of the resources and reinforces of others" (Merrick 2016). Power can for instance be legitimized by moral superiority. The motive of affiliation represents social components of motivation – both the hope of social acceptance and the fear of social exclusion. "Affiliation refers to a class of social interactions that seek contact with formerly unknown or little known individuals and maintain contact with those individuals in a manner that both parties experience as satisfying, stimulating, and enriching" (Merrick 2016). Thereby subtypes of each motivation can be identified (Merrick 2016). Prestige, social status, and social security can be seen as submotives of the motive for affiliation.

"The key idea (of employing game theoretical approaches) is to model attackers/defenders to have multiple levels of attack/defence strategies that are different in terms of effectiveness, strategy costs, and attack gains/damages. Each player adjusts his strategy based on the strategy's cost, potential attack gain/damage, and effectiveness in anticipating of the opponent's strategy" (Attiah et al. 2018). Different game theoretical approaches can thereby be classified according to the involved players. In cyber risk management, single-player games (also called games against nature) can be used to evaluate the security of a specific state of a system (de Gusmão et al. 2018) or decide on the optimal spending on cyber security measures (Kissoon 2020; Panaousis et al. 2014). However, if beliefs get important or long-term equilibria should be analyzed, two- to n-player games get more feasible.

2.2.3 Cyber threat intelligence

Cyber threat intelligence is structured, actionable, evidence-based information on past attacks (Elitzur et al. 2019). It enables to gain a deeper understanding of the threat landscape and may help to gain a holistic view on the threat landscape. Cyber threat intelligence can be acquired by victims of a cyberattack by recording the attack and extracting knowledge over this attack. Since cyber threat intelligence is information on experienced attacks, each defender can only acquire a limited set of knowledge which represents a limited perspective. That is, an important feature of cyber threat intelligence is its shareability (Elitzur et al. 2019). By sharing cyber threat intelligence between different parties, each party can gain a holistic view on the current threat landscape. A major obstacle of cyber threat intelligence is that the information is oftentimes provided in various different formats depending on the preferences of the respective source. To encounter this obstacle, the US Department of Homeland Security's Office of Cybersecurity and Communications and MITRE developed and established a standardized language for sharing cyber threat intelligence (Structured Threat Information eXpression). However, other cyber threat intelligence languages exist as well. These include OpenIOC, Incident Object Description Exchange Format and proprietary languages. Yet, Sauerwein et al. (2017) provide evidence that Structured Threat Information eXpression can be seen as de facto standard language of cyber threat intelligence sharing. Cyber threat intelligence furthermore is shared by many platforms (e.g. Malware Information Sharing Platform, OpenCTI, Collective Intelligence Framework, Anomali STAXX, and Open Threat Exchange platform). An understanding of the specific benefits as well as the weaknesses of these different formats of cyber threat intelligence sharing, respectively, the different languages and platforms (de Melo e Silva et al. 2020) can be helpful. In the research paper, they provide a comprehensive evaluation of a set of those different cyber threat intelligence languages and platforms. Additionally, information regarding vulnerabilities is shared. MITRE provides for this purpose the common vulnerability enumeration. Furthermore, for understanding cyber threat intelligence, a profound understanding of the procedures used during cyberattacks need to be established. Therefore, the Cyber Kill Chain was developed by Lockheed Martin Corporation. It describes on a generic level the steps an offender needs to take to achieve a specific attack goal. Hence, Cyber Kill Chain helps in understanding the threat landscape and establishes a means of understanding attack vectors as an attack strategy that is followed by an attacker. The Cyber Kill Chain includes seven steps of attacker action taking. It can be closely aligned to the tactics presented in various cyber threat intelligence languages. Cyber threat intelligence has proven to be a helpful means for forensic operations, attack hypothesis generation (Elitzur et al. 2019), attack forecasting and for increasing the efficiency of intrusion detection systems and many other approaches in cyber risk mitigation, e.g. threat hunting. However, using cyber threat intelligence within game theoretical models for quantifying cyber risks and specifying game models is only rarely researched.

2.3 GAME THEORETICAL MODEL ON WEIGHTED ATTACK GRAPHS CONSIDERING BEHAVIORAL FACTORS

Cyber risks can be represented and analyzed in the form of game theoretical models. Here, attackers and defenders compete against each other in a game. The benefits of the game for the attacker can be of different nature. The motivating incentives can be understood according to different computational models of motivation (see e.g. Merrick 2016) and describe the transition from a game theory model based primarily on monetary values to behavioral game theory. Thus, in the game between defender and attacker, different attack strategies lead to different benefits (payoffs) depending on the type (different motivations) of the attacker.

In the simplest case, the game involves a defender i and an attacker j playing against each other. Let the defender's utility and the attacker's utility be given as follows, where Ψ is the probability of success of an attack a, I is its impact and V is its value to the attacker (here, the specification of utility can be done according to the motivating factors which means that V will be different for different attacker types).

$$U_i = -\Psi_a \cdot I_a \tag{2.1}$$

$$U_j = \Psi_a \cdot V_a \tag{2.2}$$

For a first analysis, strategic interactions between the attacker and the defender can be abstracted from this point. In the sense of decision theory or a single-player game, the analysis is limited to the execution of the attack (the choice of an attack strategy by the attacker). In this way, a risk analysis can be performed for a given system. The probability of success of an attack is determined by the existence of exploitable vulnerabilities for this attack. It is assumed that the attacker has complete information (the attacker's subjective beliefs about the network structure and its backups correspond to the real state of the system).

For the analysis of real systems, an attack graph is created based on cyber threat intelligence, which includes information about the attack strategies (e.g. use of a special malware), the strategic actions (used attack techniques of the malware which represent the nodes), vulnerabilities that exploit the strategic actions, the products in which the vulnerabilities occur and the processes in which the products are used. A schema of the attack graph is presented in Figure 2.1. It is valid that if no attack technique is prevented

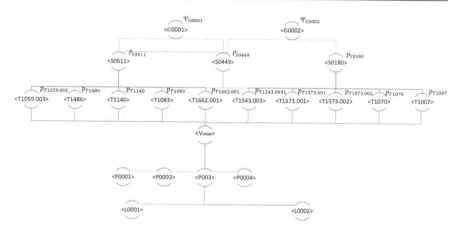

Figure 2.1 Exemplary attack graph with two targets and three possible attack paths.

or hindered and there is a vulnerability for the attack technique, the attack will be successful. However, if a technique is prevented (by a suitable countermeasure being taken by the defender), the attack will be unsuccessful. In the structure of the attack graph, the different targets of the attackers are specified at the top level. Different types of attackers can be guided by different goals. For example, we could distinguish between a Byzantine player (the one who is solely interested in destruction possibly as a punishing power according to a power motive) and a Tullock player (sees hacking as a game and is interested in challenging himself and being the first to hack a system that is considered secure according to achievement motives). In the attack tree, the nodes now represent those critical points that the attacker wants to reach (successfully mastering a subgoal of his attack, such as gaining initial access to the system). For an insecure system (a system with known vulnerabilities), the attacker can achieve this goal with negligible effort.

Given complete information, the attacker will now choose the attack that (I) will be successful (i.e., possible with a given infrastructure) and (II) promises the greatest benefit. The game can be solved as a simple single-player game with a large size of the attack graph using backward induction.

Under incomplete information, the attacker can only form a subjective belief about the actual effects of an attack and its probability of success. In this case, the attacker will not be able to form an exact picture of the benefits of the attack strategies and will choose the attack strategy that promises the highest benefit based on this subjective perception. This case can be represented as a Bayesian game, where the attacker does not know which defensive measures have been implemented and consequently which parts of the system are vulnerable. To understand the game, this makes the strategic interactions between attacker and defender important. Thus, if the system is secure in the sense that there are no known vulnerabilities (either because the attacker has no information about the defender's chosen security measures or because the system is zero-day secure), effort must be spent by the attacker (to find existing or new vulnerabilities). We describe this effort with the variable x. Specifically, x_{21} represents the attack intensity at node 2 expended by attacker 1. Attack intensities or attack effort have a cost associated with them (constant variable cost κ). A defender may also expend effort to keep the system secure (search for and close any vulnerabilities itself). The defender expends intensity/deployment d_k of defense resources at node k. Deployment with defense resources also has a cost (constant variable cost c_d). This creates a competition between the defender and attacker to see who can find a vulnerability first and close or exploit it. This can lead to an arms race between attacker and defender.

At the nodes, the respective attack intensities and defense intensities now determine the probabilities that the nodes can be overcome (an attack technique is successful and thus a partial goal of an attack can be achieved). The probability that node k can be overcome by attacker (type) j using the attack strategy a (the technique encoded in the node can be successfully applied) is given as p_{akj}.

$$p_{akj} = \frac{x_{akj}}{x_{akj} + d_k}\left(\text{node probability}\right) \qquad (2.3)$$

$$P_{akj} = \prod_k p_{akj}\left(\text{strategy success probability}\right) \qquad (2.4)$$

From these node probabilities (represented with a small p), the success probabilities of different strategies can be derived (the latter are represented with a large P). The node probabilities can thus be conceptualized as beliefs. Thus, P_1 is the probability that attack strategy 1 (of attacker type 1) will succeed. Ψ_1 is now the probability that an attack target will be reached. This can be determined now again from the success probabilities of the strategies. Here it must be noted that targets can be reached under the use of different strategies (OR condition). For a simple example with two different targets and three strategies, where strategy 1 can be used to reach target 1 as well as target 2, it follows:

$$\Psi_1 = P_{11} + P_{21} - P_{11} \cdot P_{21} \text{ and } \Psi_2 = P_{12} + P_{32} - P_{12} \cdot P_{32} \left(\text{target probability}\right) (2.5)$$

We now turn to the defender's objective function. In a more complicated but interesting version, the defender's objective can take into account the impact of digitization investments. A simpler version ignores digitalization investments and just focuses on the outcomes of the pure attack-defense interaction. This results in two variants of the game. Whereby taking into account the digitization investments, trade-offs are made between increased productivity due to the digitization investments, on the one hand, and increased vulnerability due to the rising attack surface and increased attractiveness for many attacker types (due to the greater impact of an attack), on the other.

Without consideration of digitalization investments and their effect on the utility of each player, the defender's objective function could be given as follows.

$$\prod_D (d_k) = z \cdot q - c_q \cdot q - c_d \cdot \sum_k d_k - \sum_a \Psi_a(d_{ak}) \cdot L_a$$

$$= z \cdot q - c_q \cdot q - c_d \cdot \sum_{k=1}^{3} d_k - \sum_{a=1}^{2} \Psi_a(d_{ak}) \cdot L_a \qquad (2.6)$$

When digitization investments are taken into account, the target function expands as follows:

$$\prod_D (d_k) = z \cdot q \cdot (1+\gamma y) - c_q \cdot q \cdot (1-\eta y) - c_d \cdot \sum_k d_k - c_y \cdot y - \sum_a \Psi_a(d_{ak}) \cdot y \cdot L_a$$

$$= z \cdot q \cdot (1+\gamma y) - c_q \cdot q \cdot (1-\eta y) - c_d \cdot \sum_{k=1}^{3} d_k - c_y \cdot y - \sum_{a=1}^{2} \Psi_a(d_{ak}) \cdot y \cdot L_a$$

$$(2.7)$$

where z is the product price, q is the quantity of product sold, y is the amount of digitization investment, c_q is the cost parameter for producing quantity q, c_d is the cost parameter for defense units d, c_y is the cost parameter for digitization investment, Ψ_1 is the probability that attacker type 1 reaches its target, L_1 is the defender's loss if attacker reaches target 1, Ψ_2 is the probability that attacker type 2 reaches its target (target 2) and L_2 is the defender's loss if attacker reaches target 2.

In general, the attacker follows the following logic:

$$\max_{a \in \{n\}} \Psi_{aj}(x_{akj}, d_k) \cdot v_j - c(x_j) \qquad (2.8)$$

In the example used above, the objective function of the Tullock player T as well as the Byzantine player B can thus be represented as follows:

$$u_T = \Psi_{aT}(x_{akT}, d_k) \cdot v_T - c(x_T) = \Psi_1(x_{11}, x_{21}, d_1, d_2) \cdot M_1 - \kappa_1(x_{11} + x_{21}) \quad (2.9)$$

M represents the value of the game for the Tullock player (non-monetary value of the achievement). The attacker's gain does not correspond to the defender's loss (in this case, reputation among his customers):

$$u_B = \Psi_{aB}(x_{akB}, d_B) \cdot v_B - c(x_B) = \Psi_2(x_{12}, x_{32}, d_1, d_3) \cdot \beta \cdot L_2 - \kappa_2(x_{12} + x_{32}) \quad (2.10)$$

In the following, we determine the optimal decision of the attackers and the optimal reaction of the defenders. For this purpose, we determine the reaction functions of the attackers and insert them into the target probabilities.

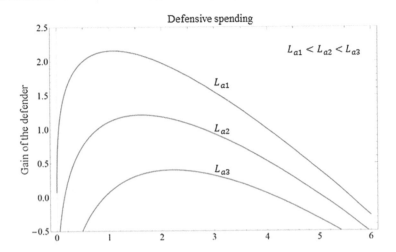

Figure 2.2 Defenders gain in dependence on defensive spending.

From the target function of the defenders, this results in the optimal defense strategy (amount of defense expenditure) shown in Figure 2.2 as a function of the amount of damage.

Figure 2.2 shows that the defender's profit decreases with increasing expected damage of the defender, since the defense expenditure is higher (parametric variation among three values for the resulting damage). Correspondingly, a higher expected damage also results in a higher defense level. The model shows here that information technology monocultures (the attacker will be able to cause greater damage by attacking such a system than in a heterogeneous system) are particularly vulnerable to attacks, require higher defensive spending and are thus suboptimal for the defender. This is because these systems appear particularly attractive to an attacker. The attacker will therefore make a greater effort to crack these systems and their defense will require correspondingly more resources.

In the present case with three nodes to be defended (three attack techniques to be prevented) as well as the two attack targets, the optimal resource allocation for the defender as well as the optimal attack intensity for the attacker (Nash equilibria) can be determined and, on the basis of these, the risk of an attack can also be determined. The formal mathematical solution of the game is given in the Appendix. At this point, only the solution of the game presented at the beginning shall be presented (see Figure 2.3).

2.4 CONCLUSION

The presented quantitative approach on cyber risk management presents a systematic approach for analyzing the state of security (single-player game) as well as investments to alter a specific state (two-player game). A significant contribution of our work is that the game can be calibrated relying on

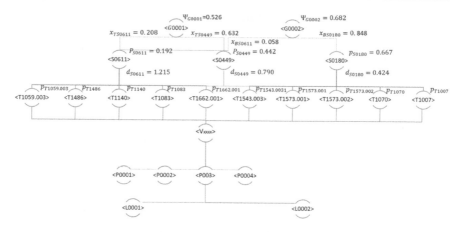

Figure 2.3 Numerical solution for the presented game within an exemplary firm.

the available information on past attacks. That is, the game can be updated automatically to enable an up-to-date risk estimation. For this purpose, the approach can easily be implemented as an algorithm enabling automated risk assessments for a priori attack risk estimations. A further benefit of using the presented methodology is the familiarity of many decision-makers with the established concept of game theory. Furthermore, to the best of our knowledge, this approach is the first of its kind demonstrating the possibility of extending quantitative risk estimations with behavioral aspects in the decision-making of attackers giving relief to the high burdens of oversimplified attacker modeling in risk quantification (Kaiser et al. 2022). That is, the presented approach can support security professionals in their daily work providing quantitative security measures. The model thereby considers interdependencies between attackers and defenders; yet, the game does not consider interdependencies between different defenders as potential targets of an attack nor between different attackers (e.g. assume an attacker that is motivated by breaching a system as the first one). Extending the model to include these effects between defensive spending of different defenders on target selection of attackers would provide substantial improvements to the model and should therefore be considered as a promising extension.

APPENDIX

Formal mathematical solution of the game:

$$d_1^* = \frac{L_1^3 \cdot \kappa_1^2 + 2\, L_1^{\frac{3}{2}} \cdot \sqrt{L_2} \cdot M \cdot \kappa_1 \cdot \kappa_2 + L_2 \cdot M^2\, \kappa_2^2}{27\, c \cdot d^3 \cdot M^2}$$

$$d_2^* = \frac{L_1^3 \cdot \kappa_1^2 + 2\,L_1^{\frac{3}{2}} \cdot \sqrt{L_2} \cdot M \cdot \kappa_1 \cdot \kappa_2}{27\,c \cdot d^3 \cdot M^2}$$

$$d_3^* = \frac{L_1^{\frac{3}{2}} \cdot \sqrt{L_2} \cdot \kappa_1 \cdot \kappa_2 + L_2 \cdot M^2\,\kappa_2^2}{27\,c \cdot d^3 \cdot M}$$

$$x_{11}^* = \frac{-\dfrac{\left(L_1^{\frac{3}{2}} \cdot \sqrt{L_2} \cdot M \cdot \kappa_1 \cdot \kappa_2\right)^2}{c \cdot d^3} + \dfrac{3M^{\frac{7}{3}} \cdot \left(\dfrac{L_1^{\frac{3}{3}} \cdot \kappa_1 \cdot \left(L_1^{\frac{3}{2}} \cdot \sqrt{L_2} \cdot M \cdot \kappa_1 \cdot \kappa_2\right)}{c \cdot d^3 \cdot M^2}\right)^{\frac{1}{3}} \cdot \left(\dfrac{\left(L_1^{\frac{3}{2}} \cdot \sqrt{L_2} \cdot M \cdot \kappa_1 \cdot \kappa_2\right)^2}{c \cdot d^3 \cdot M}\right)^{\frac{1}{3}}}{\kappa_1^{\frac{1}{3}}}}{27M^2}$$

$$x_{21}^* = -\frac{L_1^3 \cdot \kappa_1^2 + L_1^{\frac{3}{2}} \cdot \sqrt{L2} \cdot M \cdot \kappa_1 \cdot \kappa_2}{27c \cdot d^3 \cdot M^2} + \frac{M^{\frac{1}{3}} \cdot \left(\dfrac{L_1^{\frac{3}{3}} \cdot \kappa_1 \cdot \left(L_1^{\frac{3}{2}} \cdot \sqrt{L_2} \cdot M \cdot \kappa_1 \cdot \kappa_2\right)}{c \cdot d^3 \cdot M^2}\right)^{\frac{1}{3}} \cdot \left(\dfrac{\left(L_1^{\frac{3}{2}} \cdot \sqrt{L2} \cdot M \cdot \kappa_1 \cdot \kappa_2\right)^2}{c \cdot d^3 \cdot M}\right)^{\frac{1}{3}}}{9\kappa_1^{\frac{1}{3}}}$$

$$x_{32}^* = -\frac{\left(L_1^{\frac{3}{2}} \cdot \kappa_1 + \sqrt{L_2} \cdot M \cdot \kappa_2\right)^2}{27\,c \cdot d^3 \cdot M^2} + \frac{3L_2^{\frac{1}{3}} \cdot \left(\dfrac{\left(L_1^{\frac{3}{2}} \cdot \kappa_1 + \sqrt{L_2} \cdot M \cdot \kappa_2\right)^2}{c \cdot d^3 \cdot M^2}\right)^{\frac{1}{3}} \cdot \left(\dfrac{L_1^{\frac{3}{2}} \cdot \sqrt{L_2} \cdot \kappa_1 \cdot \kappa_2 + L_2 \cdot M \cdot \kappa_2^2}{c \cdot d^3 \cdot M}\right)^{\frac{1}{3}}}{9\kappa_2^{\frac{1}{3}}}$$

$$x_{32}^* = \frac{-L_1^{\frac{3}{2}} \cdot \sqrt{L2} \cdot \kappa_1 \cdot \kappa_2 + L_2 \cdot M \cdot \kappa_2^2 - \dfrac{3c \cdot d^3 \cdot L_2^{\frac{1}{3}} \cdot M \cdot \left(\dfrac{\left(L_1^{\frac{3}{2}} \cdot \kappa_1 + \sqrt{L_2} \cdot M \cdot \kappa_2\right)^2}{c \cdot d^3 \cdot M^2}\right)^{\frac{1}{3}} \cdot \left(\dfrac{L_1^{\frac{3}{2}} \cdot \sqrt{L_2} \cdot \kappa_1 \cdot \kappa_2 + L_2 \cdot M \cdot \kappa_2^2}{c \cdot d^3 \cdot M}\right)^{\frac{1}{3}}}{\kappa_2^{\frac{1}{3}}}}{27\,c \cdot d^3 \cdot M}$$

By inserting them into the target probability and the utility function, respectively, the attack probabilities that arise in the Nash equilibria as well as payoffs and thus the resulting risk of the defender can be determined.

REFERENCES

Anwar, A. H., & Kamhoua, C. (2020). Game theory on attack graph for cyber deception. *International Conference on Decision and Game Theory for Security*, 445–456. Springer, Cham.

Anwar, A. H., Leslie, N. O., Kamhoua, C., & Kiekintveld, C. (2020). A game theoretic framework for software diversity for network security. *International Conference on Decision and Game Theory for Security*, 297–311. Springer, Cham.

Attiah, A., Chatterjee, M., & Zou, C. C. (2018). A game theoretic approach to model cyber attack and defense strategies. *2018 IEEE International Conference on Communications (ICC)*, 1–7. IEEE.

Beyerer, J., & Geisler, J. (2016). A framework for a uniform quantitative description of risk with respect to safety and security. *European Journal for Security Research*, 1(2), 135–150.

Buldas, A., Laud, P., Priisalu, J., Saarepera, M., & Willemson, J. (2006). Rational choice of security measures via multi-parameter attack trees. *International Workshop on Critical Information Infrastructures Security*, 235–248. Springer, Berlin, Heidelberg.

de Gusmão, A. P. H., Silva, M. M., Poleto, T., e Silva, L. C., & Costa, A. P. C. S. (2018). Cybersecurity risk analysis model using fault tree analysis and fuzzy decision theory. *International Journal of Information Management*, 43, 248–260.

de Melo e Silva, A., Costa Gondim, J. J., de Oliveira Albuquerque, R., & García Villalba, L. J. (2020). A methodology to evaluate standards and platforms within cyber threat intelligence. *Future Internet*, 12(6), 108.

Do, C. T., Tran, N. H., Hong, C., Kamhoua, C. A., Kwiat, K. A., Blasch, E., Ren, S., Pissinou, N. & Iyengar, S. S. (2017). Game theory for cyber security and privacy. *ACM Computing Surveys (CSUR)*, 50(2), 1–37.

Durkota, K., Lisý, V., Bošanský, B., Kiekintveld, C., & Pěchouček, M. (2019). Hardening networks against strategic attackers using attack graph games. *Computers & Security*, 87, 101578.

Elitzur, A., Puzis, R., & Zilberman, P. (2019, November). Attack hypothesis generation. *2019 European Intelligence and Security Informatics Conference (EISIC)*, 40–47. IEEE.

Ingoldsby, T. R. (2010). *Attack Tree-based Threat Risk Analysis*. Amenaza Technologies Limited, Canada, 3–9.

Kamdem, G., Kamhoua, C., Lu, Y., Shetty, S., & Njilla, L. (2017, June). A Markov game theoretic approach for power grid security. *2017 IEEE 37th International Conference on Distributed Computing Systems Workshops (ICDCSW)*, 139–144. IEEE.

Kissoon, T. (2020). Optimum spending on cybersecurity measures. *Transforming Government: People, Process and Policy*.

Merrick, K. E. (2016). *Computational Models of Motivation for Game-Playing Agents*. Springer International Publishing.

Nguyen, T. H., Wright, M., Wellman, M. P., & Baveja, S. (2017). Multi-stage attack graph security games: Heuristic strategies, with empirical game-theoretic analysis. *Proceedings of the 2017 Workshop on Moving Target Defense*, 87–97.

Panaousis, E., Fielder, A., Malacaria, P., Hankin, C., & Smeraldi, F. (2014). Cybersecurity games and investments: A decision support approach. *International Conference on Decision and Game Theory for Security*, 266–286. Springer, Cham.

Rass, S., König, S., & Schauer, S. (2017). Defending against advanced persistent threats using game-theory. *PloS one*, 12(1), e0168675.

Sauerwein, C., Sillaber, C., Mussmann, A., & Breu, R. (2017). Threat intelligence sharing platforms: An exploratory study of software vendors and research perspectives. *Proceedings of 13th International Conference on Wirtschaftsinformatik*, February 12–15. St. Gallen, Switzerland

Veksler, V. D., Buchler, N., LaFleur, C. G., Yu, M. S., Lebiere, C., & Gonzalez, C. (2020). Cognitive models in cybersecurity: Learning from expert analysts and predicting attacker behavior. *Frontiers in Psychology*, 11, 1049.

Verma, S., Gruber, T., Schmittner, C., & Puschner, P. (2019). Combined approach for safety and security. *International Conference on Computer Safety, Reliability, and Security*, 87–101. Springer, Cham.

Wang, L., Islam, T., Long, T., Singhal, A., & Jajodia, S. (2008). An attack graph-based probabilistic security metric. *IFIP Annual Conference on Data and Applications Security and Privacy*, 283–296. Springer, Berlin, Heidelberg.

Wang, L., Jajodia, S., Singhal, A., Cheng, P., & Noel, S. (2013). k-zero day safety: A network security metric for measuring the risk of unknown vulnerabilities. *IEEE Transactions on Dependable and Secure Computing*, 11(1), 30–44.

Woods, D. W., & Böhme, R. (2021). Systematization of knowledge: Quantifying cyber risk. *IEEE Symposium on Security & Privacy*.

World Economic Forum. (2022). The Global Risk Report 2022. World Economic Forum.

Zarreh, A., Wan, H., Lee, Y., Saygin, C., & Al Janahi, R. (2019). Risk assessment for cyber security of manufacturing systems: A game theory approach. *Procedia Manufacturing*, 38, 605–612.

Zeller, G., & Scherer, M. (2021). A comprehensive model for cyber risk based on marked point processes and its application to insurance. *European Actuarial Journal*, 12, 153.

Chapter 3

NetFlow-based botnet detection in IoT edge environment using ensemble gradient boosting machine learning framework

D. Santhadevi and B. Janet

CONTENTS

3.1 INTRODUCTION

The Internet of Things (IoT) can alter the future by bringing global objects into our hands. Because of the smart services, anybody can obtain, connect, and save their data from anywhere. Even though IoT connects everyday routines to the digital realm through connected devices and makes things more accessible, more comfortable, smoother, to care for its services, security has become a significant concern in IoT systems. As a result, the IoT becomes more widespread; issues and security have emerged as a lucrative study area that must be tackled with novel solutions and new action decisions for uncertain threats in the system.

Understanding IoT traffic is critical for multiple reasons [1], including improving performance such as latency, reliability, loss reduction, availability, and mode of broadcasting, all of which can influence various applications.

DOI: 10.1201/9781003269144-3

The most convincing cause for analyzing IoT traffic is always to improve cyber security. IoT devices are simpler to penetrate by design, and every month new reports emerge about how IoT devices have indeed been infiltrated and utilized to mount massive assaults [2] conducted a survey on IoT security challenges; studies have suggested internet backbone security measures that monitor traffic data to detect threats. These techniques' effectiveness depends on thorough knowledge about whatever constitutes a "typical" IoT traffic characteristic.

As per the desired purposes [3], smart devices are created with restricted software and hardware. They are unable to allocate resources for security due to their limited resources. Because security standards differ between nations and brands, such circumstance results in weaknesses and loopholes in IoT devices' security, making them more vulnerable to cyber assaults. IoT devices can be attacked and utilized as a weapon for other activities in operations. Botnet infections are the most common IoT device attacks.

In [4], it is mentioned that the Mirai Botnet assault in 2016 is one of the most dangerous attacks using IoT devices. Cyberattacks on IoT devices can make the machine inaccessible, conceal the customer's data, or control the devices for other purposes. Following the acquisition of IoT devices' control, those devices are directed to DDoS attacks. The number of devices involved in DDoS assaults is significant. The number of devices deployed in the attack influences the DDOS attack's effectiveness.

Ref. [5] explained the IoT exploits, which have three phases: monitoring/scanning, contamination, and attack. The monitoring stage entails acquiring "ownership" of the device to get root access using the default credential. To take control of the devices, they use brute-force attacks using device vulnerability. The intruder then "gears up" the machine to contaminate it by executing actions. The botmaster that performs these actions is called command and control (C&C) server. C&C server installs the needed malware and takes control of the machine. Most common IoT attacks include installing malware onto the device during the "configure" step. Some assaults may even bypass the phase and continue straight to the attacking phase. Attack Phase, performing Denial of Service (DoS), coordinated DDoS, ransomware, cryptocurrency mining, and malicious device activities.

Ref. [6] claims that botnet activity has been divided into four phases: scanning, controlling, infecting, and attacking. The vulnerability is found in IoT devices during the scanning step. The virus is then implanted in the second step, which takes advantage of the vulnerability. The third step seizes root access control and attempts to locate more susceptible devices in the same network as the information is sent to the botmaster. In the fourth step, an army of bots is created to assault the victim machine. In this circumstance, it must secure the IoT devices, and monitoring the network behavior is critical. Some ways to prevent similar attempts using machine learning (ML) have been described in the literature. These techniques can be classified as signature-based, anomaly-based, or hybrid-based, applied in various combinations.

Ref. [7] applied the signature-based strategy; a database is created that contains the traffic patterns of previous malicious behavior in the network.

The arriving traffic pattern is compared to previously observed traffic patterns. If an unfamiliar pattern happens in the network, it will not be detected. The anomaly-based approach is based on the abnormal behavior of network events. It also identifies unknown malware. The hybrid method is a blend of both, based on the needs of the network. The suggested model's approach is based on an edge computing artificial intelligence-assisted network activity analysis.

Ref. [8] suggested edge computing benefits, including decreased latency and bandwidth savings, as well as safety-by-default and by-design following recent privacy laws that allow sharing only the bare minimum of data. Edge computing necessitates local data processing rather than moving it to the cloud and running ML there.

3.2 LITERATURE SURVEY

Ref. [9] conducted study on campus and smart cities, which have 20 IoT devices. The IoT devices network traffic is collected based on signal patterns, activities, burst time, and data transfer rate. IoT devices are mainly made for a specific purpose and send data to their specified servers. The number of communicating servers is also limited, which helps identify the connectivity patterns. The use of protocols is also limited, which has been taken as another parameter. Traffic generated by IoT devices are short bursts, so the mean value of the rate of transfer is considered. The rate of data transfer is considered another important feature because non-IoT devices produce high data transfers than IoT devices, which helps distinguish IoT device traffic. The authors used KNN for IoT attribute clustering to identify the fingerprint of the IoT devices. IoT device classification is identified using a random forest (RF) algorithm.

Ref. [3] used ML to find the botnet attacks on the IoT devices. This chapter applied a feature reduction technique to improve the classification accuracy of finding IoT Botnet traffic. They have used supervised learning models for detecting the Botnet traffic. Ref. [10] conducted a study on a network-based IoT botnet detection. The decision tree technique is utilized for supervised learning. The decision tree method J48 is used in their study. The decision tree algorithm uses rules to divide input from root to leaf levels. Ref. [11] developed the network intrusion detection model for network traffic analysis. The author used the associative rule mining technique to reduce the dimensionality and compare the result analysis of conventional ML algorithms like XGBoost (eXtreme Gradient Boosting).

Ref. [12] developed a framework SDN to detect and mitigate DDoS attacks. Ports in software-defined boundary switches are utilized to gather packet transmission rates. They determined the threshold value of similar vectors in each packet. The threshold value is used to identify the DDoS assault and subsequently prevents additional attacks on that port. Ref. [13] built a ML model to examine network forensics. A network forensic approach is used for hunting out harmful activities on a network. Using ML techniques, they discovered botnet activity in the IoT ecosystem. Ref. [14] suggested an attack detection approach that relied on distributed ML technique. At the edge, data from online network traffic are gathered and analyzed. They discovered that edge computing offered efficient computation for identifying real-world threats. Ref. [15] performed a study on network intrusion detection system. They used the XGBoost feature selection method and applied SVM, KNN, logistic regression, ANN, and decision tree for intrusion detection.

3.3 METHODOLOGY

The two primary IoT services and security solutions are centralized cloud-based and distributed fog-based/edge-based. Ref. [16] performed a survey and found that recent development in security measures provides security for the interconnected network through a centralized cloud architecture. Cloud service providers have ultimate responsibility for the information and IDS service. The benefits of such services include more deployment and administration versatility, reduced infrastructure costs, improved performance, and central control. The distributed structure of an IoT environment includes many devices and produces a high volume of data, low-latency needs, ad hoc settings, and user privacy issues, all of which are not scalable. The significant workload of cyber security is managed at the edge-based security architecture. It takes place at the end device instead of in the cloud. Cloud computing services have been used as an extra protection above the edges.

3.3.1 IoT edge security framework

The proposed edge-based security architecture is shown in Figure 3.1. The first part of the structure is collecting the network traffic flow of IoT sensor data through the IoT gateway. Gathered data are sent to the pre-processing stage because the traffic data may contain numerical and categorical types. The ML models take only numeric input. The input data must be preprocessed before training the ML model with this input data. Pre-processing has the following steps: removing null values/missing values, encoding, and scaling. Dataset used in this chapter does not have any null values or missing values.

3.3.2 Pre-processing dataset

Encoding: The ML model needs all input and output data in numeric form. Before fitting and evaluating the model, data should be encoded. One-Hot Encoding is one of the methods used in this work to convert categorical data to numeric. In this dataset, the attributes have a categorical value: protocol, service, and state. In One-Hot Encoding, for each level of categorical data, a new variable is created. That new variable is mapped with a binary value of 0 or 1. 1 represents the presents of categorical data, and 0 represents the absence of the categorical data.

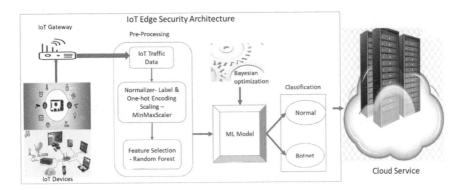

Figure 3.1 The proposed approach of edge-based intelligent botnet detection system framework.

3.3.2.1 Normalization

The dataset contains a different range of data in each feature. It needs normalization of all features to fit the model; it is the process of scaling numeric values in different ranges in different columns that are replaced with standard scales without information loss. MinMax scalar is used here to scale the data. It normalizes the columns linearly and rescales (calibrates) each feature in the range between 0 and 1. For discovering new scaled values, Equation (3.1) is used for determining the maximum and minimum values of the respective function column.

$$Z = \frac{x - \min(x)}{\left[\max(x) - \min(x) \right]}$$

$$(3.1)$$

3.3.3 Feature selection – random forest method

The feature selection algorithm is combined as part of the ML. Embedded methods encounter the drawbacks of filter and wrapper methods and merge their advantages.

The RF technique was employed in this work. It also offers feature significance to select features. In RF, while splitting a node, it looks for the best feature from a random group of features rather than an essential feature. It is simple to calculate the relative relevance of each feature on the prediction. Using the Sklearn tool, the relevance of a feature is calculated, from which it is possible to minimize feature impurity across all trees. The significant feature score is computed automatically during training and the findings are scaled such that the total of all important feature score equals one. Feature score is used to pick which features to select if they contribute enough to the prediction process. In general, the more characteristics there are in ML, the more likely it will suffer from overfitting.

Feature importance indicates which features are more essential in influencing the target feature. Figure 3.2 depicts the selection of the ten greatest

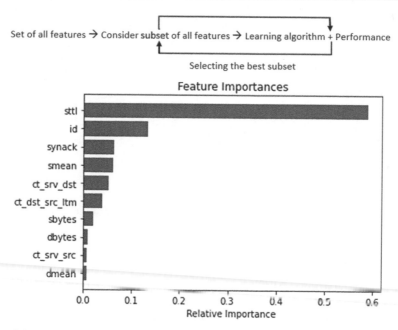

Figure 3.2 Best ten feature selection using random forest.

attributes. This chosen best ten feature outperforms all other features, as mentioned in the section on result analysis. Figure 3.3 depicts the value of each feature histogram. Figure 3.4 depicts the RF correlation matrix. In this chapter, only the top ten features for this model are identified.

3.3.4 Ensemble ML model – XGBoost

XGBoost is an advanced boosting technique using gradient boosting. The advanced feature of this technique is speed, improving the model's accuracy, providing regularization which will avoid overfitting, flexibility in terms of applying optimization, and criteria for evaluation. It has in-built cross-validation (CV), which helps find the exact number of boosting iterations needed. It allows splitting up to a specified maximum depth; after that, it will start pruning the tree backward. While pruning, it removes the extra trees when a negative loss is encountered. It can be used as an additional training model over an existing model.

Instead of eagerly scanning through all the split points, XGBoost employs an approximation approach, weighted quantile sketch, to determine the possible splitting points. Shrinkage η is the learning rate employed in addition to regularization. It causes a reduction of each tree and provides room for subsequent trees to develop, resulting in finer boundaries and improved generalization. Column subsampling is also utilized, which decreases overfitting and accelerates computing.

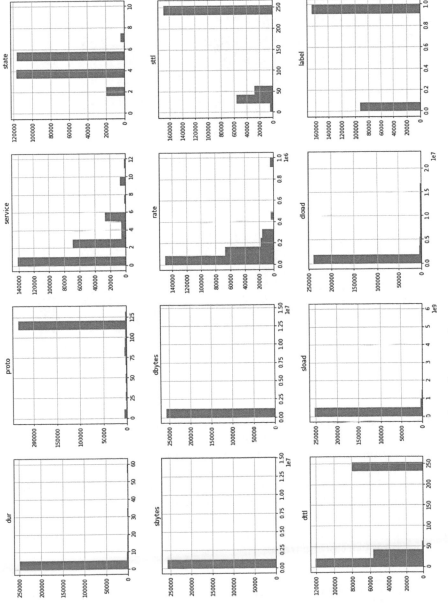

Figure 3.3 Histogram representation of random forest feature selection.

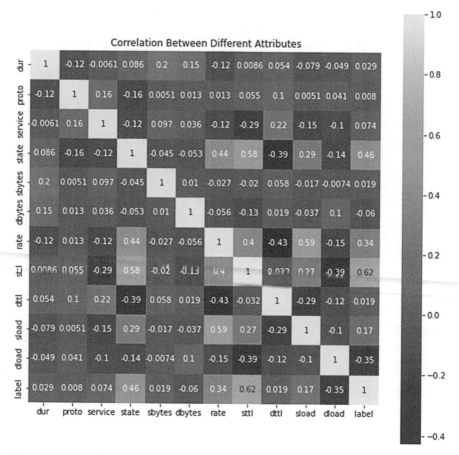

Figure 3.4 Correlation matrix of the best ten features.

The dataset is represented with n instances and m features as DS = $\{(x_1, x_2, \ldots x_i) (y_1, y_2, \ldots y_i)\} (|DS| = n, x_i \in R_m, y_i \in R)$. The ensemble XGBoost tree prediction is represented in Figure 3.5 that uses K addictive process to find the output.

The regularized gradient boosting tree model's objective function (OF) performance is based on training loss and regularization, which is represented in Equation (3.2). Training loss is used for measuring the model, and how well it fits the given training data. Regularization is used for measuring the complexity of the trees.

$$OF = \sum_{i=1}^{n} |(y_i, \hat{y}_i)| + \sum_{k=1}^{K} \Omega f(k) \qquad (3.2)$$

$$Loss \ L(\theta) = \sum_i (\hat{y}_i - y_i)^2 \qquad (3.3)$$

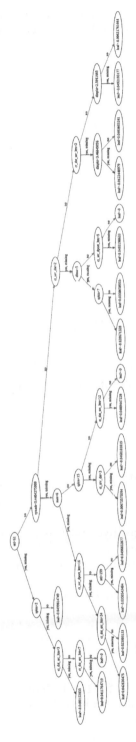

Figure 3.5 Ensembled boosting tree – sum of predictions of each tree on the UNSW_NE 15 dataset.

The complexity of the tree is represented in Equation (3.4) by two parameters like the number of leaves and L_2 norms of leaf scores:

$$\Omega\left(f_t\right) = \gamma\, T + \frac{1}{2}\,\lambda\sum_{j=i}^{T} w_j^2 \tag{3.4}$$

where γ *and* λ *are hyper parameters*. The additive boosting generalized model function is represented in Equation (3.5).

$$\hat{y}_i^{(t)} = \sum_{k=1}^{t} f_k\left(x_i\right) = \hat{y}_i^{(t-1)} = f_t\left(x_i\right)$$

$$\uparrow \qquad\qquad \uparrow \qquad\quad \uparrow$$

Final Model   Previous Model   New Model   (3.5)

The OF of loss for the new addictive model is represented below:

$$obj\ L^{(t)} = \sum_{i=1}^{n}\left(y_i\hat{y}_i^{(t-1)} - f_t\left(x_i\right)\right) + \Omega(f_t) \tag{3.6}$$

We applied Taylor approximation in addictive model to get a traditional optimized OF. The Taylor approximation is represented in Equation (3.7) and the OF in Equation (3.8).

$$f\left(x+\Delta x\right) \simeq f\left(x\right) + f'\left(x\right)\Delta x + \frac{1}{2}\,f''\left(x\right)\Delta x \tag{3.7}$$

$$Obj\ L^{(t)} \simeq \sum_{i=1}^{n}\left[L(y_i,\hat{y}_i^{(t-1)}) + g_i f_t\left(x_i\right) + \frac{1}{2}\,h_i f_t^2\left(x_i\right)\right] + \Omega\left(f_t\right) \tag{3.8}$$

Here, g_i is the first-order derivative and h_i is second-order derivative. It represents the values of each tree.

The higher order of second-order derivatives has been taken in the XGBoost model.

The simplified OF is represented below:

$$Obj\ L^{(t)} \simeq \sum_{j=1}^{T}\left[G_j\,w_j + \frac{1}{2}(h_j + \lambda)w_j^2\right] + \gamma T \tag{3.9}$$

where $G_j = \Sigma_{i\in I_j}g_i\ H_j = \Sigma_{i\in I_j}h_iG_j$ & H_j, which represents the value of the entire tree structure-function. For each quadratic function, the need to find the optimal weight w_j is defined below:

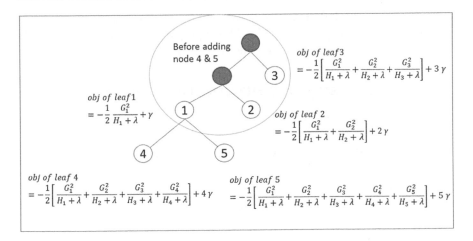

Figure 3.6 Example for working of XGB objective function calculation.

$$w_j^* = \frac{G_j}{II_j + \lambda} \tag{3.10}$$

Substituting Equation (3.10) in Equation (3.9), we get a minimal OF, represented below:

$$\text{Min Obj } L^{(t)} = -\frac{1}{2}\sum_{j=1}^{T}\frac{G_j^2}{H_J + \lambda} + \gamma\, T \tag{3.11}$$

where γ is the complexity cost calculated on the addictive tree when it reaches to do not split state. Working of XGB objective function calculation is depicted in Figure 3.6.

3.3.5 Hyperparameter tuning – Bayesian optimization

Hyperparameter tuning is one of the important processes in the ML-supervised models. Input parameters are different from the hyperparameters. Each ML algorithm has different hyperparameters. If the hyperparameters are not tuned, then the default values are used. Suppose the model accuracy is not good, then it needs to tune the hyperparameters. Hyperparameters are the best parameter to fit the model that is obtained with the optimization technique. There are many techniques available: grid search, random search, Bayesian, and swarm-based optimization.

Grid search is an exhaustive search because the search space is sequential. It takes more time to compute when the search space is larger. Hyperparameters are offered in the statistical distribution in a random search. Random search can regulate or limit the number of possible combinations. In Bayesian optimization, a probabilistic model is created. Hyperparameters are used to map the probability score of OFs. The hyperparameters are prioritized. It requires fewer iterations than the other two searches.

BAYESIAN OPTIMIZATION ALGORITHM

Input function $F(x)$, and data is f.

Step I:

   Start with a small number of sample points randomly chosen (called as Bagl)

Step 2:

   Computer surrogate function using Bagl.

Step 3:

   Iteration in loop:

      Find acquisition function – add additional points to Bagl.

      Re-evaluate surrogate function

      Continue the loop until

         surrogate function does not change

         Or variance goes below the threshold

         Or f is exhausted

   End loop

3.4 PERFORMANCE EVALUATION

3.4.1 Dataset description

The authors in [17] created the dataset UNSW-NB15, which is used for evaluating the proposed model. It was developed by the Australian Cyber Security Centre (ACCS) cyber range lab using the IXIA PerfectStorm tool. This was done to produce a mixture of very real modern regular operations and synthetic attack behaviors. TCP dump tool used to detect raw traffic of 100 GB data (e.g., Pcap files). Around nine types of attacks were included in this dataset: Worms, Fuzzers, DoS, Generic, Backdoors, Reconnaissance, Analysis, Exploits, and Shellcode. The Argus and Bro-IDS programs were used to build the class label to produce 49 features. The ground truth training and testing datasets are concatenated, around 175,341 and 82,332 records, respectively, on different forms as attack and normal. The dataset is in the form of binary classification; detailed description is shown in Figure 3.7.

3.4.2 Experimental setup

The experimental setup used in this research is Google Colab, Anaconda Environment with Python 3.8 Notebook to develop the ML models.

Categories	Training Set	Testing Set	Total dataset
Normal	56,000	37,000	93,000
Analysis	2,000	677	2,677
Backdoor	1,746	583	2,329
DoS	12,264	4,089	16,353
Exploits	33,393	11,132	44,525
Fuzzers	18,184	6,062	24,246
Generic	40,000	18,871,	40,000
Reconnaissance	10,491,	3,496	3,496
Shellcode	1,133	378	1,511
Worms	130	44	174
Total records	1,75,341	82,332	2,57,673

Figure 3.7 UNSW-NB15 dataset description.

The models are trained and tested in the hardware environment of the Windows 10 operating system with an i7 processor with GPU, 6 cores of CPU, 8GB RAM. The dataset, which was used in this work, has 257,673 total records. Running all the records sequentially takes more time. If the system has more cores, the process can be parallelized, reducing the computation cost. This system was developed at the edge of the IoT system to detect malicious activities happening in the IoT network.

3.4.3 Model evaluation metrics

The most important part of model development is evaluating the model with performance metrics. The most used metric is accuracy. Sometimes, it may not provide good results when evaluated with logarithmic loss or any extra metric. Accuracy is used to measure only the classification performance of the model. However, this is not enough to thoroughly evaluate the model. Various evaluation metrics have been used to assess the recommended model: Confusion Matrix, F1-score, Precision, Recall, and Area Under Curve (AUC). The Confusion Matrix enables to capture the complete model performance in a matrix representation as shown in Table 3.1.

Table 3.1 Confusion matrix

Actual/predicted label	Normal	Botnet
Normal	No/No (TN)	No/Yes (FN)
Botnet	Yes/No (FP)	Yes/Yes (TP)

There are two classes in a binary classification problem, Yes or No; here, "Yes" means a binary representation of 1 which means malware, "No" means a binary representation of 0 that is benign. There are four important terms in the confusion matrix:

- **True Positives (TP):** The packets which are predicted as malware (i.e., YES) and the actual output were also labelled as malware (i.e., YES).
- **True Negatives (TN):** The packets which are predicted as benign (i.e., NO) and the actual output were also labelled as benign (i.e., NO).
- **False Positives (FP):** The packets which are predicted as malware (i.e., YES) and the actual output were labelled as benign (i.e., NO).
- **False Negatives (FN):** The packets which are predicted as benign (i.e., NO) and the actual output were labelled as (i.e., YES).

The confusion matrix constitutes the basis for the metrics of precision, recall, F1-score, and accuracy, which are calculated using the following equations

$$Accuracy = \frac{TP + FP}{TP + TN + FP + FN} \tag{3.12}$$

$$Precision = \frac{TP}{TP + FP} \tag{3.13}$$

$$Recall = \frac{TP}{TP + FN} \tag{3.14}$$

$$F1 = 2 * \frac{Precision * Recall}{Precision + Recall} \tag{3.15}$$

Area Under Curve [18] is an extensively used metric for analysis of the classification problem (binary). It is a graphical representation of the plot between the true-positive rate (TPR) and the false-positive rate (FPR) ratio. It would be in the range of [0,1].

- FPR/sensitivity

$$FPR = \frac{Total\ predicted\ benign\ as\ malware}{Total\ predicted\ benign\ as\ benign + Total\ predicted\ benign\ as\ malware} \tag{3.16}$$

- TPR/specificity

$$TPR = \frac{Total\ predicted\ malware\ as\ malware}{Total\ predicted\ malware\ as\ malware + Total\ predicted\ benign\ as\ malware} \tag{3.17}$$

Table 3.2 Performance metrics of UNSW_NB 15 dataset with all and best ten features

Class	Normal		Malware	
Features/metrics	All feature	Best 10	All feature	Best 10
Accuracy	0.93	0.97	0.93	0.97
Precision	0.92	0.96	0.93	0.97
Recall	0.87	0.95	0.96	0.97
F1-Score	0.89	0.95	0.94	0.97

3.5 RESULT ANALYSIS

The model's performance is assessed using the UNSW_NB15 dataset. The performance metrics are computed using all features and the top ten features from the test dataset, as shown in Table 3.2. This selected feature model outperforms the testing with the best ten features model. When comparing all features model to the best ten features model, accuracy improves by 4%, precision improves by 5%, recall improves by 1%, and F1-score improves by 3%. The average time required for training and testing the model is shown in Table 3.3. The best ten features model requires less time for training and testing, which is four times less than the time required for all features training.

Figure 3.8 depicts the malware classification confusion matrix on the IoT network traffic dataset. Model is created using the top ten features, predicts the malware, and regular traffic is categorized more accurately. The false alert rate is higher in all features model, implying that regular traffic is misclassified as malware. The network administrator is burdened because of this misclassification. Figure 3.9 demonstrates the performance metric difference between predicting malware and regular traffic using all features and the best ten features. There will be a need to improve accuracy and eliminate false alarms; therefore, the authors used the optimization approach known as Bayesian optimization. The optimization strategy essentially improves accuracy by tuning the model's hyperparameter. Table 3.4 shows the hyperparameters of the XGBoost model. The parameters are as follows: the number of estimators, the maximum tree depth, the minimum child weight, the number of booster rounds, alpha, beta, and gamma values. The learning rate is 0.01, and the booster is a gradient booster tree. The total number of

Table 3.3 Execution time with all and best ten features

Dataset split	Training	Testing
Instances	180,371	85,033
All features execution time (average)	41 (s)	0.30 (s)
Best ten features execution time (average)	11 (s)	0.23 (s)

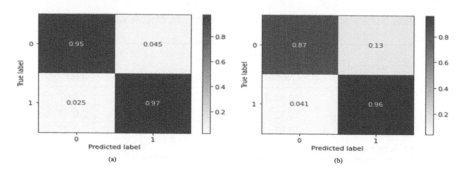

Figure 3.8 Confusion matrix of malware classification using best ten features and all features of UNSW_NBl5 dataset. (a) Confusion matrix of ten best features and (b) confusion matrix of all features.

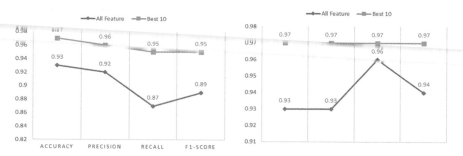

Performance Metrics of Normal Traffic   Performance Metrics of Malware Traffic

Figure 3.9 Performance metrics of proposed approach with all and best ten features.

iterations is 15, and the early stop option is enabled, which allows the model to be stopped from further processing and avoids overfitting.

It is essential to evaluate optimization techniques by performance metric, which is usually measured through CV. Twofold and fivefold CVs are used here to assess the model's performance in predicting botnet traffic in

Table 3.4 Hyperparameters tuned with Bayesian optimization

Hyperparameters	Range of values	Best value at CV = 2	Best values at CV = 5
n_estimators	(10, 100)	13	39
max_depth	(5, 40)	38	38
reg_alpha	(0.0, 0.1)	0.09419	0.06862
reg_lambda	(0.0, 0.1)	0.02411	0.06951
min_child_weight	(1, 10)	5	9
num_boost_round	(100, 1000)	999	453
gamma	(0, 10)	1.035	0.4835
early stop	20	4	2

Iteration	Target	gamma	max_depth	min_child	n_estimator	Num_boost_round	reg_alpha	reg_lamda
1	0.9955	7.372	39.05	7.198	69.22	445.6	0.05664	0.001172
2	0.9951	9.069	21.09	1.562	83.76	973.4	0.07615	0.07305
3	0.994	6.426	9.278	9.001	10.93	104.6	0.04138	0.0216
4	0.9961	1.035	38.35	5.4	13.95	999.4	0.09419	0.02411
5	0.9945	3.938	10.18	9.404	11.31	997.8	0.09555	0.07854

Figure 3.10 Bayesian optimization result of twofold CV on UNSW_NB15 dataset.

Iteration	Target	Gamma	max_depth	min_child	n_estimator	Num_boost_round	reg_alpha	reg_lamda
1	0.9915	4.61	6.841	2.082	47.04	646.1	0.09273	0.0015
2	0.9962	0.4835	38.98	9.385	39.59	453.7	0.06862	0.06951
3	0.9948	3.204	10.95	8.756	95.13	101.4	0.05575	0.08004

Figure 3.11 Bayesian optimization result of fivefold CV on UNSW_NB15 dataset.

the network. The results of the CV are shown in Figures 3.10 and 3.11 for twofold and fivefold CV, respectively.

In twofold CV, boost rounds are double to achieve higher accuracy than fivefold CV. Maximum depth is the same in both validations. Estimators are approximately 14 in twofold and 40 in fivefold CV. The maximum iteration is set as 15; the fivefold CV converged in the second iteration; twofold converged in the fourth iteration. Both CV has achieved almost the same accuracy, 99.61 and 99.62, respectively, for twofold CV and fivefold CV, respectively. Based on other hyperparameters, fivefold CV performed well and took lesser iteration.

Figure 3.12 represents ROC_AUC (Receiver-Operating Characteristic – Area Under Curve) curve for predicting the malware traffic that occurred in the IoT network. The TPR is plotted against the FPR to create the ROC-AUC. TPR and FPR values can range from 0 to 1. As a result, the ROC's maximum area is 1 for the ten best features used for predicting the botnet traffic and the maximum area is 0.983 in all features used for botnet traffic detection. The accuracy of the model increases as the area under the curve increases. It observed that our proposed approach achieves maximum value for predicting the botnet at the edge of the IoT network.

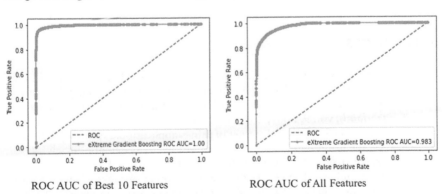

ROC AUC of Best 10 Features   ROC AUC of All Features

Figure 3.12 ROC_AUC of malware classification using the best ten features and all features of UNSW_NB15dataset.

Table 3.5 Comparison of state of art model with existing model tested on the UNSW_NB 15 dataset

Ref. papers	Algorithm	Accuracy (%)
[11]	Random Forest	88
[15]	KNN	82.66
[19]	Hybrid deep random neural network (HDRNN)	99.19
Proposed	XGBoost +RF feature selection +Bayesian optimization	99.62

3.6 CONCLUSION

Vulnerabilities in IoT devices are exploited by various malware attacks, resulting in large-scale botnet assaults. This research developed a unique technique for detecting IoT botnet-related attacks using edge computing architecture. It will reduce the computation cost, latency, and increase the availability compared to the cloud-based approach. The existence of malware at the IoT network's edge is recognized using XGBoost-supervised ensemble ML model. The random forest algorithm is used to identify the relevant attributes that contribute to detecting network traffic behavior. It uses the top ten features as input to the model, which is then compared to the all-features model. Furthermore, the model's performance is improved with hyperparameters, tuning done by the Bayesian optimization method. The final optimized model got an accuracy of 99.62%. The state of art model's accuracy is compared with other models in Table 3.5, which shows that the proposed model performs better in predicting the botnet behavior in the IoT network and reduces the computation cost by doing the process at the edge. At the same time, it declines the false alarms. The future direction of this research is to apply a hybrid approach to increase the model performance.

REFERENCES

[1] J. Asharf, N. Moustafa, H. Khurshid, E. Debie, W. Haider, and A. Wahab, 'A review of intrusion detection systems using machine and deep learning in internet of things: Challenges, solutions and future directions', *Electronics (Switzerland)*, vol. 9, no. 7, 2020, doi: 10.3390/electronics9071177.

[2] N. Mishra and S. Pandya, 'Internet of things applications, security challenges, attacks, intrusion detection, and future visions: A systematic review', *IEEE Access*, vol. 9, pp. 59353–59377, 2021, doi: 10.1109/ACCESS.2021.3073408.

[3] C. Okur and M. Dener, 'Detecting IoT Botnet Attacks Using Machine Learning Methods', *2020 International Conference on Information Security and Cryptology, ISCTURKEY 2020 - Proceedings*, pp. 31–37, 2020, doi: 10.1109/ISCTURKEY51113.2020.9307994.

[4] M. Antonakakis *et al.*, 'Understanding the Mirai Botnet This paper is included in the Proceedings of the Understanding the Mirai Botnet', *USENIX Security*, pp. 1093–1110, 2017, [Online]. Available: https://www.usenix.org/conference/usenixsecurity17/technical-sessions/presentation/antonakakis.

[5] A. O. Prokofiev, Y. S. Smirnova, and V. A. Surov, 'A Method to Detect Internet of Things Botnets', *Proceedings of the 2018 IEEE Conference of Russian Young Researchers in Electrical and Electronic Engineering, ElConRus 2018*, vol. 2018-Janua, no. January 2018, pp. 105–108, 2018, doi: 10.1109/EIConRus.2018.8317041.

[6] C. D. Mcdermott, A. V Petrovski, and F. Majdani, 'Towards Situational Awareness of Botnet Activity in the Internet of Things', *2018 International Conference On Cyber Situational Awareness, Data Analytics And Assessment (Cyber SA)*, no. 2018 International Conference On Cyber Situational Awareness, Data Analytics And Assessment (Cyber SA), pp. 1–8, doi: 10.1109/CyberSA.2018.8551408.

[7] J. Lloret, L. Parra, M. Taha, and J. Tomás, 'An architecture and protocol for smart continuous eHealth monitoring using 5G', *Computer Networks*, 2017, doi: 10.1016/j.comnet.2017.05.018.

[8] K. Dolui and S. K. Datta, 'Comparison of Edge Computing Implementations: Fog Computing, Cloudlet and Mobile Edge Computing', GIoTS 2017 – Global Internet of Things Summit, Proceedings, 2017, doi: 10.1109/GIOTS.2017.8016213.

[9] A. Sivanathan *et al.*, 'Characterizing and Classifying IoT Traffic in Smart Cities and Campuses', *2017 IEEE Conference on Computer Communications Workshops, INFOCOM WKSHPS 2017*, pp. 559–564, 2017, doi: 10.1109/INFCOMW.2017.8116438.

[10] Y. Meidan *et al.*, 'N-BaIoT: Network-based detection of IoT botnet attacks using deep autoencoders', *IEEE Pervasive Computing*, vol. 13, no. 9, pp. 1–8, 2018, [Online]. Available: http://arxiv.org/abs/1805.03409.

[11] A. Husain, A. Salem, C. Jim, and G. Dimitoglou, 'Development of an Efficient Network Intrusion Detection Model Using Extreme Gradient Boosting (XGBoost) on the UNSW-NB15 Dataset', *2019 IEEE 19th International Symposium on Signal Processing and Information Technology, ISSPIT 2019*, 2019, doi: 10.1109/ISSPIT47144.2019.9001867.

[12] D. Yin, L. Zhang, and K. Yang, 'A DDoS attack detection and mitigation with software-defined internet of things framework', *IEEE Access*, vol. 6, no. Mcc, pp. 24694–24705, 2018, doi: 10.1109/ACCESS.2018.2831284.

[13] N. Koroniotis, N. Moustafa, E. Sitnikova, and B. Turnbull, 'Towards the development of realistic botnet dataset in the internet of things for network forensic analytics: Bot-IoT dataset', *Future Generation Computer Systems*, vol. 100, pp. 779–796, 2019, doi: 10.1016/j.future.2019.05.041.

[14] R. Kozik, 'Distributed System for Botnet Traffic Analysis and Anomaly Detection', *Proceedings - 2017 IEEE International Conference on Internet of Things, IEEE Green Computing and Communications, IEEE Cyber, Physical and Social Computing, IEEE Smart Data, iThings-GreenCom-CPSCom-SmartData 2017*, vol. 2018-Janua, pp. 330–335, 2018, doi: 10.1109/iThings-GreenCom-CPSCom-SmartData.2017.55.

[15] S. M. Kasongo and Y. Sun, 'Performance analysis of intrusion detection systems using a feature selection method on the UNSW-NB15 dataset', *Journal of Big Data*, vol. 7, no. 1, 2020, doi: 10.1186/s40537-020-00379-6.

[16] P. Kumar, G. P. Gupta, and R. Tripathi, 'An ensemble learning and fog-cloud architecture-driven cyber-attack detection framework for IoMT networks', *Computer Communications*, vol. 166, no. October 2020, pp. 110–124, 2021, doi: 10.1016/j.comcom.2020.12.003.

[17] N. Koroniotis, N. Moustafa, E. Sitnikova, and B. Turnbull, 'Towards the development of realistic botnet dataset in the internet of things for network forensic analytics: Bot-IoT dataset', *Future Generation Computer Systems*, 2019, doi: 10.1016/j.future.2019.05.041.

[18] M. Hasan, M. M. Islam, M. I. I. Zarif, and M. M. A. Hashem, 'Attack and anomaly detection in IoT sensors in IoT sites using machine learning approaches', *Internet of Things*, vol. 7, p. 100059, 2019, doi: 10.1016/j.iot.2019.100059.

[19] Z. E. Huma *et al.*, 'A hybrid deep random neural network for cyberattack detection in the industrial internet of things', *IEEE Access*, vol. 9, pp. 55595–55605, 2021, doi: 10.1109/ACCESS.2021.3071766.

Chapter 4

Exploring the possibility of blockchain and smart contract-based digital certificate

P. Ravi Kumar, P. Herbert Raj, and Sharul Tajuddin

CONTENTS

4.1 INTRODUCTION

Currently, digital certificates are produced by certificate authority (CA) using X.509 standard which provides trust between a client and a server [1, 2]. This X.509 standard defines the format of the Public Key Infrastructure (PKI), and it is adapted to the internet in RFC5280 which forms the foundation for Hypertext Transfer Protocol Secure (HTTPS) [3]. A digital certificate is an electronic document that proves the authenticity of a client, device, program, server, or any entity by using cryptographic protocols and PKI [4]. It ensures that only trusted entities are allowed to connect to the network or website and allowed to access any resources. Digital certificates contain identifiable information like username, company name, department, device IP number or serial number, and the public key of the user. It binds the identity to a public key using a digital signature. Digital certificates provided by CA in the wired networks and internet environment use the concept of centralized CA [5, 6].

DOI: 10.1201/9781003269144-4

Secure Sockets Layer (SSL)/Transport Layer Security (TLS) is the de facto protocol used to secure the communication and the digital infrastructure on the internet for more than 25 years. SSL/TLS is one of the most deployed cryptographic protocols in information security [7]. Authentication, confidentiality, and integrity are the three important security services provided by TLS by using appropriate cryptographic protocols. The last version of the SSL protocol is deprecated in 2015 [8] and the TLS protocol is the current standard now. TLS is the security protocol that is used on top of the HTTP protocol to protect the end-to-end communication of applications used on the internet. This secured protocol is called HTTPS and it is shown by using a lock symbol in the URL of a browser. TLS protocols are also used on top of other application-layer protocols like File Transfer Protocol (FTP), Simple Mail Transfer Protocol (SMTP), Post Office Protocol (POP3), Internet Message Access Protocol (IMAP), and Session Initiation Protocol (SIP) to secure communication [8]. The different components that contribute to producing the X.509 TLS digital certificate are shown in Figure 4.1

Blockchain is one of the highly sought research topics in recent times due to its technical advantages and to prevent the users from double-spending. Blockchain is an immutable, peer-to-peer, distributed digital ledger, consists of multiple nodes containing replicated information, and operates in a decentralized manner. Satoshi Nakamoto developed blockchain technology (BCT) in 2008 from the work done by Stuart Haber and W. Scott Stornetta back in 1991 in their research on the timestamp on digital documents [9, 10]. Bitcoin is the first application using BCT [11]. Based on the Bitcoin framework, centralized and decentralized cryptocurrencies were developed [12]. BCT is initially started as a distributed public digital ledger for transactions using Bitcoins. The applications of BCT have been

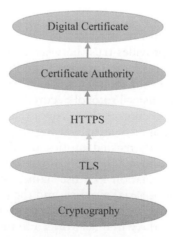

Figure 4.1 Components involved in the X.509 digital certificate.

escalating to different domains. According to Baiod et al., blockchain is getting popular in the Finance, Accounting, Insurance, Supply chain management, Energy, Advertising and Media, Legal, Real Estate, Healthcare, and Internet of Things (IoT) domains [13].

The smart contract idea was introduced by American cryptographer Nick Szabo in 1994 [14]. He also conceptualized a digital currency called Bit Gold in 1998 [15]. Smart contracts are automatically executable codes that run on top of blockchain to enable, execute, and impose an agreement between two or more parties without the need or supervision of central authority [16, 17]. In smart contracts, all the requirements, agreements, and trust relations are programmed into automated transactions without the supervision of a central authority such as real estate agencies, banks, or notaries [17, 18]. These transactions are transparent and traceable.

All the above technologies use cryptography algorithms either directly or indirectly. For example, TLS protocol uses directly symmetric and asymmetric key cryptographic algorithms. Cryptography plays an important role in a digital certificate, blockchain, and smart contract. X.509-based digital certificates use public key cryptography algorithms and digital signatures to provide three security services: message integrity, message authentication, and non-repudiation (with the support of CA) [19]. Confidentiality can be provided by using symmetric key cryptography algorithms after authentication. Hash and digital signature are the two essential cryptographic primitives used in the blockchain which provide tamper-proof global digital ledger, public verifiability, and consensus mechanism [12]. According to Wan et al., ring signature, accumulators, and zero-knowledge proofs (ZKP) are the optional cryptographic primitives used in the blockchain [12]. This research explores the possibility of using blockchain and smart contracts to provide digital certificates in the web environment. This chapter provides the following contributions, especially to young researchers in the digital certificate process and blockchain:

- Study the current X.509-based PKI, TLS digital certification process, and its weaknesses.
- Study the functionalities of CA, and problems facing the CA, and find out the possibilities of using blockchain for the TLS digital certificate process.
- Propose a framework for blockchain-based CA for TLS digital certificates.

The rest of this chapter is organized as follows: Section 4.2 provides the background study on the current method of the PKI-based CA which includes PKI, CA, digital certificate, and TLS protocol. It also introduces the smart contract. Section 4.3 provides the weaknesses and vulnerabilities of the current digital certificate ecosystem. Related works in this area are covered in Section 4.4. Section 4.5 is dedicated to our proposed blockchain-based CA. Section 4.6 analyses our proposed framework and provides the advantages, challenges, and future research areas in this field. This chapter is concluded in Section 4.7 with the future research direction.

4.2 BACKGROUND STUDY

Figure 4.2 shows the current method of validation performed by a CA when a client wants to connect securely to a website in the web environment.

The CA is a third party, and all the personal details of the client are stored in the CA that is used during validation when a client wants to connect securely to a website. The validation is done using PKI as per the X.509 framework in the form of a digital certificate. PKI, CA and digital certificate, and TLS are the three important entities in the current HTTPS ecosystem.

4.2.1 Public key infrastructure

Currently, PKI is the key entity in providing secured online communication using the internet, email, social networking, cloud computing, IoT, and many others which rely on certificate-based authentication [20]. X.509-based PKI consists of five important components: end entity, CA, registration authority (RA), validation authority (VA), and certificate revocation list (CRL) [21]. PKI manages policies regarding the digital certificate and allows using of the correct public key cryptography algorithms [20]. PKI is often called PKIX because it uses the X.509 standard of the Internet Engineering Task Force (IETF) [21]. CAs are the authorized third party to issue a digital certificate based on the X.509 standards and authenticate the validity of the certificate holder. When digital certificates are issued for a website, it is called an SSL/TLS certificate because it uses the SSL/TLS protocol (the current standard is TLS). An empirical analysis of PKI problems and the methodologies to improve the problems was conducted in [22].

Client   CERTIFICATE   Server
                       AUTHORITY

Figure 4.2 CA validation of a website.

4.2.2 Certificate authorities and digital certificates

CA is the key component in the PKI framework which issues digital certificates, authenticates certificates, and manages the issued certificates, including the revocation of the certificates [23]. CAs act as a trusted organization (third party) between the certificate holder and the other party relying upon the certificate [24]. According to Durumeric et al., modern operating systems and browsers are shipped with trusted certificates called root certificates [24]. The root authorities can assign and sign intermediate authorities and so on to create a chain of trust in CA. If any of the chains in the trust is compromised or weak then it can jeopardize the trust. There are thousands of CAs currently in the market and they provide digital certificates. The format of the certificate is based on the X.509 standard by the International Telecommunication Union (ITU) and that is why it is also called X.509 certificate. CA has five important functions. They are:

- Entity verification.
- Certificate issue.
- Certificate validation.
- Certificate revocation.
- Certificate monitoring and maintenance.

The main objective of our research is how to provide the above functions using blockchain and smart contract technologies and propose a framework based on these technologies. There are eight types of digital certificates based on PKI [25]: TLS certificates, TLS client certificates, code signing certificates, email certificates or S/MIME certificates, Europay, MasterCard, and Visa (EMV) certificates, qualified certificates, chain certificates, and self-signed certificates. The TLS certificate has three types of certificates: domain validation (DV), organizational validation (OV), and extended validation (EV) [26]. Figure 4.3 shows the current market share of the top six certificate providers [27]:

Figure 4.3 Current market share of the top certificate providers.

4.2.3 TLS protocols

TLS protocols are used to secure communication using cryptographic primitives. TLS protocols are under constant attack because it is one of the most popular security protocols used in business and commercial applications. TLS protocol provides three important security services: authentication, confidentiality, and integrity using cryptographic primitives. Both symmetric key and asymmetric key cryptography protocols are used by TLS to provide the three security services. The current version of TLS, version 1.3, uses authenticated encryption rather than just encryption to authenticate the encrypted message to avoid replay attacks. It does not have backward compatibility with the older versions of TLS/SSL. TLS 1.3 has reduced the number of supported cipher suites to five to mitigate the attacks [28]. Even though TLS 1.3 mitigates many security attacks, it is susceptible to attacks like the Selfie attack [29] and Bleichenbacher attack [30].

4.2.4 Smart contract

Most of the smart contract platforms support irreversible, but platforms like Hyperledger Fabric support updatable smart contracts [18]. There are plentiful smart contract platforms available on the market and Ethereum stands tall among them due to its open source, security features, standards, support, and decentralization [31]. Ethereum is a Turing-complete language, and it has its advantages and disadvantages [32]. According to Singh et al., there are numerous smart contract programming languages; some are domain-specific languages such as Solidity on Ethereum, and other general-purpose programming languages like Java and Go are also used to write smart contract programs [18]. Parizi et al. did an empirical vulnerability study on the usability and security of Solidity, Pact, and Liquidity smart contract languages implemented and compared them [33]. According to them, Solidity did better among the three. More comparisons of smart contracts can be found in [34–36] with pros and cons.

4.3 THREATS AND VULNERABILITIES IN THE DIGITAL CERTIFICATE ECOSYSTEM

PKI, CA, and TLS are the three important components or entities involved in the digital certificate ecosystem. Vulnerabilities can occur in the TLS ecosystem due to CA, TLS protocols, and the cryptography algorithms used. A complete study of the PKI and its known incidents was presented in [37]. There is a detailed study on the TLS ecosystem, and its security flaws are given in the thesis by [8].

One of the largest commercial CA providers, Comodo CA, was hacked in 2011 and forced to issue fraudulent certificates [38]. DigiNotar CA from

Dutch was compromised in July 2011 and issued 531 fraudulent certificates, including google.com [38]. The challenges of centralized CA are listed in [6]. According to this chapter, transparency and security are the major concerns with centralized CA. The important challenge of the centralized CA is identity management because all the user's information related to identity management is with them, and if the organization (CA) is compromised, all the user's information under the organization is also compromised [39]. An organization can leak the information if they wish due to the lack of standards and security auditing currently in the CA process. CA-based PKI has three main challenges: a trusted third-party, cost, and a single point of failure [40]. There is a weakness in the validation of the domains by the CA because the CA issues a certificate to any domain without verifying the actual relationship between the domain and the domain owner [41]. Domain validation is done by sending an email to the CA with an authentication link. Table 4.1 summarizes the weaknesses/vulnerabilities of CA and the TLS protocol [20, 29, 42–47].

4.4 RELATED WORK

There are many research initiatives to find alternative ways to produce TLS digital certificates to mitigate security and privacy issues. Jayaraman et al. proposed a two-party certificate signing using Elliptic Curve Digital Signature Algorithm (ECDSA) to implement decentralized CA [44]. Rastegari et al. proposed a Certificate Less Designated Verifier Signature (CL-DVS) to overcome the PKI and ID-based settings [48]. Certificate Transparency (CT) by Google has helped to detect fraudulent certificates and the certificate logs are accessible by auditors and monitors [49]. Kubilay et al. proposed a blockchain-based PKI model with certificate transparency called CertLedger to eradicate the split-word attacks and provide transparency in certificate issues and revocation [38]. An enhanced validation framework for PKI is proposed which studies the current PKI validation process and suggested an enhanced method which includes the CA [50]. A blockchain-based PKI for the web is proposed by Fredriksson using a custom federation blockchain relying on an honest majority [51]. A decentralized PKI transparency (DPKIT) is proposed by Boyen et al. to rectify the PKI trust issues without changing the underlying hierarchical PKI [52]. Hwang et al. proposed a blockchain-based semi-decentralized PKI architecture that can prevent a single point of failure [53]. Adja et al. proposed a blockchain-based certificate revocation and status verification based on *Namecoin*, implemented, and compared with other blockchain-based revocation methods [54]. Eisenstadt et al. developed a Covid-19 antibody/vaccination certificate using a decentralized and consortium Ethereum-based blockchain [55].

An experimental open-source blockchain-based technology called *Namecoin* claims that it can offer solutions in identity management (one of the problems

Table 4.1 Summary of vulnerabilities in the digital certificate ecosystem

Entity	Weaknesses/attack	Description
CA	• Self-signed wildcard certificates	Lead to host malicious websites and phishing
	• Forged CA certificate	Can compromise the trust and masquerade attack
	• CA compromise	Can lead to man-in-the-middle attacks
	• Fake CA	Can lead to issue of fake certificates and lead to man-in-the-middle attacks
	• Delay in CRL issuing	Can lead to a fake server
	• Expired certificate	Can lead to DNS spoofing and man-in-the-middle attacks
	• Single point of failure	This occurs when the CA's private key is compromised
SSL/TLS	• SSL renegotiation attack	Due to the vulnerability in the SSL renegotiation procedure, can lead to HTTPS connection hijack
	• SSL/TLS downgrade attacks	Padding Oracle On Downgraded Legacy Encryption, if TLS connection fails then it will try to connect using SSL (SSL downgrade)
	• POODLE	
	• FREAK	Factoring RSA export keys, due to weak export cipher suites
	• Logjam attack	Attacker can intercept an HTTPS connection and downgrade to a 512-bit connection
	• Truncation attack	An attacker can block the user's logout request and make the account active without the user's knowledge
	• Sweet32 attack	This attack happens due to the 64-bit block cipher used in the CBC mode
	• Man-in-the-middle attack	Many ways, MiTM attack can be done, for example compromising the SSL/TLS private keys
		It is like a MiTM attack and collects user credentials and payment-related data
	• SSL stripping attacks	Also called session or cookie hijacking
	• SSL hijacking attacks	
	• SSL/TLS vulnerability attacks	Browser Exploit Against SSL/TLS, is a type of MiTM attack, TLS 1.0, exploits the vulnerability of CBC cipher
	• BEAST attack	Compression Ratio Info-Leak Made Easy, exploits the compression algorithm
	• CRIME attack	Browser Reconnaissance and Exfiltration via Compression of Hypertext, exploits the compression mechanism of HTTPS
	• BREACH attack	Decrypting RSA with Obsolete and Weakened Encryption, happened in SSL 2.0
	• DROWN	Happened due to a flaw in using Open SSL, a data breach
	• HEARTBLEED	It is a type of reflection attack in TLS 1.3, a kind of eavesdropping and MiTM attack, breaking the mutual authentication
	• Selfie attack	
	• Raccoon attack	In TLS 1.2 and below, the type of timing side-channel attack

with the current CA) and domain name system (DNS) [56]. There is another blockchain-based decentralized technology called REMME that provides solutions to issue SSL certificates for smartphones and other IoT devices [57].

4.5 PROPOSED FRAMEWORK

Figure 4.4 shows our simple model of the proposed blockchain-based digital certificate process. In our proposed methodology, BCT along with smart contract does the role of CA.

This research proposes a blockchain-based digital certificate issue, verification, and validation process to avoid data breaches and information leaks by the CAs either accidentally or deliberately. Apart from that, this proposed method can avoid most of the CA's weaknesses mentioned in Table 4.1.

Figure 4.5 shows the general process of digital certificate issues and verification using blockchain. When an end entity wants to get a certificate, it can contact a blockchain-based CA. The CA will verify the identity of the end entity and generate a private and public key pair. The CA returns the certificate (signed by the CA's private key) with the end entity's identity and the public key to the entity. The private key is kept confidentially by the end entity. Users also can generate private and public key pairs using tools and send certificate signing request (CSR) to CAs.

Our proposed blockchain-based CA certificate issue and validation framework are shown in Figure 4.6. Only a sample of three nodes is shown in the framework. There are five important sequences of steps in this proposed method. The first one is to define all the requirements and the conditions of the smart contract. It is used to establish the trust between identified parties (CA) and the anonymous parties (end entities). In the second step, the end entities like domains can request a digital certificate. The third step is to verify the identity of the end entity which is the same entity that requests the certificate. The fourth step is to issue the certificate if the end entity is found genuine after verification. The fifth step is that when the relying parties want to have a secure connection with end entities, they can check the validity of their certificate. This is the most challenging part

Client   Server

Figure 4.4 Blockchain-based digital certificate.

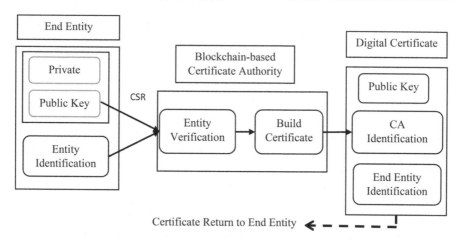

Figure 4.5 The general process of a blockchain-based digital certificate issuance.

because it involves many levels of validation, the validity of the signature, time validity, genuineness of the certificate, and improper use of the certificate. Currently, most browsers keep all the popular CAs root certificates in their trust store.

Digital certificates are added to all the nodes in the blockchain in the form of transactions. All the nodes are having a copy of all the digital certificates. In this way, it provides resilience in the form of fault tolerance.

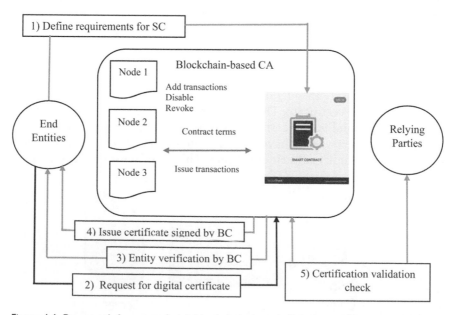

Figure 4.6 Proposed framework of blockchain-based digital certificate issuance and validation.

Table 4.2 Comparing the current CA functions with the proposed blockchain technologies

Current CA functions	Equivalent blockchain functions
End entity verification	Hybrid blockchain can be used to verify the end entity
Digital certificate issuance	Decentralized blockchain with smart contract
Certificate validation	Decentralized blockchain with smart contract
Certificate revocation	Decentralized blockchain with smart contract
Certificate monitoring and maintenance	Decentralized blockchain with smart contract

Different types of digital certificates are issued depending on the nature of the business. Extended validation requires a thorough checking of the end entity because it requires the highest level of authentication like banks, shopping carts, and login pages. This proposed blockchain-based validation has advantages in terms of security, data protection, transparency, no single point of failure, and less fees. Based on this research, a public hybrid blockchain is more appropriate for implementation.

4.6 RESEARCH OUTCOME

Based on our research, issuing digital certificates through blockchain is possible. Table 4.2 shows the important functions currently provided by CA and the proposed blockchain technologies.

Only for entity verification, a hybrid blockchain approach is required. Table 4.3 summarizes our research in terms of benefits, challenges, and the areas where more research is required to make blockchain-based CA in real use.

4.7 CONCLUSION AND FUTURE RESEARCH

We have initiated and studied the current digital certificate issued by CA based on the X.509 standards. In this, X.509-based PKI framework is studied, and the functions of CA are identified. The cryptographic support and the security services provided by TLS protocols are analyzed. Weaknesses/vulnerabilities of the current digital certificate process are summarized with a focus on the CA and the TLS protocol. This proposed framework is presented and the equivalent blockchain technologies that provide the CA functionalities are identified. The advantages, challenges, and future research requirements in this area are also summarized. Based on our research, blockchain along with smart contracts can be used to provide the services of CA. A hybrid public blockchain can be used for the implementation because public blockchains provide transparency and decentralization and the hybrid technology is proposed to verify the end

Table 4.3 Advantages, challenges, and areas of more research required in blockchain-based CA

Advantages	Challenges	More research requires
Avoid single point of failure	Scalability	Extended validation of domains
Immutable	Expensive computational power	Validation of the chain of trust
Eliminate rogue certificate issues by CAs	Standards are lacking	Certificate revocation needs to be explored
Certificate Transparency (CT)	Security challenges	Forks handling (if it doesn't handle properly can lead to security attacks)
Reduce certificate frauds	Legalizing blockchain because of the illegal activities of cryptocurrencies	Type of consensus algorithm for this blockchain-based CA
No third party is involved so MiTM type of attacks can be avoided		Backward compatibility
Supports auditability		
Automation of certificate issuance, validation and revocation, and cheaper		
Resiliency because blockchain supports fault tolerance		

entities in a non-decentralized way. Still, more research is required in the areas like consensus algorithm, extended validation of domain, and entity verification. Ethereum is to be used for implementation purpose because it is an open-source platform with lots of development support.

REFERENCES

[1] Chokhani, S., & Ford, W [Internet]. Internet X.509 Public Key Infrastructure Certificate Policy and Certification Practices Framework. *RFC2527*; 1999; [cited 2021 Nov 2]. Available from: https://datatracker.ietf.org/doc/html/rfc2527.

[2] Berkowsky, J.A., & Hayajneh, T. Security Issues with Certificate Authorities. *Proceedings of the 2017 IEEE 8th Annual Ubiquitous Computing, Electronics and Mobile Communication Conference (UEMCON)*; 2021 Nov 03; New York, USA. 2017.

[3] Gruschka, N., Lo Iacono, L., & Sorge, C. Analysis of the Current State in Website Certificate Validation. Security and Communication Networks. Wiley Online Library, United States, 7, 2014; 865–877. https://onlinelibrary.wiley.com/doi/epdf/10.1002/sec.799.

[4] Fortinet. [Internet]. What Is a Digital Certificate; [cited 2021 Nov 2]. Available from: https://www.fortinet.com/resources/cyberglossary/digital-certificates.

[5] Masdari, M., Jabbehdari, S., Ahmadi, M.R., Hashemi, S.M., Bagherzadeh, J., & Khadem-Zadeh, A. A Survey and Taxonomy of Distributed Certificate Authorities in *Mobile Ad-hoc Networks. EURASIP Journal on Wireless Communications and Networking.* 2011; 112: 1–12.

[6] Habr [Internet]. PKI Decentralization: Proposed Approaches to Security Improvement. ENCRY; 2019. [cited 2021 Nov 03]. Available from: https://habr.com/en/post/473548/.

[7] Madala, D.S.V., Jhanwar, M.P., & Chattopadhyay, A. Certificate Transparency using Blockchain. IACR. 2018. https://eprint.iacr.org/2018/1232.pdf.

[8] Levillain, O. A Study of the TLS Ecosystem. [Doctoral Dissertation]. France: *Institut National des Télécommunications*; 2016. https://tel.archives-ouvertes.fr/tel-01454976/document.

[9] Iredale, G. [Internet]. History of Blockchain Technology: A Detailed Guide. 101Blockchains; [cited 2021 Nov 4]. Available from: https://101blockchains.com/history-of-blockchain-timeline/.

[10] Zhang, R., Xui, R., & Liu L. Security and Privacy on Blockchain. *ACM Computing Surveys*, 2019; 1(1): 1–35. https://dl.acm.org/doi/pdf/10.1145/3316481.

[11] Capece, G., Ghiron, N.L., & Pasquale, F. Blockchain Technology: Redefining Trust for Digital Certificates. *Sustainability MDPI*, 2020; 12(21): 8952. https://doi.org/10.3390/su12218952.

[12] Wang, L., Shen, X., Li, J., Shao, J., & Yang, Y. Cryptographic Primitives in Blockchains. *Journal of Network and Computer Applications.* Elsevier, 2019; 127: 43–58.

[13] Baiod, W., Light, J., & Mahanti, A. Blockchain Technology and its Applications Across Multiple Domains: A Survey. *Journal of International Technology and Information Management.* 2021; 29(4): 78–119. https://scholarworks.lib.csusb.edu/jitim/vol29/iss4/4.

[14] Petersson, D. [Internet]. How Smart Contracts Started and Where They Are Heading. (Forbes.com); 2018. [cited 2021 Nov 5]. Available from: https://www.forbes.com/sites/davidpetersson/2018/10/24/how-smart-contracts-started-and-where-they-are-heading/?sh=615e51a837b6.

[15] Cointelegraph. [Internet]. What Are Smart Contracts? A Beginner Guide to Automated Agreements; [cited 2021 Nov 5]. Available from: https://cointelegraph.com/ethereum-for-beginners/what-are-smart-contracts-a-beginners-guide-to-automated-agreements.

[16] Buterin, V. [Internet]. A Next Generation Smart Contract & Decentralized Application Platform. 2014; [cited 2021 Nov 6]. Available from: https://blockchainlab.com/pdf/Ethereum_white_paper-a_next_generation_smart_contract_and_decentralized_application_platform-vitalik-buterin.pdf.

[17] Khan, N.H., Loukil, F., Ghedira-Guegan, C., Benkhelifa, E., & Bani-Hani, A. Blockchain Smart Contracts: Applications, Challenges and Future Trends. *Peer-to-Peer Networking and Applications*, 2021; 14: 2901–2925. https://doi.org/10.1007/s12083-021-01127-0.

[18] Singh, A., Parizi, R.M., Zhang, Q., Choo, K.W.R., & Dehghantanha, A. Blockchain Smart Contracts Formalization: Approaches and Challenges to Address Vulnerabilities. *Computers & Security.* Elsevier, 2020; 88: 101654. https://doi.org/10.1016/j.cose.2019.101654.

[19] Stallings, W. Cryptography and Network Security: Principles and Practice (7th ed.). Pearson Publishers, United States; 2017, 25–30.

[20] Talamo, M., Arcieri, F., Dimitri, A., & Schunck, S.H. A Blockchain Based PKI Validation System based on Rare Events Management. *Future Internet, MDPI*. 2020; 12(2): 40. https://doi.org/10.3390/fi12020040.

[21] Cooper, D., Santesson, S., Farrell, S., Boeyen, S., Housley, R., & Polk, W. [Internet]. Internet X.509 Public Key Infrastructure Certificate and Certificate Revocation List (SRL) Profile. RFC5280. 2008; [cited 2021 Nov 7]. Available from: https://www.rfc-editor.org/rfc/pdfrfc/rfc5280.txt.pdf.

[22] Holz, R.G. Empirical Analysis of Public Key Infrastructures and Investigation of Improvements. [Doctoral Dissertations]. Germany: Technischen Universität München; 2013. https://d-nb.info/1058450808/34.

[23] Kehe, W., Wei, C. & Yueguang, G. The Research and Implementation of the Authentication Technology based on Digital Certificates. *Proceedings of the 4th International Conference on Computational and Information Sciences*; 2021 Nov 7; Chongqing, China; 2012.

[24] Durumeric, Z., Kasten, J., Bailey, M., & Halderman, A.J. Analysis of the HTTPS Certificate Ecosystem. *Proceedings of the 13th Internet Measurement Conference (IMC' 13)*; 2021 Nov 7; Barcelona, Spain; 2013.

[25] Arun K.L. [Internet]. What is a PKI Certificate? What Are the Different Types of PKI Certificates? TheSecMaster; [cited 2021 Nov 7]. Available from: https://www.thesecmaster.com/what-are-the-different-types-of-pki-certificates/.

[26] Digicert [Internet]. How to Choose the Right Type of TLS/SSL Certificate; [cited 2021 Nov 8]. Available from: https://www.digicert.com/blog/how-to-choose-the-right-type-of-tls-ssl-certificate.

[27] W3techs. [Internet]. Usage Statistics of SSL Certificate Authorities for Websites; [cited 2021 Nov 10]. Available from: https://w3techs.com/technologies/overview/ssl_certificate.

[28] Warburton, D. [Internet]. The 2021 TLS Telemetry Report. (F5 Labs). Application Threat Intelligence; [cited 2021 Nov 12]. Available from: https://www.f5.com/labs/articles/threat-intelligence/the-2021-tls-telemetry-report.

[29] Drucker, N., & Gueron, S. [Internet]. Selfie: Reflections on TLS 1.3 with PSK. IACR; 2019. [cited 2021 Nov 15]. Available from: https://eprint.iacr.org/2019/347.pdf.

[30] Jager, T., Schwenk, J., & Somorovsky, J. On the Security of TLS 1.3 and QUIC Against Weaknesses in PKCS#1 v1.5 Encryption. *Proceedings of the 22nd ACM SIGSAC Conference on Computer and Communication Security*; 2021 Nov 16; New York, USA; 2015.

[31] Crunch, C. [Internet]. The Top Five Smart Contract Platforms. Medium.com; [cited 2021 Nov 17]. Available from: https://medium.com/coinmonks/the-top-five-smart-contract-platforms-november-2021-72a9128a2b4f.

[32] Rolfe, T. [Internet]. Turing Completeness and Smart Contract Security. Medium.com; [cited 2021 Nov 17]. Available from: https://medium.com/kadena-io/turing-completeness-and-smart-contract-security-67e4c41704c.

[33] Parizi, R.M., Amritraj, & Dehghantanha, A. Smart Contract Programming Languages on Blockchains: An Empirical Evaluation of Usability and Security. In: Chen, S. et al. editor. Blockchain –ICBC, Lecture Notes in Computer Science, Springer, Cham; 2018. p. 75–91.

[34] Xu, Y., Chong, H.Y., & Chi, M. Review of Smart Contract Applications in Various Industries: A Procurement Perspective. Advances in Civil Engineering. Hindawi, 2021: 5530755: 1–25. https://doi.org/10.1155/2021/5530755.

[35] Bartoletti M., & Pompianu L. An Empirical Analysis of Smart Contracts: Platforms, Applications, and Design Patterns. In: Brenner M. et al. editors. Financial Cryptography and Data Security: Lecture Notes in Computer Science, Springer, Cham; 2017. p. 494–509.

[36] Hu, B., Zhang, Z., Liu, J., Yin, J., Lu, R., & Lin., X. A Comprehensive Survey on Smart Contract Construction and Execution: Paradigms, Tools, and Systems. *Patterns, Cell Press*, 2021; 2(2): 1–51. https://doi.org/10.1016/j.patter.2020.100179.

[37] Serrano, N., Hadan, H., & Camp, L.J. A Complete Study of P.K.I. (PKI's Known Incidents). *Proceeding s of the 47th Research Conference on Communications, Information and Internet Policy*; 2021 Nov 18; Washington, USA; 2019.

[38] Kubilay, M.Y., Kiraz, M.S., & Mantar, H.A. CertLedger: A New PKI Model with Certificate Transparency Based on Blockchain. *Computers and Security*. Elsevier, 2019; 85: 333–352.

[39] Soltani, S.Z. Improving PKI – Solution Analysis in Case of CA Compromisation. [Master's Dissertations]. Utrecht, Netherlands: Utrecht University; 2013.

[40] Salman, T., Zolanvari, M., Erbad, A., Jain, R., & Samaka, M. Security Services Using Blockchain: A State of the Art Survey. *IEEE Communications Surveys and Tutorials*, 2019; 21(1): 858–880. https://ieeexplore.ieee.org/stamp/stamp.jsp?tp=&arnumber=8428402.

[41] Internet Society [Internet]. TLS Basics; [cited 2021 Nov 20]. Available from: https://www.internetsociety.org/deploy360/tls/basics/.

[42] Venafi. [Internet]. Common SSL Attacks: SSL & TLS Key Vulnerability; [cited 2021 Nov 21]. Available from: https://www.venafi.com/education-center/ssl/common-ssl-attacks.

[43] Teiss. [Internet]. What Happens When a Certificate Authority is Compromised? Teiss; [cited 2021 Nov 22]. Available from: https://www.teiss.co.uk/what-happens-when-a-certificate-authority-is-compromised/.

[44] Jayaraman, B., Li, H., & Evans, D. [Internet]. Decentralized Certificate Authorities. Cornell University Research Publications; 2017 [cited 2021 Nov 23]. Available from: https://arxiv.org/abs/1706.03370.

[45] Ikbal, A. [Internet]. Reduce Your Risks: SSL/TLS Certificate Weaknesses; [cited 2021 Nov 24]. Available from: https://perspectiverisk.com/multiple-ssl-tls-certificate-weaknesses/.

[46] Davies, N. [Internet]. Recent SSL/TLS Certificate Attacks Show the Importance of Updating Your Encryption Protocols; [cited 2021 Nov 25]. Available from: https://www.globalsign.com/en/blog/recent-ssltls-certificate-attacks-show-importance-updating-your-encryption-protocols.

[47] Encryption Consulting [Internet]. What Kind of Attack Does SSL Prevent?; [cited 2021 Nov 25]. Available from: https://www.encryptionconsulting.com/education-center/ssl-attacks/.

[48] Rastegari, P., Susilo, W. & Dakhilalian, M. Certificateless Designated Verifier Signature Revisited: Achieving a Concrete Scheme in the Standard Model. *International Journal of Information Security*, 2019; 18: 619–635. https://doi.org/10.1007/s10207-019-00430-5.

[49] Laurie, B., Langley, A., & Kasper, E. [Internet]. Certificate Transparency. RFC6962. 2013; [cited 2021 Nov 27]. Available from: https://datatracker.ietf.org/doc/html/rfc6962.

[50] Danquah, P., & Adade H.K. Public Key Infrastructure: An Enhanced Validation Framework. *Journal of Information Security*, 2020; 11(4): 241–260. doi: 10.4236/jis.2020.114016.

[51] Fredriksson, B. A Distributed Public Key Infrastructure for the Web Backed by a Blockchain. [Master's Dissertations]. Stockholm, Sweden: KTH Royal Institute of Technology; 2017.

[52] Boyen, X., Herath, U., McKague, M., & Stebila, D. Associative Blockchain for Decentralized PKI Transparency. Cryptography, MDPI, 2021, 5: 14: 1–27. https://doi.org/10.3390/cryptography5020014.

[53] Hwang, G.H., Chang, T.K., & Chiang, H.W. A Semidecentralized PKI System Based on Public Blockchains with Automatic Indemnification Mechanism. *Security and Communication Networks*. Hindawi, 2021: 7400466. https://doi.org/10.1155/2021/7400466.

[54] Adja, Y.C.E., Hammi, B., Serhrouchni, A., & Zeadally, S. A Blockchain-based Certificate Revocation Management and Status Verification System. *Computers and Security*, Elsevier, 2021; 104: 102209.

[55] Eisenstadt, M., Ramachandran, M., Chowdhury, N., Third, A., & Domingue, J. Covid-19 Antibody Test/Vaccination Certification: There's an App for That. *IEEE Open Journal of Engineering in Medicine and Biology*, 2020; 1: 148–155. doi: 10.1109/OJEMB.2020.2999214.

[56] Namecoin [Internet]. Decentralized All the Things; [cited 2021 Nov 28]. Available from: https://www.namecoin.org/.

[57] Curtis, H. [Internet]. Hype Aside: Can Blockchain Really Replace SSL?; [cited 2021 Nov 29]. Available from: https://www.venafi.com/blog/hype-aside-can-blockchain-really-replace-ssl.

Chapter 5

Senso Scale

A framework to preserve privacy over cloud using sensitivity range

Niharika Singh, Ishu Gupta,
and Ashutosh Kumar Singh

CONTENTS

5.1 INTRODUCTION

According to a *New York Times* survey, it was found that children of today's generation are technically becoming smarter and extraordinary. In the early stage, they urge to handle electronic devices, and as some years pass they start using the internet. They don't hesitate to share their personal information like name, contact, social security number (if they know in case) on social networking. Unawareness regarding the multiple positive

DOI: 10.1201/9781003269144-5

and negative issues from sharing personal information may lead to some severe changes for the kid or the family. Such examples render us to initiate methods for protecting data and providing convenient user accessibility. According to the survey, a very popular social networking website surpassed 1 billion users giving a rush to big data content. Awareness of data privacy allows a minimum age of 15 years to sign in to the social networking [1].

In today's era of distributed network communication, sharing, computing, and storing data through online resources has become common [2]. Thus, in the field of network security, one of the biggest issues is preserving data privacy [3]. Due to third party involvement in cloud computing, outsourcing a huge amount of data to reduce costs and ease of access makes privacy perseverance a crucial task. Data is stored as private or public for which various searching measures are available. Confidential data is usually stored using encryption techniques so that only authenticated users can access respective data [4, 5].

Today, being an emerging strategy big data has set a trend on a worldwide stage. When compared to machine learning, small data, microdata, computerized database, and many more modern technologies, big data inspires to handle massive amounts. Big data can produce diverse and analytic information for further proceedings [6]. This systematic approach to handle a large amount of data is largely dependent on the combination of various tools, technology, and algorithms. It handles raw data for tangible results and also needs to assign authorized accessibility to the users (defining who may use what data) [7]. The data sharing tendency provides us many opportunities and benefits, but sometimes it may become a way for intruders to alter, leak, or regenerate private data. That is why data owners and other cloud communities demand high levels of privacy that can be conducted by following privacy-preserving algorithms and effective schemes [8, 9]. Big data ensures the presence of massive variability in the data and introduces a high level of complexity in data handling. To solve such issues and fully understand the concept of data sensitiveness, the cloud requires a more promising and exponent technique. Hence, the proposed work concentrates to encourage data sensitivity, effectiveness, and analysis privileges [10, 11]. Now, the issue is that all kinds of important/sensitive data are measured at the same standard. If we decide to use the strongest privacy algorithm for preserving privacy, it would create information loss much more than required. In that case, information utility helps users in determining data authorization [12]. Until one would not know how sensitive the data is, it is quite difficult to predict and provide "data accessibility" authority to various users. In concern, we focus on dividing the data sensitivity into parts and set the information utility level. Thus, this chapter helps in dividing the data defined as the sensitivity scale to measure data sensitivity with logical calculations that are further used to preserve privacy using privacy perseverance architecture.

5.2 KEY CONTRIBUTION

5.2.1 Sensitiveness accessibility

In [9], authors have designed a privacy-aware framework to address the challenges of data privacy with the support of sensitive data segregation on hybrid clouds. They have modeled data sensitivity in a dynamic and comprehensive manner using a set of tagging mechanisms by including (a) coarse-grained file-level tagging (b) fine-grained line-level tagging (c) temporal and spatial tagging. In some other work, the authors divided the data sensitivity range into two categories and recommended over data criticality at three levels. The measures were defined at the institution level for the electronic resource classification [13]. Sai Teja Peddinti and authors used behavioral data to determine the content sensitivity, in [11], via clues given by users to know what information they consider to be private, public, or sensitive through their parametric values. They have performed a large-scale analysis for user anonymity choices during activity on a question-answer site, Quora.

The authors assure that findings validate the viability of the proposed approach toward automatic assessment of sensitiveness and also advance machine learning over behavioral data that can be effectively used to develop product features to help keep users safe. The design was introduced to estimate global sensitivity indices from the given simulation input-output data at some minimum computational cost. The problem solution is based on the L1-norm that formally defines corresponding consistency theorems. The strategy is applied in the identification of key drivers of the uncertainty in complex computer code developed at NASA to assess the risk of lunar space missions. The symmetry result was introduced enabling global sensitivity measure estimation to datasets that were produced externally [14, 15].

5.2.2 Filtering and validation-related privacy schemes

Many novel models have been proposed to validate improvement in privacy protection from generality and other similarity attacks, likewise, deployment of biometric-based verification systems, the evolution of privacy algorithms, or proposing some trust-awareness privacy frameworks. Though encryption not only helps in protecting the confidentiality of user data but also initiates a challenging problem in practically efficient secure search functioning over the encrypted data. Getting inspired by the problem [16], Wenhai Sun proposed a multi-dimensional algorithm to enhance searching privacy. Further, two secure index schemes, the Ciphertext model and the known background model, were also proposed meeting stringent privacy requirements under the strong threat models. Table 5.1 gives a technical description of three famous encryption algorithms comparing the best functioning and also what kind of attacks can be seen when the algorithms

Table 5.1 Modified cryptography algorithms comparison

Algorithm	Modified version release	Secure bit size	Superiority over	Possible attacks
Modified RSA	2012	>2048	Encryption	Timing Attack
DSA	1991	>2048/3072	Decryption	Key Recovery
Modified ELGamal	2011	4096	Decryption	Man-in-middle

are applied [17]. Keeping in mind the advancement of data storage and privacy communications, modified versions of encryption algorithms are supposed to be preferred for evaluation and simulation over the latest configured cloud environments [18].

To take care of the privacy issue in the cloud architecture, a semi-administered privacy-preserving clustering algorithm is proposed. The distribution of original data is changed using the multiplicative perturbation technique. This results in preserving privacy while providing high availability of data [19]. Table 5.2 gives a reliable comparison of some famous hashing algorithms. Authentication mechanisms are used lately to protect the data from unauthorized access. An authentication model is proposed using Petri Nets. It authenticates tags and readers in the cloud environment [20, 21]. Strong elliptical curve cryptography (ECC) is used to protect the server. The proposed model is robust to handle different attacks such as replay and tracking attacks, eavesdropping, and cloning [21].

To take care privacy of the medical records is the biggest concern in cloud architecture. However, this risk can be reduced by applying methods such as maintaining the uniqueness of the records up to a certain level [22]. Data exchange-based anonymous authentication is considered a must for organizations that deal with data sharing. A protocol for anonymous just-in-time secure data exchange is proposed using pairing-based cryptography. A session key is produced dynamically for each data exchange session. The researchers also tested their proposed model against diverse attacks, for example, target-oriented and message manipulation attacks [23]. More unique records will provide high successful chances of data leakage. Re-identification risks are also considered a measure by many researchers

Table 5.2 Available hash algorithms comparison

Algorithm	Version release	Digest size	Rounds	Max. message size	Possible attacks
SHA-0	1993	160	80	$2^{64}-1$	Collision
SHA-1	1995	160	64 or 80	$2^{64}-1$	Collision
SHA-2	2001	224, 384, 512	24	$2^{128}-1$	Pre-image
MD5	2009	128	80	$2^{64}-1$	Differential collision
SHA-3	2014	512, Arbitrary	64	Unlimited	Not yet found

to preserve the privacy of the EMRs. It proposed a combination of ano-nymization techniques such as l-Diversity, t-Closeness [24], k-Anonymity [25], and δ-Presence is applied through the ARX anonymization tool. One of its developments is attribute-based encryption (ABE) that is utilized to scramble the Electronic Health Record (EHR) information and metadata with the help of private and public keys [26, 27]. A Trusted Authority (TA) manages these keys with access rights to all encoded EHRs. Symmetric key cryptography is used to encrypt the data. To provide access to these keys with limited users, ABE is used. A trust-aware privacy evaluation framework was proposed, called TAPE. It aims to address information pri-vacy threatened by social networking. It is a function of users' privacy risk awareness that also protects personal information related to their nearby profiles with outperforming strategies. Hence, to ensure sensitivity and pri-vacy in the cloud, some new protection methods are required to be imple-mented for the betterment of accessibility issues [28].

5.3 SYSTEM ARCHITECTURE AND DESIGN GOALS

5.3.1 Problem statement and threat model

The workflow is motivated from the foundation of sharing scenarios between the three parties over the cloud, which can be illustrated from Figure 5.1, including data owner, data user, and cloud service provider. The four types of clouds (public, private, community, and hybrid) play a big role in users' privacy because it also restricts the accessibility of the users. However, the design goals of the proponent model are to give a brief range of scal-ability effectiveness of the data sensitivity. It prohibits cloud servers (CS)

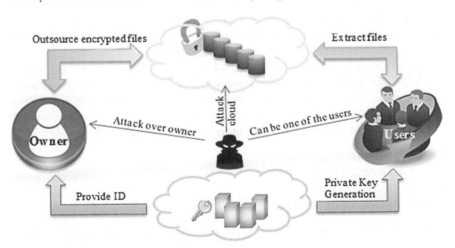

Figure 5.1 Data communication and accessibility environment.

from breakthrough or learning the users' data content. The content being shared over the internet is concerned with the effectiveness of the access privilege. Finally, to ensure parameters like, how much sensitivity percentage the data reinforces and how the data can preserve privacy, can be resolved using of sensitiveness scale.

In some parts, cloud computing is directly proportional to data sharing in a virtual but distributed environment. In the cloud, exploring the transformation uncertainty in the data accessibility often indicates the risk of data being hacked by some intruder [29, 30]. Thus, the sharing of data demands for categorization of data accessibility and authorization of data confidentiality for various kinds of data. It is worthwhile to measure the input datasets and consequent parameters even if they rarely serve any kind of distinctions. Concerned with such issues, it is required to maintain privacy perseverance for all kinds of data, whether it is raw, processed, confidential data, or of some other kind. In concern, it is better to scale datasets taking the sensitivity factor as a priority. It encourages the prediction and analysis of accessibility and policy authority for a number of users [31].

5.3.2 Architecture description

Following workflow, description is included to depict the flow completeness and encourage ease in the reader's understanding of the heterogeneity of different sections of this chapter. This chapter is divided into seven sections demonstrating the effectiveness of data sensitivity scaling, where Section 5.1 introduces about data sensitivity of large amounts of data stored over the internet and why it is important to understand such terms. Section 5.2 contributes to explaining the proposed concept and is divided into three subsections, where first subsection is presenting the scaling criteria (what is apt to make ordered sensitivity scale subdivisions). The second subsection gives an idea over the privacy terms to be included in the implementation scenario and for the justification of the problem domain, also the third subsection predicts the dynamicity of access criteria setup. In the fourth subsection, the proponent model study is explained, which includes an architecture framework design. Further, Section 5.3 gives a deep study over the experimental justification of the work. It announces the resulting evaluation analysis of achieving factors in Section 5.4. Lastly, in the conclusion section, overall study analysis of the problem domain including external factors is explained.

5.4 PROPOSED SCHEME

5.4.1 Proponent model

The process flow starts with the data collection at the owner's place from various servers (may belong to any kind of database storage industry). It can be depicted in Figure 5.2, where the owner divided data into distributed

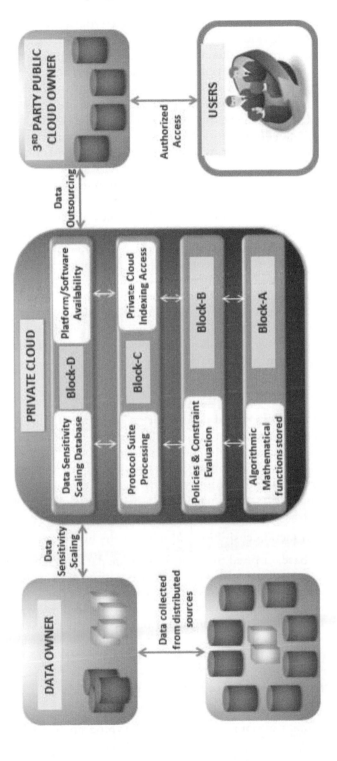

Figure 5.2 Senso Scale architecture design of workflow model.

ranges defined according to the proposed data type sensitivity range. It incorporates a private cloud having distributed working blocks. Each block is assigned different working criteria and work base. It is defined as the A-block layer having privacy algorithms defined and also access criteria policies for data categorization. The policies are defined over data prediction factors that may include government/non-governmental data sensitivity clauses, policies, social policies and regulations, user-defined personal data access factors, etc.

In the private cloud repositories, say, $r_1, r_2, \ldots, r_n$ are maintained and are overseen by the data manager, who matches data and constraints for moving data to repositories. According to the sensitivity range privacy, policies are applied in such a way that most of the data analysis factors must be preserved such as privacy, efficiency, speed. The data is now ready to be sent over the public cloud generating the petrified issues of data being manipulated by intruders or leaked by a third party. To reduce this concern, a Data Sharing Agreement is signed with the third party. Recipients can collect data according to the requirements and may decrypt using the identified algorithm and scheme. As asking or collecting data from any other recipient node is strictly against the privacy perseverance rule. Thus, in concern to the privacy achievement, no recipient/users are allowed to ask for data from the neighbor user node but always request using a token to the third party or service provider. The following subsections explain the data accessibility and algorithmic preliminaries.

5.4.2 Access policy

In cloud, data usually is stored in four forms: structured, semi-structured also the well-defined unstructured and unstructured. If we define the scale in these three terms, it would be arranged this way: For the structured, consider $[m \times n]$ matrix with m number of datasets containing values $i_1, i_2, \ldots, i_m$ and n number of column attributes $j_1, j_2, \ldots, j_m$ decoded as $[a_{ij}]$. To store unstructured data, files like images are stored in a slightly compressed format that is based on the discrete cosine transform in terms of building blocks, the function $\cos[\frac{\pi}{n}(i + \frac{1}{2})k]$. One of the hybrid practices, semi-structured database, inspired from the foundation data storage (structured) type can be stored as binary file system incorporating mapping techniques, based on *associations*, these associations are defined as pairs$(o, \cdot) \in oid \times (oid \cup int \cup string)$. The other, well-defined unstructured, is inspired from unstructured databases, which promotes binary data that is well-defined on binary operation * on a set S. this set function maps S using $S \times S$. For each (ordered pair)$(a, b) \in S \times S$, it denotes the element *$((a, b)) \in S$ as $a * b$.

5.4.3 Preliminaries/privacy requirements

Some methods have been proposed to achieve privacy over the different sensitive ranges of data. Considering a cryptographic hash function algorithm SHA-3, perceived to be more secure than MD-5, SHA-0, SHA-1, and MD-5, is a sponge function family that uses permutation as a building block. Permutation involves 24 rounds indexed as i_r, from 0 to 23, where each round R incorporates five steps, resulting into $R = \iota° \pi° \theta° \chi° \rho$, where the basic block permutation function builds over the number of iterations, i.e. $12 + 2l$. The five sub-rounds run using the following notations.

- I – Exclusive-OR is a round constant, into one word of the state and to be precise in the round n, for $0 \leq m \leq l$, $a[0][0][2^m - 1]$ is exclusive-OR with the bit $m + 7n$ of a degree-8 LFSR sequence. This breaks symmetry that is preserved by the other sub-rounds.
- Π – Permutation of 25 words in a fixed pattern, i.e. $a[j][2i + 3j] \leftarrow a[i][j]$.
- Θ – Compute parity of each of the $5w$ (320, where $w = 64$) 5-bit columns and exclusive OR (that into two nearby columns regular pattern). To be precise for parity P, here considered as $a[i][j][k] \leftarrow a[i][j][k] \oplus P(a[0...4][j-1][k] \oplus P(a[0...4][j+1][k-1])$
- X – Bitwise combine rows along by confederacy using $a \leftarrow a \oplus (\neg b$ and $c)$. To be very precise, $a[i][j][k] \leftarrow a[i][j][k] \oplus \neg a[i][j+1][k]$ and $a[i][j+2][k]$. This is the only non-linear operation in hash algorithm SHA-3.
- P – Bitwise rotates each of the 25 words with a different triangular number likewise $\{0,1,3,6,10,...\}$. To be precise, $a[0][0]$ is not rotated and thus for all $0 \leq t < 24$, $a[i][j][k] \leftarrow a[i][j][k-(t+1)(t+2)/2]$, where $$\begin{pmatrix} i \\ j \end{pmatrix} = \begin{pmatrix} 3 & 2 \\ 1 & 0 \end{pmatrix}^t \begin{pmatrix} 0 \\ 1 \end{pmatrix}.$$

Another approach included in our scheme is ABE and dynamic consideration of the performance evaluation of the ELGamal cryptosystem. This considers the concept of public-key cryptography serving as Key Policy-Attribute-Based Encryption (KP-ABE) and Ciphertext Policy-Attribute-Based Encryption (CP-KBE). The policy is based upon a bilinear map that assumes two cyclic groups G_1 and G_2 of prime order p_1 and G_1 generated by g_1 (known as a generator). Thus, bilinear mapping e: $G_1 \times G_1 \rightarrow G_2$ must satisfy the following:

- **Bi-linearity property:** for all $y,z \in G_1$ and $a,b \in Z_p$, where $Z_{p1} = \{0,1,...,p_1 - 1\}$, we are having $e(y^a, z^b) = e(y,z)^{ab}$
- **Computability property:** for any, $y,z \in G_1$ there is a polynomial time algorithm to compute the mapping $e(y,z) \in G_2$
- **Non-degeneracy property:** $e(g1, g1) \neq 1$.

These preliminaries and access policies combine to predict a particular sensitivity level to maintain privacy. Division identification can be predicted using the following scale segment description.

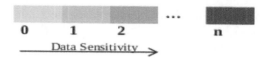

Figure 5.3 Scale compliance.

5.4.4 Scale compliance

This chapter proposes a privacy architecture that announces the data sensitivity range scale as shown in Figure 5.3. This scale distributes a date range into equivalent slots, here we intend sensitivity range with $n = 9$ that is demonstrated as *enum {non-confidential = 0, public access, resilient, quasi, unregulated, moderate, regulated, private access, confidential, restricted data}* as shown in Table 5.3. It should be noticed that the n can be any value depending upon the owner. The scale depicts how sensitive the data is, keeping in mind whether it is public/private/policy-oriented or any other free form of data, etc. Sensitivity can be divided up to two or three scales but it would not provide the precision to predict the level of information utility on the next step.

In concern to privacy parameters, the prominence of the notion is that the sensitivity distribution of dataset values senses to check the sensitive nature of related data by using a diverse scale range. If privacy outputs vary significantly, then output is sensitive to the specification of input dataset distributions. Hence, a moderately simple but diversified sensitivity analysis can be defined with care. A sensitivity coefficient might be used to analyze or measure the magnitude of change in an output dataset. Output dataset variable V, per unit change in the magnitude of an input sensitive parameter value I from the base value I_0. Let S_{VS} be the sensitivity prediction for an output dataset variable V with respect to a change ΔI in value of the input variable I from its base value I_0. Noting that assessment of the output dataset $V(P)$ is a function of I, thus sensitivity prediction can be defined using Eq. (5.1).

$$S_{VS} = [V(I_0 + \Delta I) - V(I_0 + \Delta I)] / 2\Delta I \tag{5.1}$$

Other sensitivity predictions can be defined by letting prediction p is representing a decrement and q is representing an increment in privacy parameter values from the base value S_0, the sensitivity prediction S_{VS} for privacy parameter S and output variable V can be defined using Eq. (5.2) or Eq. (5.3).

$$S_{VS} = \left\{ |(V_0 - V_i) / (S_0 - S_i)| + |(S_0 - S_j) / (S_0 - S_j)| \right\} / 2 \tag{5.2}$$

$$S_{VS} = \max \left\{ |(V_0 - V_i) / (S_0 - S_i)|, |(V_0 - V_j) / (S_0 - S_j)| \right\} \tag{5.3}$$

Table 5.3 Senso Scale divisions for sensitivity level analysis

Scale	Type	Description	Importance	Application	Sensitivity (%)
0	Raw Data	Data (any type) that does not require certain privacy protection and is publically available for any use.	To extract useful content/information subjects from the raw data.	• Data-warehouse • Functions of public nature • Social networking publically accessible online posts etc.	0–5
1	Public Access	Data is prepared and disseminated to provide full scope access to any particular public area (may be community based)	Provides easy access to related audience reaching toward required data.	• Consent of data subject • Social media • News etc.	5–10
2	Resilient Data	An approach to secure Application-oriented type data that requires locality-aware scheduling.	Achieves automatic fault-tolerance and data scalability over working sets.	• Log-based data • Query handling etc.	10–20
3	Quasi Data	Data that only can be identified when integrated to some other data thus requires to keep partial privacy.	Transforms unstructured data into a form that may be utilized.	Different data aggregators: • E-mail • Social media • Web pages • Contact forms etc.	15–30
4	Unregulated Data	Data that cut downs the regulatory overheads being not subjected to any legal restrictions.	Offers a scope in regards to the mobile users.	• Property tax records • Online searches/descriptions • Proprietary sources	25–35
5	Moderate Data	This type of data concerned to file/directory related data that adores many partial privacy accessing algorithms.	Protection is implied over the network.	• Non-public contracts • Server storing records (like student) • Phone directories etc.	35–50

(Continued)

Table 5.3 Senso Scale divisions for sensitivity level analysis (Continued)

Scale	Type	Description	Importance	Application	Sensitivity (%)
6	Regulated Data	Information surrounded with strong legal protection measures to safeguard protected data.	Positively impacts over how businesses interact over consumer data.	• Insurance under writers • Banking industries • The financial institutes like real estate appraisers etc.	50–60
7	Private Access	This perimeter is concerned to the personal records/information of individuals.	Specifies personal records to be protected.	Individual's records like: • Customer's record • Patient medical data etc.	60–70
8	Confidential Data	Data that requires protection from unauthorized user and is not suitable to store online/shared publically.	Predicted as moderately sensitive information.	• Sensitive research • Recommendation letters etc.	65–80
9	Restricted Data	Predicts to be most sensitive information necessitates highest level of privacy through all legal/regulatory aspects.	Provides limited authorization for super sensitive data privacy protection.	• SSN/license/IDs • Credit card/financial details • Military communication tracks • Medical records etc.	80–100

For document-based no-SQL datasets of sensitivity are sensed as sensitivity key, SK_{VS}, that measures a relative change in the output dataset variable V for a relative change in input S can be defined using Eq. (5.4).

$$SK_{VS} = [S_0 / V(S_0)]S_{VS} \qquad (5.4)$$

We define sensitivity as the probability that the data requires privacy access to handle different types of data. The data has the essence of various external consideration factors. To predict the sensitivity percentage influence over data, one needs to calculate the ratio of the total number of dataset variables S_D, where S_D includes dataset variables that need privacy access S_P and variables that don't demand any privacy access S_N resulting into the sensitivity measure S_M^+ using Eq. (5.5).

$$P(S_M^+) = \frac{S_P}{S_P + S_N} \qquad (5.5)$$

When it is required to predict the non-sensitivity, one must know the dataset variables that don't need any kind of privacy and might be freely available for public use. So, the non-sensitivity measure S_N^- is computed using Eq. (5.6).

$$P(S_N^-) = \frac{S_N}{S_P + S_N} \qquad (5.6)$$

However, it might create conflict at a screening time to achieve 100% sensitivity in some cases, but the sensitivity percentage changes according to some external factors and the type of data to be processed.

5.4.5 Progressive algorithm

The proponent model is the architectural study of the projected scenario that can be explained as a process using Algorithm 1. The *PROCESS_MAIN*() algorithm includes the outline of the progressive workflow. It starts with the initializing terms to be used following a call for server setup at work. It builds a hybrid structure as the base for communication. Further, data distribution is done, which gives numerals to the scale divisions and follows a call for dataset variables that are divided into S_P and S_N. When the scale division is done, datasets are calculated over the percentage scale. This leads to computing the sensitivity and non-sensitivity measure over which privacy protection algorithms are implemented and introduces user accessibility.

ALGORITHM 1: PROGRESSIVE ALGORITHM

1: Initialize matrix $a[i][j]$, files $F = \{d_1, d_2, \ldots, d_n, d_{n+1}, \ldots, d_m\}$
2: Set $arr[0 : i - 1][0 : j - 1]$;
3: **for each** document d in folder F **do**
4: Divide $d = \begin{cases} 1 \text{ to } n, & \text{stores government policies} \\ n+1 \text{ to } m, & \text{stores non-government \& other rules} \end{cases}$
5: **end for**
6: Call $SERVER\_HANDSHAKE\_SETUP()$;
7: Call $DISTRIBUTION\_DATA()$;
8: Set $total\_dataset\_variable$ $S_D = \{v_1, v_2, \ldots, v_m\}$;
9: Map $M_i = (d_k, arr[p][q])$; //using matching algorithm
10: **if** M_i requires privacy **then**
11: ASSIGN S_P
12: **else**
13:    ASSIGN S_N
14: **end if**
15: Divide $SENSITIVITY\_SCALE$ range $(0 - 100\%)$
16: Calculate S_M^+ \& S_N^-
17: Sensitivity measure $P(S_M^+) = \dfrac{S_P}{S_P + S_N}$;
18: Non-Sensitivity measure $P(S_N^-) = \dfrac{S_N}{S_P + S_N}$
19: Call $SENSITIVITY\_SCALE()$;
20: Call $PRIVACY\_PROTECTION()$;

Here we notice that in PROCESS_MAIN() algorithm we have called some functions that are depicted in Algorithms 2–5. *SETUP_SERVER_ HANDSHAKE*() in Algorithm 2 manage server set up calls using a 3-way handshake. Then *DATA_DISTRIBUTION*() in Algorithm 3 helps in dividing data on sensitivity scale and assigns numeral value to it that helps in predicting sensitivity. *SENSITIVITY_SCALE*() in Algorithm 4 maps sensitivity measure with data distributions. *PRIVACY_PROTECTION*() in Algorithm 5 divides implementation algorithms into several cases, which can be used in association with the required sensitivity scale measure.

5.5 IMPLEMENTATION SCHEME

The implementation scheme consists of two modules, i.e. system environment and platform computation. Where the system environment discusses the hardware and software required components. Also the utilities for machine-level computation. On the other hand, platform computation is

ALGORITHM 2: SERVER HANDSHAKE

1: **function** *SERVER_HANDSHAKE_SETUP*
2:   Install *INTERFACE_SERVER*;
3:   **for** TCP & UDP; Create *SOCKET* **do**
4:     *DNS* servers status check
5:     Read $(X.X.X.X)$ *MAC* address for *UDP DESTINATION*
6:     Binding of *SOCKET* to *TARGET_PORT_TCP*
7:     **for each** *HANDSHAKE 3 − WAY* **do**
8:       Client call: sends (SYN) call to synchronize
9:       *SOURCE_PORT REQUEST* from
10:       Server call: *DESTINITION_PORT* read request
11:       Formulate *REPLY*
12:       Client call: receive *REPLY* at *SOURCE_PORT*
13:       Receive (ACK) to Acknowledge
14:     **end for**
15:   **end for**
16: **end function**

ALGORITHM 3: DATA DISTRIBUTION

1: **function** *DISTRIBUTION_DATA*
2:   **for** $i = 0$ to n **do**
3:     Assign *NUMERICALS* to *SENSITIVITY_SCALE*
4:     enum $\{non - confidential = 0, publicaccess,$
        $resilient, quasi, unregulated, moderate, regulated,$
        $privateaccess, confidential, restricteddata\}$
5:     *PREDICT_SENSITIVITY*
        using $S_{VS} = [V(I_0 + \Delta I) - V(I_0 + \Delta I)]/2\Delta I$
6:   **end for**
7: **end function**

ALGORITHM 4: SENSITIVITY SCALE

1: **function** *SENSITIVITY_SCALE*
2:   Assign *KEY_SENSITIVITY* $(S_{ui} = [S_0 / V(S_0)]S_{ui})$
3:   Call *DISTRIBUTION_DATA()*
4:   Map S_M^+ & S_N^- : *DISTRIBUTION_DATA()*
5: **end function**

ALGORITHM 5: PRIVACY PROTECTION

```
 1:  function PRIVACY_PROTECTION
 2:     if SENSITIVITY_SCALE then
 3:        case 1 : 0%
 4:           Print(FREELY AVAILABLE FOR ACCESS)
 5:        case 2 : 1 – 20%
 6:           Apply DELTA_PRESENCE
 7:        case 3 : 21 – 40%
 8:           Apply MD-6
 9:        case 4 : 41 – 60%
10:           Apply SHA-3
11:        case 5 : 61 – 80%
12:           Apply ELGamal
13:        case 6 : 01 – 100%
14:           Apply RSA
15:     end if
16:  end function
```

self-explanatory to confer the technical details for the proposed Senso Scale effectiveness.

5.5.1 System environment

The proposed scheme probably doesn't disclose or reveal any attribute of any user attribute set to the CS. We preserve and sense a wide variety of datasets in the form of big data analytics. Time being the cloud has no clue about users' secret keys S_{ui} that might not possess and derive access of data-sensitive slabs at its own place. In the cloud, the process is done at the data owners' place who evaluate the effectiveness. It works upon the defined policies to discover the data scaling. Keeping in mind, here the system setup including Table 5.4 depicts the technical details of the minimum requirement for implementing the proposed scheme. This contributes as a strong machine to create an archetype model for designing a hybrid cloud to satisfy our working criteria.

5.5.2 Database prediction

For the experiment on our progressive algorithm, we have considered a distributed EMR environment, where for each EMR some 60 attributes are picked for the implementation. The securing values are considered for the 0.5 lacks datasets. These 60 attributes are separated into two packets,

Table 5.4 Technical details of implementation environment

Setup phase	Technical attributes	Configuration
Setup of the environment	Capacity of RAM	8 GB
	Operating system	Windows 7 ultimate
	Details of Processor	Intel(R) Core(TM) i7 CPU Q 740 @ 1.73 GHz Turbo up to 1.93 GHz
	Graphic card (if required)	NVIDIA GeForce GT 425 M-2 GB
	Hard-disk	1 TB

i.e. attributes containing patient information PI and medical information MI of each patient. Table 5.5 lists out attributes containing sensitive and non-sensitive (including quasi-identifiers). It is a hypothetically predicted medical dataset.

Table 5.6 depicts sample datasets for banking database creation that is scheduled in two different categories and stored as $[a_{ij}]$ using MySQL, document form having n number of files for different processes $\{f_1, f_2, f_3, ..., f_m\}$ and policy documents for data attribute comparison are processed through MongoDB. MongoDB can be replaced with OrientDB that reflects each of the unstructured, well-formed unstructured, and semi-structured data values and files. Dataset considers two different domains, i.e. banking sector details and medical sector details, that separate two kinds of storage information of a single person (who may be a highly confidential/general bank customer or a patient suffering from a mild/severe trauma). This enriches the sensitivity percentage scale implementation concept for dividing sensitive range.

Table 5.5 Describing medical attribute used for implementation

Patient information		Medical information	
Patient ID	Gender	Diagnosis Name	Patient Lifestyle
Name	Doctor Code	Prescription	Medical History
DOB	Nation	Diagnosis Code	Family History
Address	Clinic Code	Dosage	Blood Pressure
Email	Race	Purchase Quality	Blood Type
Contact No.	No. of Offspring	Cost	Height
Credit Card no.	State	Treatment	Weight
Salary	City	Endoscopy Report	Appointment Mode
ZIP code	PIN code	Pathology Report	Communication Mode
Marital Status	Education	Insurance verification	Eyesight
Social Security No.	Duration	Discharge summary	Dosage Range
Corresponding address	Job(temp./ permanent)	Admission Date	Emergency Relationship
Office ID	Continent	Hospital Address	Smoke/Drink
Nearest Landmark	Work	Hospital Contact	Protein Intake
Occupation	Languages Known	Emergency Contact	No. of Teeth

Table 5.6 Describing banking dataset attribute used for implementation

Customer details		Bank details	
Customer ID	Last login date	Merchant id	Customer Insurance Code
Name	Transaction password	Debt	Bank contact
Contact	Current balance ($)	Currency	Bank Address
E-mail	Insurance ID	Branch head code	City Code
Date acc open	Gender	Branch name	Country Code
User id	Customer Address	Account type	ZIP
Login password	Country	Customer type	Bank contact
Last login date	Zip code	Customer credit ID	Customer Insurance Code

5.5.3 Platform computation

For the validation, the owner must revoke a protected evaluation and some tangible results for achieving optimized and justified deliveries. Table 5.7 gives environmental and experimental details for the implementations of the cloud setup. This setup preserves the privacy for the implementation and preserving the privacy at variable data sensitivity and for range effectiveness. Here the criteria say, the authors have taken six privacy algorithms that would be known as users' part only who is responsible for encrypting the data at its place and put the results over the cloud for the users' access. For the scale 0–4 sensitivity, it needs to achieve 0–50% user sensitiveness accessibility defining the effective authority. This may get by following the hashing and moderate level privacy algorithms. When we input 60,000 dataset variables at time t_1, the algorithm scheme is being followed in the subsequent order, language variation/generalization, delta presence and MD-6. Now for the range, 5–9 on the scale, the sensitivity level complexity of our scheme can be maintained through secret keys s_{ui} concept that follows the high-level privacy maintenance algorithms as follows, RSA, ELGamal, and SHA-3. The database we are using considers SQL, NoSQL, and NewSQL data pretending to store structure, unstructured, and semi-structured. It can also use well-formed unstructured data content, with the help of MongoDB and MySQL platform application.

Table 5.7 Experimental technical configuration details of implementation setup phase

Setup phase	Technical attributes	Configuration
Experimental setup	EMR size	790 MB
	EMR attributes	60
	Datasets	0.1 million
	Encryption algorithm	RSA, ELGamal
	Other privacy algorithms	Attribute-based encryption, SHA-3, MD-6
	Database	SQL, NoSQL, NewSQL
	Platform	MongoDB, MySQL
	Infrastructure	Open Source Server Oriented

Table 5.8 Server-oriented details

Setup state	Source	Server type	Configuration
Validation setup	Block-A	Apache	80 PORT
		Master	Open-Source Platform, WAMP SERVER
		MySQL	3306 PORT
	Block-B	Apache	8180 and 8081 PORT
		Master	Open-Source Platform, WAMP SERVER,
		MySQL	3309 PORT
	Block-C	Apache	443 and 9090 PORT
		Slave	Open Source, XAMPP SERVER-1
		Language	Perl, Php
		MySQL	MySQL Server
	Block-D	Apache	8181 and 8080 PORT
		Slave	Open Source, XAMPP SERVER-2
		Language	Perl, Php
		MySQL	3308 PORT

Further, Table 5.8 helps readers to identify and get information about the server-oriented open-source platform description. This evaluates the information about the server type and its configuration by dividing the process into a block-level scenario. The classification is done as technically there are three chunks to define server workings and query processing, which is defined in the table sub-sequences.

5.6 EVALUATION ANALYSIS

Here, in this section, our scheme gives details about the data modification for privacy purposes. The sensitivity scale approaches six different and effective encryption algorithms to increase the flexibility of the significant add-ons. Taking the $S_D = 0.6$ million dataset variables, along with the external consideration factors, compute the S_M^+ sensitivity probability measure using the formula $P(S_M^+) = \dfrac{S_P}{S_P + S_N}$; & $P(S_N^-) = \dfrac{S_N}{S_P + S_N}$; here we take $S_P = 35\%$ and thus for the same process the non-privacy access required datasets variables $S_N = 45\%$ giving the computational evaluation and results keeping the values dynamic in all variations in Table 5.9.

The Senso Scale has $n = 9$ divisions. Figure 5.4(a)–(e) represents individual results for a few of the scale divisions to understand their behavior

Table 5.9 Formula validity evaluation through examples

S_D (in million)	S_M^+ sensitivity measure	S_N^- non-sensitivity measure
0.6	0.438	0.563
0.65	0.782	0.427

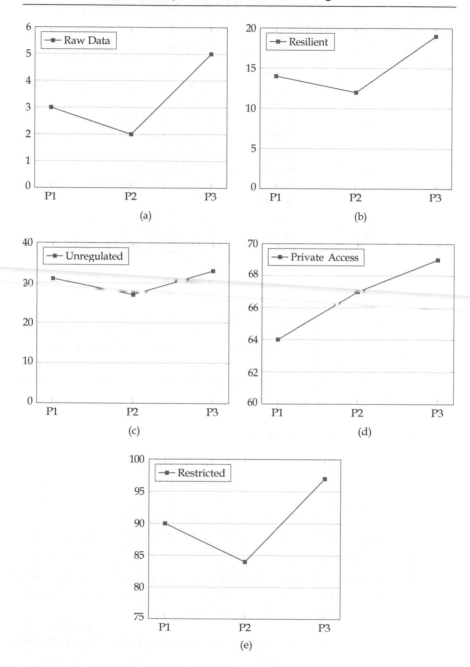

Figure 5.4 Senso Scale sensitivity percentage evaluation. (a) For raw data (scale 0), (b) for resilient data (scale 2), (c) for regulated data (scale 4), (d) for private data (scale 7), (e) for restricted data (scale 9).

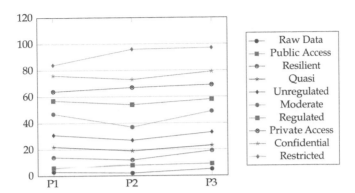

Figure 5.5 Sensitivity percentage evaluation for scale division.

for different processes. In the row, Figure 5.5 evaluates the sensitivity. Also, the privacy measure for the six different encryption and hashing schemes is discussed in the platform computation section. It may be used for the most effective results concerning to generalized level. Figure 5.5 depicts that there are six data sensitivity variations and each of them lias to different algorithms. The evaluation cost is not consistent but is depicted strongly to give the reduced overhead optimizations. The datasets and the access policy consider medical and banking dataset records for the implementation. These datasets are used for the validity of the variable big data considerations and access policies. The users are might aware of the fact that the data is being hacked or leaked at any instant when it is shared with the third party, thus for the medical and banking sectors, the patient and customer personal details are required to be maintained safely and protected. The dataset itself depicts the complexity and variability in the privacy access for the sensitiveness divisions.

The measures such as sensitivity prediction, sensitivity probability range, also privacy perseverance, are calculated to depict the significant approaches. Algorithms i.e. Delta-presence, MD-6, SHA-3, ELGamal, RSA algorithms are defined in a way that makes it feasible to protect data requiring 20–100% of the privacy accessibility. Algorithms impact on data sensitiveness is represented in Figure 5.6(a)–(e). From Figure 5.7, it is evaluated how these protection algorithms respond against different processes over privacy percentage. This handles frequent ups and downs because of variability in the data processing. Here, the figure predicts an experimental result in concern to the total static number of datasets with respect to sensitive percentage, which gives an ideology for the scaling effectiveness. This effectiveness is for ten different privacy accessible data-sensitive predictions. It shows the combined results from implementing algorithm scenarios of variable trends followed by the analyses of algorithmic comparison.

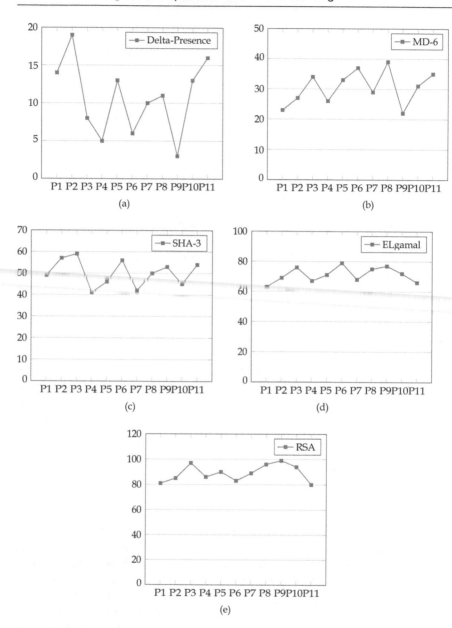

Figure 5.6 Privacy percentage scale for implemented algorithms. (a) Privacy percentage scale of delta presence, (b) privacy percentage scale of MD-6, (c) privacy percentage scale of SHA-3, (d) privacy percentage scale of Modified ELGamal, (e) privacy percentage scale of modified (RSA).

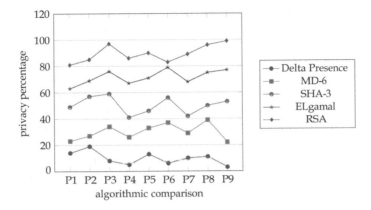

Figure 5.7 Privacy percentage comparison of the algorithms used.

Now further, Figure 5.8 gives an interactive scenario for computation by taking different kinds of databases that are processed under big data analytics. The privacy evaluation is described by taking sub-sequent values in concern to time and datasets. The privacy is different for different kinds of data but in concern to the fact, the result is found when RSA and ELGamal are applied to the variable databases for judging their reflexive behaviors.

5.7 CONCLUSION

The need of handling petabyte and zettabytes of big data analytics and preserve privacy in a cloud environment is increasing. In apprehension, this chapter presented a Senso Scale sensitivity range criteria that divided data sensitivity into categories and computational analysis ensured data privacy for different kinds of databases. These databases consider variable user accessibility scenarios for the data. Furthermore, it initiated privacy

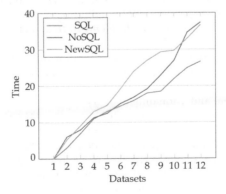

Figure 5.8 Database-based privacy evaluation.

validation for each layer in a hybrid cloud. It depends upon proven encryption and hashing privacy algorithmic schemes. The work introduced a comparison structure for multiple privacy algorithms for privacy protection. The proposed model calculated the sensitivity percentage of the data and initiated to analyze privacy accessibility for different users. In this chapter, a number of attributes from different datasets used for work evaluation have also been introduced. We have used SQL, NoSQL, and NewSQL types of data to support the variability of big data integrated into hybrid cloud. The results showed that the proposed work manages to achieve efficient privacy by optimizing and minimizing the complexity of data encryption and decryption using data sensitivity and sensitiveness probability percentage analysis. In addition, our framework demonstrated better scalability by increasing the data sensitivity range.

ACKNOWLEDGEMENTS

This work is supported by the University Grants Commission (UGC), Ministry of Human Resource Development (MHRD), Government of India under the scheme of National Eligibility Test-Junior Research Fellowship (NET-JRF) with Grant No.– F.15-9(JUNE 2015)/2015(NET).

REFERENCES

[1] Jenna Wortham. Toward a childproof internet. *The New York Times*, 2014. http://bits.blogs.nytimes.com/2014/09/13/toward-a-childproof-internet/.

[2] Ishu Gupta, Niharika Singh, and Ashutosh Singh. Layer-based privacy and security architecture for cloud data sharing. *Journal of Communications Software and Systems (JCOMSS)*, 15(2), 173–185, 2019. ISSN 1846-6079.

[3] Deepika Saxena, Ishu Gupta, Jitendra Kumar, Ashutosh Kumar Singh, and Xiaoqing Wen. A secure and multiobjective virtual machine placement framework for cloud data center. *IEEE Systems Journal*, 16(2), 3163–3174, 2021.

[4] Alptekin Küpçü. *Efficient Cryptography for the Next Generation Secure Cloud: Protocols, Proofs, and Implementation*. Lambert Academic Publishing, San Jose, CA, 2010.

[5] Ashutosh Kumar Singh and Ishu Gupta. Online information leaker identification scheme for secure data sharing. *Multimedia Tools and Applications*, 79 (41), 31165–31182, November 2020.

[6] Syed A. Ahson and Mohammad Ilyas. *Cloud Computing and Software Services*. CRC Press, Boca Raton, 2011.

[7] Niharika Singh and Ashutosh Kumar Singh. Data privacy protection mechanisms in cloud. *Data Science Engineering*, 3, 24–39, 2018.

[8] Zhuo Hao, Sheng Zhong, Nenghai Yu. A privacy-preserving remote data integrity checking protocol with data dynamics and public verifiability. *IEEE Transactions on Knowledge and Data Engineering*, 23(9), 1041–4347, 2011.

[9] Xiangqiang Xu and Xinghui Zhao. A framework for privacy-aware computing on hybrid clouds with mixed-sensitivity data. In *IEEE 12th International Conference on Embedded Software and Systems (ICESS)*, IEEE 7th International Symposium on Cyberspace Safety and Security (CSS), 1344–1349. 2015.

[10] Oded Goldreich. *Foundations of Cryptography*, volume 1. Cambridge University Press UK, 2011.

[11] Sai Teja Peddinti et al. Cloak and swagger: understanding data sensitivity through the lens of user anonymity. In *IEEE Symposium on Security and Privacy (SP)*, San Jose, CA, 2014.

[12] Ishu Gupta, Rishabh Gupta, Ashutosh Kumar Singh, and Rajkumar Buyya. MLPAM: a machine learning and probabilistic analysis based model for preserving security and privacy in cloud environment. *IEEE Systems Journal*, 15 (3), 4248–4259, 2021.

[13] Jason Clause, Data classification is key to effective cybersecurity, 2022. https://www.jasonclause.com/data-classification-cybersecurity/

[14] Elmar Plischke, Emanuele Borgonovo, and Curtis L. Smith. Global sensitivity measures from given data. *European Journal of Operational Research*, 226 (3), 536–550, 2013. ISSN 0377-2217.

[15] Qingchen Zhang, Zhikui Chen, Ailing Lv, Liang Zhao, Fangyi Liu, and Jian Zou. A universal storage architecture for big data in cloud environment. *IEEE International Conference on Green Computing and Communications*, 476–480, 2013.

[16] Elisa Bertino and Ashish Kundu. Privacy-preserving authentication of trees and graphs. *International Journal of Information Security*, 12, 467–494, 2013.

[17] Jordi Nin and Javier Herranz. Secure and efficient anonymization of distributed confidential databases. *International Journal of Information Security*, 13, 497–512, 2014.

[18] Douglas R. Stinson and Colleen M. Swanson. Extended results on privacy against coalitions of users in user-private information retrieval protocols. *International Journal of Information Security*, 7, 415–437, 2014. Cryptography and Communications.

[19] Meiyu Huang, Yiqiang Chen, Bo-Wei Chen, Junfa Liu, Seungmin Rho, and Wen Ji. A semi-supervised privacy-preserving clustering algorithm for healthcare. *Peer-to-Peer Network Applications*, 9, 864–875, 2015.

[20] Marco Casassa-Mont et al. Towards safer information sharing in the cloud. *International Journal of Information Security*, 14, 319–334, 2014.

[21] Subhas C. Misra, Rahat Iqbal, Neeraj Kumar, Kuljeet Kaur. An intelligent RFID-enabled authentication scheme for healthcare applications in vehicular mobile cloud. *Peer-to-Peer Network Applications*, 9, 824–840, 2015.

[22] Ashutosh Kumar Singh and Kapil Himanshu Taneja. Preserving privacy of patients based on re-identification risk. In *Proceedings of forth IEEE International Conference on Eco-friendly Computing and Communication Systems*, 448–454, 2015.

[23] Sk. Md. Mizanur Rahman. Privacy preserving secure data exchange in mobile P2P cloud healthcare environment. *Peer-to-Peer Network Application*, 9, 894–909, 2015.

[24] Tiancheng Li, Ninghui Li, and Suresh Venkatasubramanian. Closeness: a new privacy measure for data publishing. *IEEE*, 22, 943–956, 2010.

[25] Roberto J. Bayardo and Rakesh Agrawal. Data privacy through optimal k-anonymization. In *21st International Conference on Data Engineering*, 217–228. IEEE, 2005.

[26] Ronald Petrlic, Osman Ugus, Dirk Westhoff-Gregorio, Martínez Pérez, Félix Gómez Mármol, Christoph Sorge. *Privacy-Enhanced Architecture for Smart Metering*. Springer, Cham, 2012.

[27] Shivaramakrishnan Narayan. *Privacy Preserving AHR Systems Using Attribute Based Infrastructure*. ACM, New York, NY, 2010.

[28] Yongbo Zeng, Yan Sun, Liudong Xing, and Vinod Vokkarane. A study of online social network privacy via the tape framework. *IEEE Journal of Selected Topics in Signal Processing*, 9 (7), 1270–1284, 2015.

[29] Gouenou Coatrieux, Eric Benzenine, Francois-André Allaert, Catherine Quantina, David-Olivier Jaquet-Chiffelle. Medical record search engines, using pseudonymised patient identity: an alternative to centralised medical records. *International Journal of Medical Informatics*, 80 (2), 6–11, 2011.

[30] François-Xavier Standaert, Sonia Belaïd, Vincent Grosso. Masking and leakage-resilient primitives: one, the other(s) or both? *Cryptography and Communications*, 7(1), 163–184, 2014.

[31] Zhenfu Cao, Xiaolei Dong, Weiwei Jia, Yunlu Chen, Lifei Wei, Haojin Zhu. Security and privacy for storage and computation in cloud computing *Information Sciences*, 258, 371–386, 2014.

Chapter 6

Addressing the cybersecurity issues in cloud computing

Shivanshu Oliyhan and Chandrashekhar Azad

CONTENTS

DOI: 10.1201/9781003269144-6

6.1 INTRODUCTION

The term cloud in cloud computing refers to the servers that are accessed over a network along with the databases and software on those servers. In simple terms, we can say that the cloud consists of all the important files, application software that we have uploaded to the cloud servers at a certain point of time. Cloud computing refers to the hosting of various types of services that are offered to end users through the online platform [1, 2]. Cloud computing makes it easier for the user to access the same information from different devices in different locations with the blink of an eye. The portability cloud provides to users has enormous advantages to technology over the course of time. Cloud eliminates the need to carry a physical hardware to access information as it works as a backup copy for computing in the past before cloud started to provide its services. Users and companies do not have to manage the local servers, physical hardware and they do not have to execute applications on their machines. That is the additional benefit cloud provides to companies all over the world.

Virtualization is the technology method that allows cloud computing to work efficiently [3]. Virtualization allows the users to create a virtual computer or a "virtual machine" that simply works like a real computer device with all its own hardware. The idea of host servers in cloud computing is taken from the virtualization concept. The hardware hosting the virtual machines makes the multiple virtual machines can be run on one server and similarly multiple servers can run a single virtual machine at various network points on the internet and it became effective for various cloud service providers and organizations.

Cloud computing can be divided into three models depending on the services they offer to the users. These types are given in the following sections.

6.1.1 Infrastructure as a service (IaaS)

In this model of cloud infrastructure, an organization offers the storage and servers that are required for the end user. Here hardware resources are being shared upon requirements such as certain memory allocations, data storage, CPU processing, all in the extensive computing essentials that is required to build and work on a full-fledged machine are the part of Infrastructure as a service (IaaS) model. IaaS generally gives a platform for business to small companies and individuals from the big organizations. The usage of allocated computing resources to the end users is measured to ensure a proper service is being provided at a certain amount [4]. Examples: Google Cloud Engine, Amazon EC2.

6.1.2 Software as a service (SaaS)

In this model, service providers offer the application software that is executing on a cloud infrastructure, which is accessible from different clients by the end users through a network. While Software as a service (SaaS) eliminates the need to deploy and manage apps on end-user devices, any employee can potentially access and download content from web services. To monitor the sorts of SaaS applications accessed, usage, and cost, suitable visibility and access controls are essential. SaaS does not require any hardware installation on any type of hardware expenses. SaaS services are basically free to use services in most cases and it can vary from trial period to subscription-based services. Examples: Dropbox, Google Docs.

6.1.3 Platform as a service (PaaS)

In this model, the service provider is responsible for providing clients with IaaS, operating systems, and other facilities, as well as supporting programing languages and tools that allow customers to design, build, test, and install applications. Platform as a service (PaaS) is a cloud platform that allows for the development and deployment of web services. Development tools, middleware, and data analysis solutions are also included in the service. In this case, managing and configuring self-service entitlements and rights are critical to risk management. Examples: Microsoft Azure, Heroku Engine.

6.2 ISSUES IN PUBLIC AND PRIVATE CLOUD SECURITY

6.2.1 Attacks on the networks

The major problem in public clouds arises due to cyberattacks that happen frequently to exploit the sensitive information from a particular source [5]. In the case of private clouds, the frequency of attacks is reduced by half due to the fact that Private clouds are maintained by private enterprises that supervise all areas of cloud infrastructure security. However, in the context of public clouds, the situation is exactly the opposite. Furthermore, in order to ease the problem of infrastructure underutilization and to maximize the use of computing power and storage capacity, cloud service providers recommend virtual machines to consumers. According to this fact, there is a chance that data in the public cloud will be exploited by hackers. A hacker can steal or seize control of a virtual machine in order to host a malicious service or application in order to launch an attack against a service provider or access customer data.

6.2.2 Insecure APIs

Cloud service providers allow their Application Programming Interfaces (APIs) to software developers so that they would create applications that connect to their cloud. These APIs are freely accessible and can be used by the entire developer community if required. However, it has been discovered that the APIs provided are not secure for use in a cloud context.

This vulnerability was discovered because of third-party cloud API use. As a result, insecure APIs render the cloud vulnerable to a variety of attacks. If there are insecure APIs in the cloud infrastructure then it will surely lead to multiple issues like CIA, i.e., Confidentiality, Integrity, and Accountability. Insecure increases the risk of cloud service providers because they commonly interact with third parties for API implementation on their cloud service platform.

6.2.3 Data breaches

A data breach is a cloud security concern that occurs when sensitive and private information is accessed by an individual or non-personal account that is not allowed and authenticated to access such sensitive data. A data breach might be purposeful to get access to unauthorized data, or it can be the result of a probable defect in the system or application.

Data breaches can have a variety of commercial consequences, depending on the sensitive data exposed. When a data breach happens, the organization must pay a significant fee. Although cloud providers offer a number of security choices, the client is ultimately responsible for ensuring the safety. Availability of information can include data that is not intended to be publicly available, as well as sensitive and Personally Identifiable Information (PII).

6.2.4 Data access by government organization

The term "cloud" refers to the unpredictability of infrastructure, particularly data storage supplied by public cloud service providers. The infrastructures of large worldwide cloud suppliers are distributed across multiple countries with distinct authorities. It certainly means that data of an enterprise may be held in several countries with varying norms and laws controlling data storage and access activities. As a result, geographical data localization is an essential component of cloud computing.

6.3 A BRIEF STUDY OF CYBERATTACKS IN CLOUD COMPUTING

Now at this point after identifying various issues in cloud security, we are analyzing the factors that occurred due to vulnerabilities and threats in cloud computing. In each case, we will identify which cloud services are vulnerable and what was its impact on various security models. They use cloud resources in many of their cyberattacks.

This research provides a brief summary of the vulnerabilities as well as an indication of which cloud service models may be impacted by them. For this research, we focus mostly on technology-based vulnerabilities;

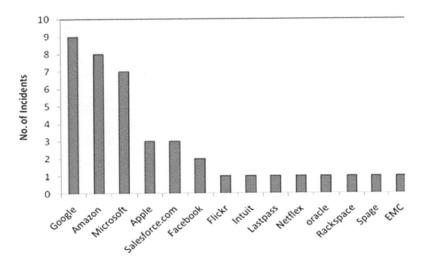

Figure 6.1 Number of incidents reported in major cloud.

nevertheless, there are additional vulnerabilities that are common to every company, however, they must be evaluated since they might have a substantial impact on the safety and security of the cloud and its underlying platform. Figure 6.1 depicts the number of incidents reported in major cloud.

As we can see, after comparing the number of attacks of various cloud service providers, the three giants Google, Amazon, and Microsoft are severely affected by most cyber incidents.

Cryptographic algorithms require ongoing aggregation to avoid vulnerability as computers become faster and failure techniques become safer. It is important to note that there is a distinction among cybercrime, cyberwarfare, and cyberattacks in general. Organizations must understand the model for each cloud vendor with which they deal and safeguard each cloud instance. If they do not, they expose themselves to cyber danger. Furthermore, standard security assessments employed in on-premises settings might be challenging to scale [6]. Figure 6.2 indicates attack incident rates as per type of industry.

Cybersecurity comprises practical techniques to secure information, networks, and data from internal and external attacks. Cybersecurity experts safeguard networks, servers, intranets, and computer systems. Cybersecurity guarantees that only authorized personnel have access to the information. To safeguard data in cloud storage, attribute-based encryption may be used to encrypt data with a specific access control policy before storage [7]. As a result, only users with access characteristics and keys may access the data. Another method for protecting data in the cloud is to employ scalable and fine-grained data access control.

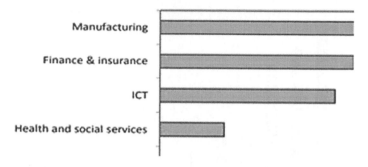

Figure 6.2 Attack incident rates as per type of industry.

6.3.1 Network security

Network security refers to the set of systems that enable companies to keep network infrastructure safe from hackers, coordinated attacks, and viruses. The security of a cloud network could be improved by implementing several security measures on the cloud network. These include using Intrusion Detection Systems (IDS) in the cloud to monitor network traffic and nodes for malicious activity. Intrusion detection and some other network security solutions must be designed and implemented with cloud efficiency, system integration, and virtualization in mind.

6.3.2 Access control

Because of access control, cloud data owners can execute some restrictive permissions to access their data carried out simultaneously to the cloud, and data owners authorized users can access cloud data, while intruders who do not have permission are not allowed. As a result of access control, cloud data is protected from modification or unauthorized disclosure of data. The growth of cloud services such as storage and computing has altered the cybersecurity environment. Migrating to the cloud not only solves many ongoing concerns of cyber insecurity for enterprises that formerly maintained their IT systems alone, but it also introduces a new set of very sophisticated, global security difficulties.

6.3.3 Denial of service (DoS)

Denial of service (DoS) cyberattacks may be avoided by having additional network bandwidth, utilizing IDS that validates network requests before they reach the cloud server, and keeping a backup for emergency situations. To avoid DoS attacks, it is critical to identify and implement all of the cloud network's core security needs, including apps, databases, and other services.

6.3.4 Cloud services unavailability

The global adoption of cloud services across all industries has been accelerated by the COVID-19 pandemic. On the other hand, health-care services around the world have seen the most sudden and rapid transition to support incompetent network and increasing collaboration while employing the same restricted IT and security resources [8]. Health-care providers have been charged with rapidly scaling their operations by employing remote access and cloud analytics. While cloud computing improves resource use in healthcare, it also introduces major hazards. This is especially true when cloud adoption occurs quicker than information security employees can do proper checks. Cyberattacks have progressed from targeting and attacking computer systems, network services, and smartphones to targeting and killing people, automobiles, railroads, planes, power grids, and an electrical pulse. Many of these items are in some manner linked to company networks, thus complicating cybersecurity [9].

6.3.5 Loss of data

Data loss is one of the major cloud security risks that are difficult to foresee and much more difficult to manage. Data breaches was the most prevalent threat action seen by IBM in hacked cloud settings outside of malware distribution during the previous year. In the case of a cloud security breach, attackers can get direct exposure to trade secrets or other personal information.

6.4 CYBERATTACKS ON THE NETWORK

6.4.1 Ransomware

Malware is software or hardware that attacks on personal devices such as computers and mobile phones, and blocks access to files, by regularly threatening irreversible data loss unless a ransom has reached to give pandemic-like situations, proportions throughout the world, and is the "go-to method of attack" for cybercriminals. Ransomware, which is currently the fastest growing and one of the most costly kinds of cybercrime, will eventually persuade corporate management to address the cyber threat more seriously. Figure 6.3 shows a scenario of attacker-target.

6.4.2 Service hijacking

Service hijacking is rather an old term in cyberattacks and it is a process in which the cloud account related to an individual or an organization is stolen or hijacked by the intruder. The affected account information is then used in multiple ways to engage in unauthorized behavior by the attacker. In any case, if the attacker gets logged in to the system by stolen information then surely they have access to the servers and all the data that

Figure 6.3 Attacker-target.

can bring a variety of security wise concerns in the organization. The risk factor service hijacking brings to the organization is huge as business is directly affected by this type of attack.

6.4.3 Cryptojacking

Cryptojacking is a relatively new type of cyberattack that may go unnoticed very easily. It focuses on the well-known activity of mining for cryptocurrencies such as Bitcoin. You require processing power to achieve this, and fraudsters have discovered ways to get access into cloud computing platforms and then use their computer resources to mine for cryptocurrencies. Cryptojacking is sometimes difficult to detect and deal with immediately. The primary issue is that even when hackers utilize system resources from your cloud system, your performance will be slowed, but (importantly) it will remain operational. This implies that it may appear as though nothing illegal is taking place and that the systems are just struggling with their computational power. Figure 6.4 shows scenario of cryptojacking.

6.4.4 Man in the cloud attack

In this type of attack, hackers decrypt and reconfigure cloud services by targeting weaknesses in the synchronization token system, such that the

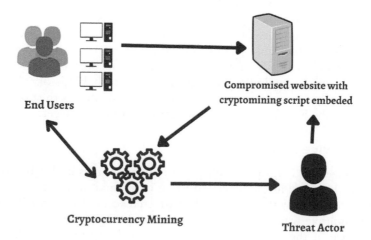

Figure 6.4 Cryptojacking.

synchronization token is changed with a new one that gives the attackers access toward the next synchronization with the cloud. Because an attacker may re-create the original synchronization tokens at any moment, clients may never be aware that their credentials have been compromised. Furthermore, there is a possibility that hacked accounts would never be retrieved.

6.4.5 Spectre and Meltdown

These two types of cybersecurity threats emerged earlier this year but have certainly established a new risk to cloud computing. Malicious actors can access encrypted system information by exploiting a design flaw in most current CPUs with the means of malicious JavaScript code. Each of Spectre and Meltdown breach the separation between programs and the operating system, allowing attackers to extract data from the kernel. This is a major challenge for cloud developers and security engineers since not all cloud users install and configure the most recent security updates.

6.5 CLOUD COMPUTING CHALLENGES

6.5.1 Security

It is obvious that the security issue has been the most serious disadvantage to Cloud computing. Without a question, placing your data and executing your programs on someone else's hard disc and utilizing someone else's CPU looks intimidating to many people. Data theft, phishing, and botnets are all well-known security vulnerabilities that represent major risks to a company's applications and software. Furthermore, the multi-tenancy model and pooled computing resources in cloud computing have generated new security concerns that necessitate the use of unique solutions to address.

6.5.2 Service level agreements (SLAs)

It is essential for consumers to acquire service delivery assurances from suppliers. This is often offered under Service Level Agreements (SLAs) agreed between suppliers and users. The first such concern is defining SLA specifications with an appropriate level of precision, namely the considerations among expressiveness and behavior, so that they can cover the majority of customer needs while remaining fairly simple to be balanced, verified, assessed, and regulated by the cloud service delivery mechanism.

6.5.3 Cybersecurity policy

The objective of the applicable regulatory body dictates the component of the security policy. In general, the objectives of the National security policy are entirely different from business or corporate security policy. The method by which these objectives became policies and the mechanism by which these guidelines are then adopted in the law vary from organization to organization. The way in which the policy is interpreted and registered shall be defined by the organizations involved in the implementation, and its approval shall be determined by the licensing body.

6.6 CONCLUSION

Cloud computing is a relatively new idea that offers a variety of benefits to its users; nevertheless, it also raises significant security concerns that may limit its use. Understanding the risks in cloud computing will assist enterprises in making the transition to the cloud. Because cloud computing makes use of several technologies, it shares potential vulnerabilities with them. Working groups are distributing draughts of their findings on major security risks and recommending various solutions. Despite the fact that several studies show that the hosted approach is more secure than what's on the cloud model. Nonetheless, many attacks target the hosted approach in order to exploit the weaknesses.

REFERENCES

[1] M. Zareapoor, S. Pourya, M. A. Alam, (2014). "Establishing safe cloud: ensuring data security and performance evaluation." International Journal of Electronics and Information Engineering, 1(2): 88–99.

[2] N. J. King, V. T. Raja, (2012). "Protecting the privacy and security of sensitive customer data in the cloud." Computer Law & Security Review 28(3): 308–319.

[3] Hofmann, Woods, (2010). "Cloud computing: the limits of public clouds for business applications." Internet Computing, IEEE 14(6): 90–93.

[4] S. Poremba, "Can the Cloud be hacked?", (2021), available at https://www.verizon.com/business/en-in/resources/articles/s/can-the-cloud-be-hacked/

[5] K. Sheridan, "Cloud Attack Analysis Unearths Lessons for Security Pros", (2021), available at https://www.darkreading.com/cloud/cloud-attack-analysis-unearths-lessons-for-security-pros

[6] M. Kazim, S. Y. Zhu, (2015). "A survey on top security threats in cloud computing." International Journal of Advanced Computer Science and Applications, 6(3): 110–111.

[7] Y. Li, Q. Liu, (2021). "A comprehensive review study of cyber-attacks and cyber security; Emerging trends and recent developments." Energy Reports, 7: 8180–8181.

[8] "Exploitable attack surface within the cloud services", (June 2020), available at https://www.securitymagazine.com/articles/92719-new-study-shows-exploitable-attack-surface-within-cloud-services-and-remote-healthcare

[9] S. Lokuge, (2020). "Security Concerns in Cloud Computing: A Review", (2020), available at https://www.researchgate.net/publication/346606684_Security_Concerns_in_Cloud_Computing_A_Review

Chapter 7

Role of medical image encryption algorithms in cloud platform for teleradiology applications

Siju John and S. N. Kumar

CONTENTS

7.1 INTRODUCTION

A great breakthrough in medical diagnosis has occurred in today's scenario due to the innovations in technology. The rapid expansion of communication networks has resulted in ever increasing volumes of interactive media information such as images, sound, and video being transmitted through insecure communication channels. Medical records typically contain both confidential and private data, thus their security must be maintained against a variety of dangerous threats, while also avoiding data loss and assuring integrity. Encryption of medical images is one of the most cost-effective methods for ensuring the security of patients' data in open networks against malicious attacks [1]. Medical image encryption is a key component in improving medical records' confirmation, respectability, non-disavowal, and attack resistance capabilities [2]. The delivery of health care and the exchange of health-care information over long distances are referred to as telemedicine. It isn't a new discipline of medicine or new technology. The term "title" comes from the Greek for "at a distance," so telemedicine is

DOI: 10.1201/9781003269144-7

essentially medicine delivered over the internet. As such, it involves the full range of medical activities, including disease diagnosis, treatment, and prevention, as well as a health-care provider and consumer continuing education, research, and assessment [3]. The interaction between the client and the expert (real-time or pre-recorded) and the sort of information being delivered are two factors that can be used to classify telemedicine episodes (e.g., text, audio, and video). Much of today's telemedicine is carried out in developed countries, such as the United States, although there is growing interest in using telemedicine in underdeveloped countries.

Telemedicine should be explored in two situations: (1) when there is no other option (for example, in crises in remote areas) and (2) when it is superior to existing traditional services (e.g., teleradiology for rural hospitals). Telemedicine, for example, is predicted to increase access to health care, as well as the quality and efficiency with which it is given. In the late 1990s, telemedicine research grew steadily, albeit the quality of the study could be better – there have been some notable exceptions [3]. Almost all countries were put on lockdown during the COVID-19 pandemic. Telemedicine is advantageous for health care since It reduces social distance. During the lockdown, this technology helps avoid visits to the doctor and hospital by providing a viable treatment alternative. It gathers medical data and information that can aid in bettering the patient's therapy. For the patient, telemedicine uses virtualized therapeutic approaches. During COVID-19 lockdown, patients can now receive better treatment without having to leave their homes [4]. The benefits of telemedicine are depicted in Figure 7.1.

Teleradiology refers to the transmission of the scientific image from one area to any other place via the cloud network. The teleradiology features prominence in the COVID-19 situation considering that the customers can have interaction through the internet-enabled nodes except journeying an area for getting a professional opinion. The teleradiology workflow is depicted in Figure 7.2.

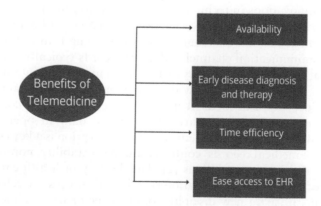

Figure 7.1 Benefits of telemedicine.

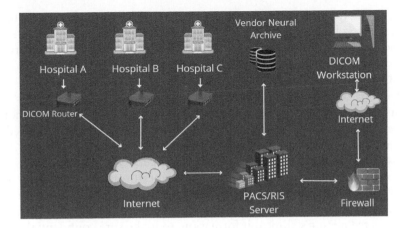

Figure 7.2 Teleradiology workflow.

The hospital can be rural or urban areas. Through DICOM routers, medical data are transferred to the cloud repository, from there data are sent to the picture archiving and communication system (PACS) of a super specialty hospital. The DICOM workstation facilitates the analysis of images and the analysis reports are also transferred through the cloud.

7.2 OVERVIEW OF MEDICAL IMAGE ENCRYPTION

Encryption is described as the procedure of changing a message into ciphertext, the contents of ciphertext are no longer comprehensible to others. Decryption is the inverse method that performs the recovery of messages from encrypted textual content [5]. The encryption procedure is depicted in Figure 7.3.

The simple concept behind image encryption is to switch the image throughout the community securely so that it can't be deciphered with the aid of an unauthorized user. The special facets of images are excessive pixel

Figure 7.3 Encryption/decryption process.

correlation, redundancy and in the state of affairs of clinical images, the file dimension is huge. A novel double random phase encryption scheme was proposed in [5], it comprises two-phase; multiplexing and Fourier transform forms the first phase, and the second phase comprises the classical Double Random Phase (DRP) scheme.

It is one of the most frequent functions of cryptographic systems, and it has to be executed with methods that take much less time and money. Varied strategies with several parameters can be used to encrypt medical images. High-speed scrambling, bitwise or diffusion, chaotic and facet maps, and different techniques can be used to encrypt clinical images. The performance metrics are used to validate the performance of the encryption algorithm by judging the quality of decrypted image. The principal purpose of clinical image encryption is to make certain the secure transmission of the affected person's clinical information, to make sure confidentiality and integrity. The transmission of images should resist the attack and poor-quality images can lead to wrong diagnosis [6]. In clinical informatics systems, medical images are viewed as crucial data. It is required to construct a tightly closed encryption algorithm for transferring scientific images with the aid of a secure network. Secrecy is the most vital attribute for transmitting the clinical image to physicians amongst the three essential traits of protection offerings (i.e., confidentiality, integrity, and availability) [7].

7.2.1 Medical image encryption techniques

Data Encryption Standard (DES) is the classical encryption utilizing a secret key of 56 bits. It was once created in 1976 at IBM [13]. The AES is based totally on the Rijndael algorithm, which is an iterated block cipher approach with variable key dimension and variable block size. The key and block sizes can be 128, 192, and 256 bits. The method's preliminary key is the 2D Henon map, whilst the non-public key is the 2D Chebyshev map, which is then used to assemble the AES spherical key. The RSA algorithm (Rivest-Shamir-Adleman) is the cornerstone of a cryptosystem that permits public-key encryption and is typically used to impervious touchy data, especially when it is transmitted over the internet.

The RSA algorithm is the next cornerstone of a cryptosystem that permits public-key encryption and is usually used to encrypt data, particularly when it is despatched over an unsecured community like the internet. In RSA cryptography, each public and private key are utilized for the encryption of the message. The decryption key is the polar contrary of the communication's encryption key. RSA is the most extensively used asymmetric algorithm due to the fact it ensures efficient data transfer with security. Medical image encryption is an accurate way to preserve clinical image security from dangers. It's one of the most crucial areas of cryptography, and it must be completed with less computation time and cost. This approach relies on pixel manipulation and has low computational complexity and security when compared with the transform domain and classical approach. An improved ElGamal encryption algorithm was proposed in [13, 14] for the medical images, the computation involved in the conversion of plain text into elliptical coordinates was eliminated. The data expansion problem was solved in this encryption model with the computation time minimized. The quality of the decrypted image was superior and validated in terms of performance metrics.

The method of disguising a scientific image inside a provider sign is acknowledged as watermarking [6, 15]. The watermarking structure consists of a watermark embedding phase, a transmission channel that may be wired or wireless, and a watermark extractor [16]. The watermark is embedded into the input image with a key and transmitted through the channel. In the extraction stage, the same key is used to recover the input image [8]. The points that are imperative for digital watermarking differ relying on the context. To make certain anonymity, the digitally watermarked image needs to be resistant to adjustments throughout transmission and a more desirable watermarking strategy ought to be applied. Watermarking can be done in spatial, transform, and hybrid domains [8]. Because the pixels in the host image are at once changed, spatial area techniques are easy to construct but have a decreased imperceptibility. Watermarking in the transform domain approach has more computational complexity than watermarking in the spatial domain, however, it affords higher security. Watermarking is a protection function that protects a clinical image by using including a layer of security. It simply provides a watermark to the facts in the scientific image; it does not degrade, compress, or exchange it in any way. A novel encryption scheme was proposed in [28] for the watermarked medical image with biometric trait also as an input for improving security. This method yields good efficiency when compared with the classical approaches. The watermarked medical images are encrypted using hyperchaotic systems; proficient results are produced with resistance to attacks [29]. A hybrid transforms domain approach comprising the continuous wavelet transform and discrete cosine transform was employed in [30] for the watermarking of images followed by encryption utilizing a chaotic system. The fuzzy logic was employed in [31] for ROI extraction, watermarking with encryption was carried out using discrete wavelet transform along with the chaotic function. The key was generated from the singular values of the encrypted image from the Singular value decomposition (SVD) algorithm.

Edge detection is a collection of mathematical methods for extracting high-contrast factors in a digital picture by using gradient functions. Edge detection is a classical segmentation approach that traces the boundary of objects in an image and gains prominence in computer vision applications also. For the first time in Edge map-based medical image encryption (EMMIE), area maps are proposed for scientific photograph encryption [9]. EMMIE comprises the following: bit-plane decomposition methods, chaotic sequence generator, and scrambling mechanism. A new permutation approach used in the process can vary both the position of bits and the values of pixels, enhancing EMMIE's security [9]. Edge maps are useful because they can be used with any sort of source image, the choice of bit-plane decomposition method is flexible, and the number of permutations is also flexible [6]. Furthermore, as compared to other encryption algorithms, edge maps provide greater security benefits. The edge maps generated from the wavelet transform of input medical images were utilized in the [32] for the encryption process. The coupled map lattice was initially applied for the generation of cipher images and it serves as input for modified genetic algorithm [33].

Chaotic logistic maps [8] are used to construct an order of subkeys, and the image was encrypted by utilizing the logistic maps' subkeys. The receiver may additionally decode the digital scientific picture the usage of the equal subkeys, and the encryption technique is evaluated using performance metrics. To alleviate the drawbacks of modern-day chaotic map networks, more than one chaotic mapping is employed. To begin, the system scrambled the simple image function by the use of Logistic-sine chaos mapping. In an adaptive photograph encryption method with more than one selection, a hyperchaotic system is used to alleviate the diffusion scarcity brought about using single encryption sequences in classical encryption algorithms. In the permutation stage, the secondary key sequences have been used to permute the rows and columns of images. The algorithm has an excessive sensible significance and software potential, and it can be used to encrypt picture transmission. The algorithm performs properly in phases of encryption and recovery, as properly as protection and attack resistance [10].

The cosine number strategy works with non-compressed images, specifically clinical images that are in DICOM format [9]. It is pretty adaptable and relies on a mathematical function. The unique feature of image encryption using cosine number transform is that, in the decoding stage, the reconstructed image quality is good and comparable with the input images. The cosine number transform coupled with the chaos was proposed in [11, 12] for the encryption of medical images. The fractional discrete cosine transform along with the chaotic function was employed in [34] for the encryption of medical images. Image encryption using discrete parametric cosine transform was highlighted in [35].

7.3 NEED FOR MEDICAL IMAGE ENCRYPTION IN TELEMEDICINE

The safety of scientific imaging is turning increasingly more necessary as the telemedicine enterprise grows. The health-care gadget is altering as a result of the employment of modern computer-based technology [14]. Recent developments in the public health-care sector have made it less difficult to retrieve a patient's fitness record, therapy history, and prescription utilization records by using cloud storage, which is integral for wonderful fitness care delivery. As malicious cyberinfrastructure attacks turn out to be greater widespread, the health-care industry's protection necessities are developing extra demanding [15]. Medical images make up a substantial component of the health-care system. There are major hazards to data including confidential information from a patient's health records in the e-health-care system [16]. Many issues regarding the safety and security of health-care data may arise during the administration and transmission of this data to third parties such as private/public or hybrid clouds. As a result, we need a method that is both efficient and reliable for ensuring secure communication [17]. Patient information, such as scientific images, is shared through the internet or mobile smartphone networks [20, 21]. Through the telemedicine network, nodes in any place can access the data through the cloud. However, the thing that should be taken care of is the cyber-attack. The encrypted data can recover only by the authorized users and the data are useless to the unauthorized users [22]. Medical image watermarking and encryption are the proven tools ensuring secured data transfer in telemedicine [36]. The DNA chaos cryptography algorithm was proposed in [37] for ensuring security in the telemedicine network.

7.4 CHAOS AND ITS ROLE IN MEDICAL IMAGE PROCESSING

Chaos is a procedure in which a nonlinear dynamical machine generates an exact pseudo-random sequence. It's non-astringent and non-periodic [23]. Chaos structures have several advantages, such as sensitivity to preliminary circumstances, deterministic random numbers, ergodicity, shape complexity, big keyspace, flexibility, and large periodicity [24]. The capability of some dynamic structures to create random sequences of integers is the basis of chaos encryption. This sequence is used to encrypt data. The initial constraints play a vital role; it influences the random generation of sequences. The minute change in the initial conditions will generate different sequences. Chaotic systems are useful for encryption because of their sensitivity to the initial situation [25].

One-dimensional (1D), two-dimensional (2D), and three-dimensional (3D) chaotic maps are the three types of chaotic maps. When compared to high-dimensional chaotic maps, the advantages of 1D [22] chaotic maps are ease of configuration and cheap computational resource requirements. Though the chaotic map offers some beneficial qualities for randomizing image data before encryption, if the underlying encryption method is not properly constructed, it can be cryptanalysis using common cryptographic attacks such as the differential attack. The 2D or 3D are widely used since they increase the security of encryption systems.

7.4.1 Arnold's cat map (ACM)

Arnold's cat map (ACM) is widely utilized in cryptography applications. The intention is to rotate the image many times till it takes on a non-visible and random form, permitting the machine to apprehend it as an image file even though it is now not seen to the bare eye (image). Chaos is a famous random variety generator strategy; it is employed in the method circulate objects in view that it is quicker and simpler to use in phrases of each storage and method object. There are solely a few parameters and features (chaotic maps) that can be used (initial conditions). The Arnold's Transform was utilized in [38] for watermarking of medical images for secure transmission.

7.4.2 Henon map

A Henon map is a discrete-time nonlinear chaotic map in two dimensions proposed it in 1976. Two awesome sequences are represented by way of the Henon chaotic map. These sequences are then utilized in the row and column diversifications of the original/plain image. To produce pixel diffusion, the skew tent map employs XOR models. Hussain's substitute field is used at the output of the system to exchange every pixel with a new random pixel. The Henon chaotic map was utilized in [18] for medical image encryption.

7.4.3 Tent map

The tent map is the simplest chaotic iterative map. The tent map is a 1D map that is also called a triangular map. The tent map was utilized in [39] for the medical image watermarking scheme for telemedicine applications. The dual encryption scheme comprising RC6 and logistic tent map was deployed in or the DICOM medical images.

7.4.4 Logistic map

It's a nonlinear, 1D, discrete-time map with quadratic nonlinearity. The use of chaos-based cryptographic algorithms [19] has proven some novel and environment-friendly strategies for growing secure image encryption systems. As telemedicine grows in popularity, a massive quantity of affected person records will be transmitted using the internet. Patients' data, on the different hand, are private records that should be saved impenetrable whilst being delivered and retained. It encrypts clinical images to maintain them safe.

7.5 HYBRID CHAOTIC ALGORITHM FOR MEDICAL IMAGE ENCRYPTION

A huge amount of medical data are generated today and the storage and transmission of medical data are a crucial one. The secured transmission of data is required in the health-care sector [23]. Cryptographic algorithms

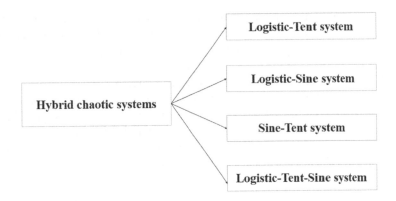

Figure 7.4 Hybrid chaotic systems.

are divided into two categories: move ciphers and block ciphers. Stream ciphers use a secret key generator to encrypt digital information bit via bit, whereas block ciphers encrypt blocks of bits. Because picture statistics requires sturdy real-time properties, common encryption schemes such as linear comments shift registers (LFSR) (stream cipher), superior encryption popular (AES), information encryption preferred (DES), triple DES (TDES) (block ciphers), and others are ineffective for image encryption. In image encryption methods, there are two sorts of chaotic maps: 1D and higher-dimensional (HD) chaotic maps. Although 1D chaotic maps have an easy shape and are easy to design, their chaotic levels and susceptibility are restricted. More statistics are on hand on HD maps. Several encryption methods have been proposed to overcome these difficulties. A new photo encryption method primarily based on the hybrid chaotic device [24] was once lately introduced. Different hybrid chaotic systems are there; however, some of the typical hybrid chaotic systems are depicted in Figure 7.4.

Each chaotic machine is a nonlinear mixing of two or three distinct chaotic maps, specifically the Logistic, Tent, and Sine maps, all of which are seed maps [24]. To generate high-quality image encryption, the aggregate of cryptographic algorithms can be utilized. This combination can be used in two ways:

1. Mix two chaotic algorithms (e.g., Logistic, Lorenz, Rossler, Henon, or Chau maps).
2. Combining usual encryption (such as DES, 3DES, or AES) with chaotic algorithms (e.g., Logistic, Lorenz, Rossler, Henon, or Chau maps).

The plaintext P is encrypted at the transmitter aspect the use of an encryption rule that makes use of a well-known manner to produce sign Z, a nonlinear characteristic to produce sign Y, and the chaotic system to produce cipher-text C. The chaotic machine is then pushed by using the scrambled output signal, enabling the chaotic dynamics to continuously evolve in a tricky manner. The variable of the chaotic device in the transmitter is then broadcast throughout the channel. At the receiver's end, the plaintext is recreated through decrypting utilizing the reverse encryption technique [26]. A novel thinking combining the number-theoretic strategy and the Henon map has been developed for impervious and environment-friendly encryption. Modular exponentiation of the primitive roots of the chosen high in the vary of its residual set is used to assemble a 2D array of keys. The key matrix, which is permuted and chaotically managed by using the Henon map, permutes and chaotically controls the encryption keys for every pixel of the DICOM picture. The recommended machine is mainly protected due to the unpredictability supplied using the aggregate of modular exponentiation key era and Henon maps for key permutation [27]. The hybrid chaotic key generation with DNA diffusion was employed in for medical image encryption. A hybrid encryption model comprising DNA masking, secure hash algorithm, and hybrid chaotic approach was utilized in for the encryption of medical images. A novel encryption scheme comprising multiple chaotic functions is deployed in for the encryption of medical images. The hybrid 2D chaotic maps comprising sine and cosine map was utilized in for the encryption of color/grayscale images. A hybrid chaotic scheme was proposed in for the body area network.

7.6 CONCLUSION

This chapter proposes the role of encryption algorithms in telemedicine. The encryption algorithms ensure the efficient transmission of data through the cloud network. The need for image encryption in telemedicine is investigated initially, followed by the overview of image encryption and medical image encryption techniques. Chaotic algorithms are gaining prominence in the encryption domain and hybrid chaotic algorithms generate proficient results than the classical chaotic technique. The future work will be the hardware implementation of the chaotic encryption algorithm for the health-care application.

REFERENCES

[1] P. Pravcenkum, R. Hemalatha, R. Uma, K. Madhunisha, K. Thenmozhi, and R. Amirtharaj, "Image encryption," Res. J. Inf. Technol., vol. 6, no. 4, pp. 368–378, 2014, doi: 10.3923/rjit.2014.368.378.
[2] C. Lakshmi, K. Thenmozhi, J. B. B. Rayappan, and R. Amirtharajan, "Encryption and watermark-treated medical image against hacking disease—An immune convention in spatial and frequency domains," Comput. Methods Programs Biomed., vol. 159, pp. 11–21, 2018, doi: 10.1016/j.cmpb.2018.02.021.

[3] J. Craig and V. Patterson, "Introduction to the practice of telemedicine," J. Telemed. Telecare, vol. 11, no. 1, pp. 3–9, 2005, doi: 10.1258/1357633053430494.

[4] S. Bahl, R. P. Singh, M. Javaid, I. H. Khan, R. Vaishya, and R. Suman, "Telemedicine technologies for confronting covid-19 pandemic: A review," J. Ind. Integr. Manag., vol. 5, no. 4, pp. 547–561, 2020, doi: 10.1142/S2424862220300057.

[5] J. M. Justin, "A survey on various encryption techniques," Int. J. Soft Comput. Eng., vol. 2, no. 2, pp. 2231–2307, 2012.

[6] V. Pavithra and C. Jeyamala, "A Survey on the Techniques of Medical Image Encryption," 2018 IEEE Int. Conf. Comput. Intell. Comput. Res. ICCIC 2018, pp. 1–8, 2018, doi: 10.1109/ICCIC.2018.8782432.

[7] M. Sokouti, A. Zakerolhosseini, and B. Sokouti, "Medical image encryption : An application for improved padding," Open Med. Inform. J., vol. 10, pp. 11–22, 2016, doi: 10.2174/1874431101610010011.

[8] R. Thanki and A. Kothari, "Multi-level security of medical images based on encryption and watermarking for telemedicine applications," Multimed. Tools Appl., vol. 80, no. 3, pp. 4307–4325, 2021, doi: 10.1007/s11042-020-09941-z.

[9] W. Cao, Y. Zhou, C. L. P. Chen, and L. Xia, "Medical image encryption using edge maps," Signal Process., vol. 132, no. October 2016, pp. 96–109, 2017, doi: 10.1016/j.sigpro.2016.10.003.

[10] Z. Hua, Y. Zhou, and H. Huang, "Cosine-transform-based chaotic system for image encryption," Inf. Sci., vol. 480, pp. 403–419, 2019 Apr 1.

[11] J. B. Lima, F. Madeiro, and F. J. R. Sales, "Encryption of medical images based on the cosine number transform," Signal Process. Image Commun., vol. 35, pp. 1–8, 2015, doi: 10.1016/j.image.2015.03.005.

[12] D. S. Laiphrakpam and M. S. Khumanthem, "Medical image encryption based on improved ElGamal encryption technique," Optik (Stuttg), vol. 147, pp. 88–102, 2017, doi: 10.1016/j.ijleo.2017.08.028.

[13] M. Usama and M. K. Khan, "Classical and chaotic encryption techniques for the security of satellite images," IEEE-Int. Symp. Biometrics Secur. Technol. ISBAST'08, 2008, doi: 10.1109/ISBAST.2008.4547663.

[14] X. Geng, C. Du, and Q. Ding, "Image encryption system of new chaotic algorithm based on DSP," Proc. 2012 2nd Int. Conf. Instrum. Meas. Comput. Commun. Control. IMCCC 2012, pp. 614–618, 2012, doi: 10.1109/IMCCC.2012.395.

[15] J. H. Collins and J. J. Moschler, "The benefits and limitations of telecommuting," Def. Acquis. Rev. J., vol. 16, no. 1, pp. 55–66, 2009. Available: http://eres.library.manoa.hawaii.edu/login?url=http://search.ebscohost.com/login.aspx?direct=true&db=aph&AN=43096390&site=ehost-live.

[16] A. Haleem, M. Javaid, R. P. Singh, and R. Suman, "Telemedicine for healthcare: Capabilities, features, barriers, and applications," Sensors Int., vol. 2, no. July, p. 100117, 2021, doi: 10.1016/j.sintl.2021.100117.

[17] T. S. Ali and R. Ali, "A novel medical image signcryption scheme using TLTS and Henon chaotic map," IEEE Access, vol. 8, pp. 71974–71992, 2020, doi: 10.1109/ACCESS.2020.2987615.

[18] F. Masood et al., "A lightweight chaos-based medical image encryption scheme using random shuffling and XOR operations," Wirel. Pers. Commun., no. 0123456789, 2021, doi: 10.1007/s11277-021-08584-z.

[19] M. Ashtiyani, P. M. Birgani, and H. M. Hosseini, "Chaos-based medical image encryption using symmetric cryptography," 2008 3rd Int. Conf. Inf. Commun. Technol. From Theory to Appl. ICTTA, 2008, doi: 10.1109/ICTTA.2008.4530291.

[20] M. Gafsi, N. Abbassi, M. A. Hajjaji, J. Malek, and A. Mtibaa, "Improved chaos-based cryptosystem for medical image encryption and decryption," Sci. Program., vol. 2020, 2020, doi: 10.1155/2020/6612390.

[21] S. Al-Maadeed, A. Al-Ali, and T. Abdalla, "A new chaos-based image-encryption and compression algorithm," J. Electr. Comput. Eng., vol. 2012, 2012, doi: 10.1155/2012/179693.

[22] S. Deb and B. Bhuyan, "Chaos-based medical image encryption scheme using special nonlinear filtering function based LFSR," Multimed. Tools Appl., vol. 80, no. 13, pp. 19803–19826, 2021, doi: 10.1007/s11042-020-10308-7.

[23] N. Sasikaladevi, K. Geetha, K. Sriharshini, and M. Durga Aruna, "RADIANT – hybrid multilayered chaotic image encryption system for color images," Multimed. Tools Appl., vol. 78, no. 9, pp. 11675–11700, 2019, doi: 10.1007/s11042-018-6711-0.

[24] A. Pourjabbar Kari, A. Habibizad Navin, A. M. Bidgoli, and M. Mirnia, "A new image encryption scheme based on hybrid chaotic maps," Multimed. Tools Appl., vol. 80, no. 2, pp. 2753–2772, 2021, doi: 10.1007/s11042-020-09648-1.

[25] S. Pan, J. Wei, and S. Hu, "A novel image encryption algorithm based on hybrid chaotic mapping and intelligent learning in financial security system," Multimed. Tools Appl., vol. 79, pp. 1–3, 2019.

[26] J. Chandrasekaran, S. J. Thiruvengadam, and D. Rey, "A hybrid chaotic and number theoretic approach for securing DICOM images," Secur. Commun. Netw., vol. 2017, 2017.

[27] S. Priya and B. Santhi, "A novel visual medical image encryption for secure transmission of authenticated watermarked medical images," Mob. Netw. Appl., vol. 9, pp.1–8, 2019 Feb.

[28] S. Zhang, T. Gao, and L. Gao, "A novel encryption frame for medical image with watermark based on hyperchaotic system," Math. Probl. Eng., vol. 2014, 2014 Apr 9.

[29] J. Liu, J. Li, J. Cheng, J. Ma, N. Sadiq, B. Han, Q. Geng, and Ai Y. "A novel robust watermarking algorithm for encrypted medical image based on DTCWT-DCT and chaotic map," Comput. Mater. Contin., vol. 61, no. 2, pp. 889–910, 2019 Feb 8.

[30] K. Balasamy and S. Suganyadevi, "A fuzzy based ROI selection for encryption and watermarking in medical image using DWT and SVD," Multimed. Tools. Appl., vol. 80, no. 5, pp. 7167–7186, 2021 Feb.

[31] S. Jeevitha and N. A. Prabha, "Novel medical image encryption using DWT block-based scrambling and edge maps," J. Ambient. Intell. Humaniz. Comput., vol. 12, no. 3, pp. 3373–88, 2021 Mar.

[32] H. Nematzadeh, R. Enayatifar, H. Motameni, F. G. Guimarães, and V. N. Coelho, "Medical image encryption using a hybrid model of modified genetic algorithm and coupled map lattices," Opt. Lasers Eng., vol. 110, pp. 24–32, 2018 Nov 1.

[33] S. Kumar, B. Panna, and R. K. Jha, "Medical image encryption using fractional discrete cosine transform with chaotic function," Med. Biol. Eng. Comput., vol. 57, no. 11, pp. 2517–2533, 2019 Nov.

[34] Y. Zhou, K. Panetta, and S. Agaian, Image encryption using discrete parametric cosine transform. In 2009 Conference Record of the Forty-Third Asilomar Conference on Signals, Systems and Computers 2009 Nov 1 (pp. 395–399). IEEE.

[35] V. Pavithra, and J. Chandrasekaran, Developing security solutions for telemedicine applications: medical image encryption and watermarking. In Research anthology on telemedicine efficacy, adoption, and impact on healthcare delivery 2021 (pp. 612–631). IGI Global.

[36] W. El-Shafai, F. Khallaf, E. S. El-Rabaie, and F. E. Abd El-Samie, "Robust medical image encryption based on DNA-chaos cryptosystem for secure telemedicine and healthcare applications," J. Ambient. Intell. Humaniz. Comput., vol. 12, 9007–9035, 2021 Mar 26.

[37] A. Umamageswari and G. R. Suresh, Security in medical image communication with Arnold's cat map method and reversible watermarking. In 2013 International Conference on Circuits, Power and Computing Technologies (ICCPCT) 2013 Mar 20 (pp. 1116–1121). IEEE.

[38] J. C. Dagadu, J. Li, E. O. Aboagye, and F. K. Deynu, "Medical image encryption scheme based on multiple chaos and DNA coding," Int. J. Netw. Secur., vol. 21, no. 1, pp. 83–90, 2019 Jan 1.

[39] V. Manikandan and R. Amirtharajan, "On dual encryption with RC6 and combined logistic tent map for grayscale and DICOM," Multimed. Tools. Appl., vol. 3, pp. 1–30, 2021 May.

Chapter 8

Machine-learning approach for detecting cyberattacks in Medical Internet of Things

Thulasi M. Santhi and M. C. Helen Mary

CONTENTS

8.1 INTRODUCTION

Human health monitoring is an important area to research, and day-to-day development is taking place based on the technological revolution and necessity. Internet of Things (IoT) is seeking the current interest in academia and industries and applied in all fields to make life easier by utilizing the power of the internet to collect and transfer data [1]. In the present COVID-19 pandemic scenario, remote patient monitoring (RPM) and disease diagnosis supported by comfortable wearable sensors became inevitable for society's well-being and IoT in the medical domain became more common. The wearable sensor senses the abnormal changes in an individual's body and alerts the user; simultaneously, the Medical Internet of Things (IoMT) triggers the alarm for the immediate attention

DOI: 10.1201/9781003269144-8

of health workers in case of an emergency. In such a way, the patient will get the first aid or advice within no time and avoid physical consultation in noncritical cases. IoMT-based wearable sensor monitoring is beneficial for the patients and can also be used for all who were imposed to hazardous environments such as soldiers, rescuers, miners, mountain climbers and sailors.

Even though the IoMT plays a vital role in the remote monitoring of a patient, the privacy and security of the sensor data are questionable. The Wireless Sensor Networks (WSN) are prone to various types of cyberattacks, as well as data transmission delay and loss are also major issues. These all data privacy and security issues have to be taken care of [2–5]. Recently, the industry and researchers are giving primary importance to these cyber threats as internet-based areas develop. But yet, a reliable method is not found.

The IoMT structure, necessity, applications, and advantages are explained briefly in Section 8.2 of this chapter. The privacy and cyber security issues involved with the data sent to the cloud are presented in the third section. Different types of cyberattacks are described in this part for a better understanding of the reader. The data from the wearable sensor is sent to the cloud after encryption for introducing privacy is explained in the fourth section. The neural network-based attack detection is elaborated and discussed next. Then the future scope of research in the cyber security point of view is briefed and concludes this chapter.

8.2 MEDICAL INTERNET OF THINGS (IoMT)

IoMT is the practical application of IoT technology in healthcare and the medical sensors, devices and tools for collecting, processing, transmitting and storing medical data in real-time diagnosing or monitoring a patient and a person in an elderly condition. It is commonly known as internet connected medical devices. To analyze the physical parameter changes, a person can also use wearable or handheld devices by himself. The utilization of software features helps to keep person health-conscious by utilizing the merits of technology. As an IoMT tool, the apps can collect and analyze a person's metrics and suggest the remedies in case of nonserious health issues such as healthy weight management, blood sugar management and water consumption requirement [6–8].

The IoMT can be classified according to its application area as:

- **In-home IoMT:** This IoMT allows the patients to be in home and monitors them and in case of any abnormality remoting the primary health-care members or doctors. The blood sugar level, pulse, blood pressure etc. are usually monitored.
- **On-body IoMT:** Wearable devices are the main category coming under on-body IoMT. The sensors are attached to the wrist bands

or clothes and continuously monitored. The service will be available when the person is inside the home or outside.

- **Community IoMT:** In a geographical area or town, the centers will be open for patient monitoring. The usage of environmental analyzers for sensing temperature, pressure etc. in health-care goods carrying logistics also comes under this category.
- **In-hospital IoMT:** The hospital management and doctors use IoT technology to assess the overall running and patient behavior.

There are different types of IoMT devices based on applications and availability. Few of the categories are as follows:

- Consumer-grade wearables.
- Medical-grade wearables.
- RPM devices.
- Personal emergency response systems (PERS).
- Smart pills.
- Point-of care devices and kiosks.
- In-clinic monitors.
- In-hospital devices.

8.2.1 Architecture of Medical Internet of Things (IoMT)

For implementing IoMT technology, the sensors and wireless network play a vital role. Different types of sensors based on the biological parameters to be measured are placed in an appropriate position on the human body. For example, for pulse or heart rate measurement, a sensor can be worn as a wrist band, electroencephalogram (EEG) signals can be taken by wearing a cap with sensors appropriately placed. We can place one or more sensors at a time as per the necessity and these signals will be collected and processed by a sensor coordinator. After the signal processing and amplification, the data is sent to the mobile apps or personal computer that is connected with strong internet. The data is pushed to the cloud after encryption for data privacy. This data is accessible to the concerned authorized person in the hospital for further action, based on the data. The basic architecture of IoMT is given in Figure 8.1.

Basic IoT has a four-step architecture as a flow from data sensing, processing and encrypting, pushing to the cloud and coming to a decision after analysis.

Step 1: The first step consists of the deployment of interconnected devices that includes sensors, actuators, monitors, detectors, camera systems etc. These devices collect the data.

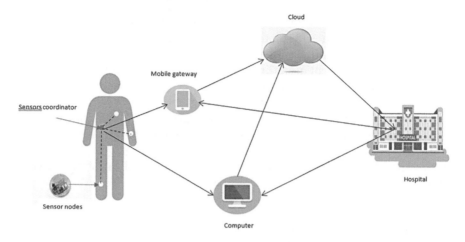

Figure 8.1 Basic architecture of IoMT-based health monitoring system.

Step 2: Usually, data received from sensors and other devices are in analog form, which needs to be aggregated and converted to digital for further data processing.

Step 3: Once the data is digitized and aggregated, this is pre-processed, standardized and moved to the data center or cloud.

Step 4: Final data is managed and analyzed at the required level. Advanced Analytics applied to this data brings actionable business insights for effective decision-making.

IoT redefines healthcare by ensuring better care, improved treatment outcomes and reduced costs for patients, and better processes and workflows, improved performance and patient experience for health-care providers.

8.2.2 Necessity and advantages of IoMT

The world is running fast, and everything needed is wrapping inside the palms nowadays. The patients, doctors and insurers are benefited from the IoMT by many merits as;

- **Increased accessibility:** The doctors, patients, their caretakers and insurers can access a patient's data who is near or far from him in real-time without asking help from any other person. In this way, the productive time is saved and human communication errors are avoided.
- **Improved efficiency:** Efficiency improvement, time-saving and cost reduction are significant merits in utilizing the IoMT. The traveling and waiting times are always matters to patients in critical stages.

First aids and care can be given to them as early as possible by easy, timeless diagnosis.

- **Faster implementation:** It is easy to use the IoMT devices and a patient or individual themselves can keep a check over their physical changes.
- **Improved treatment:** It enables physicians to make evidence-based informed decisions and brings absolute transparency.
- **Faster disease diagnosis:** Continuous patient monitoring and real-time data help in diagnosing diseases at an early stage or even before the condition develops based on symptoms.
- **Proactive treatment:** Continuous health monitoring opens the doors for proactive medical treatment.
- **Drugs and equipment management:** Management of drugs and medical equipment is a major challenge in the health-care industry. Through connected devices, these are managed and utilized efficiently with reduced costs.
- **Error reduction:** Data generated through IoT devices not only helps in effective decision-making but also ensures smooth health-care operations with reduced errors, waste and system costs.
- **Patient empowerment:** IoMT devices such as wearables and smart scales let patients take control of their vitals, giving them the information they would otherwise have to visit a doctor to get. Rather than waiting for an annual checkup, patients can now keep tabs on their health in real-time.
- **Improved patient monitoring:** Chronically and seriously ill patients need more intensive monitoring, sometimes requiring around-the-clock care. IoMT devices allow physicians to monitor patients from afar without having to rely on human caregivers, alerting them instantly if something goes awry.
- **Upgraded operations:** IoMT improves hospital's operations by giving providers and administrators easier, centralized control over their facilities. IoMT devices can provide them with more visibility into their environment and provide physicians with new technologies like robotic surgical aids and high-resolution digital imaging systems.

8.3 PRIVACY AND CYBER SECURITY ISSUES ON IoMT

The leakage of medical data can embarrass or damage the image and life of a patient and so it is treated as a criminal offense. The leaked credentials, medical data and prescriptions may be used for medical fraud activities such as getting treatment, drugs and medicines illegally. A smart pacemaker, glucose monitor and insulin pump etc. can be stopped or mishandled by the cyberattacker, which can cause potential risk to the patients. Data breaching, unauthorized accessing and hijacking, undesired sharing of data, malicious insiders, data loss, various cyberattacks, etc. are the leading privacy and security issues on any IoT-related systems. Securing personal and confidential data while preserving its privacy has paramount importance in the IoMTs [9].

- **Data breach:** Any data leakage by unauthorized access or an internal person comes under this category. Particularly in IoMTs, data breach leads to the person's privacy revealing to the world.
- **Unauthorized accessing and hijacking:** An attacker can hijack the system and access, edit and remove the data in the cloud and detecting who plays back to it is not easy.
- **Malicious insider:** The authorized insider can easily access, change and delete the available data and is very severe and difficult to detect.
- **Data loss:** Data loss creates a disturbance to the continuous monitoring of a person. At the time of any abnormality, if the data is not reached and analyzed by medical staff for proper action, the patient will be at threat.
- **Cyberattacks:** Various cyberattacks are present, especially in cyber physical systems. The properties and behavior of each attack are different and cause a high impact on the system [10].

8.3.1 Types of cyberattacks

8.3.1.1 Denial of Service (DoS) attack

In Denial of Service (DoS) attack, an attacker system sends plenty of data or requests to make the victim system unavailable or shut down, leading to massive misbehavior of the victim system, particularly in IoMT, risks the patient life.

8.3.1.2 Distributed Denial of Service (DDoS) attack

It's a type of DoS attack where several attacker systems send the data or request from different locations to the victim system to crash its regular operation. Distributed Denial of Service (DDoS) is more severe than the DoS attack. Identifying the attacker and blocking it isn't easy in DDOS compared to a DoS attack.

8.3.1.3 Man in the middle attack

In man in a middle attack, an attacker hides between the two user communication lines aiming to steal information shared by them. Identification and control of this type of attack is challenging and here, the question of privacy arises. Here the encryption of data can secure confidential information to a great extent.

8.3.1.4 Bad data injection attack

Injection attacks are many types. Injecting new data to the sent data, modifying the existing data, deleting the existing data, corrupting the available data, all of these comes under this category. Some small codes are also injected to extract information or crash the system. These are oldest and dangerous ones.

8.3.1.5 Replay attack

Replay attacks are challenging to find. In this way, the attacker who eavesdrops the communication can delay or resend the previous data to misdirect or mislead the other end. Detecting these attacks is also not easy because the data sent will be in the range of our desired values, even though the system behaves abnormally.

There are many more attacks and those are evolving day by day. It is not easy to secure data from all these attacks but following maximum measures can protect the data. Many security and detection methods are developed by the researchers are the industrialists and the study and work on it is the current focus.

8.3.2 Advanced encryption standard (AES) technique

Advanced encryption standard (AES)-128, AES-192 and AES-256 are the different encryption techniques and among that AES-256 is more complex to crack. The AES-256 technique produces 2^{256} key combinations and has more computational complexity for the key generation compared to other techniques [11]. The nonlinearity provided to the cipher by the AES method results in difficulty for finding the key and thus prevents the attacks and unauthorized actions [12].

8.3.2.1 Encryption and decryption algorithm

There are nine steps in the AES algorithm for both encryption and decryption.

ALGORITHM FOR ENCRYPTION

1. Start.
2. Input data for encryption.
3. Transform this data into a hexadecimal number.

4. Transform this hexadecimal number into rows and columns by using shift operation for encryption.
5. Transform each column into a new column by performing a mix column transformation.
6. To perform the addition of the matrix, add some round key to each column.
7. eXclusive OR (XOR) the output of the added matrix with a key.
8. Generate an encrypted message.
9. End.

ALGORITHM FOR DECRYPTION

1. Start.
2. Input data for decryption.
3. Transform this data into a hexadecimal number.
4. Transform this hexadecimal number into rows and columns by using shift operation for decryption.
5. Transform each column into a new column by performing a mix column transformation.
6. To perform the addition of the matrix, add some round key to each column.
7. XOR the output of the added matrix with a key.
8. Generate original text.
9. End.

8.4 NEURAL NETWORK-BASED ATTACK DETECTION

The best and easy way to detect the attack is by estimating or predicting the next value the IoMT system can produce based on the relative parameters we collected at the previous instant. An abnormality in the human body will never happen in a second, except in accidents. Any input parameters can show the variations and can alarm an upcoming change in the physical conditions. Utilizing these parameter changes, we can parallelly predict the next values and compare with the sensed values to point out the attack's presence.

A trained neural network can perform well in prediction. The input of the neural network is the last parameter values and the output is the current parameters [13, 14]. If we train a neural network properly, the prediction will be pretty accurate because of the hidden layer. In the proposed

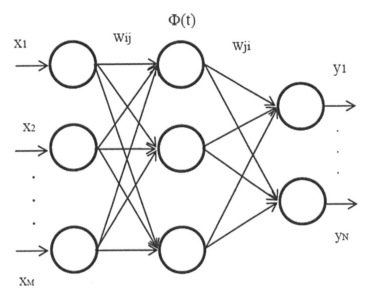

Figure 8.2 Structure of a neural network.

prediction method, a three-layer wavelet neural network is used with Mexican hat wavelet as the activation function, given by,

$$\phi\left(t\right) = \left(1 - x^{2}\right) e^{(-x^{2}/2)}$$

The structure of a wavelet neural network is given in Figure 8.2 and the predicted output is shown in Figure 8.3. The predicted values can be compared with the actual reading as shown in the block diagram Figure 8.4. If the difference exceeds a predetermined threshold based on the parameter, the presence of attack is considered. The patient can replace or maintain the wearable sensor and can take medical help for the safe side in case of doubt.

8.5 CONCLUSION

Medical Internet of Things (IoMT) is one of the flourishing technologies, especially having utter importance in the COVID-19 pandemic situation, but the system is constantly under different cyber threats and attacks. Each cyberattacks possess different nature and property making it difficult to detect. Here, a machine learning-based method is proposed that utilizes the strength of neural network in predicting future sensor data. The result shows a close relation to the actual readings and the comparison between both can indicate the system is under attack or note based on the fixed

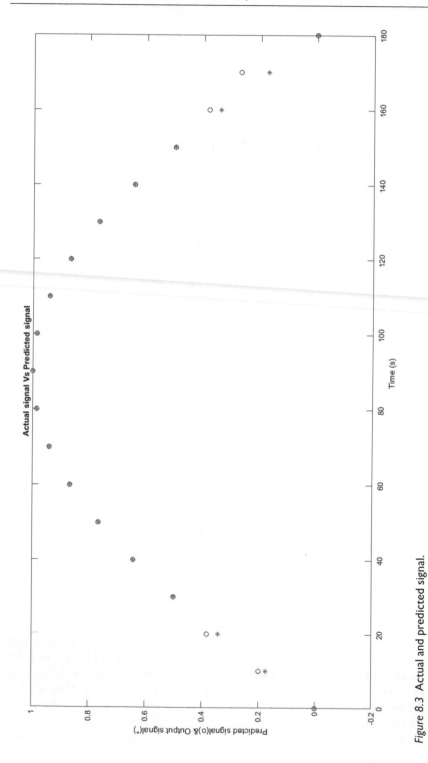

Figure 8.3 Actual and predicted signal.

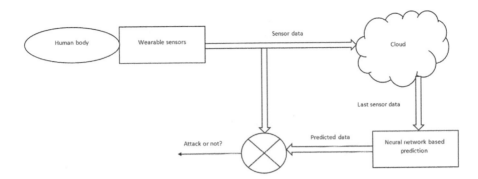

Figure 8.4 Basic block diagram of attack detection.

threshold value. If the attack is detected the patient can contact the vendor, or hospital management to rectify it by maintaining or replacing the sensor coordinate system. This chapter discusses the attacks and importance to focus on it, which acts as an eye-opener to the readers and an attack detection method that has significance in medical, industrial, vehicle, space IoTs and many other industries.

REFERENCES

[1] Syeda M. Muzammal, Raja Kumar Murugesan and Noor Zaman Jhanjhi, "A Comprehensive Review on Secure Routing in Internet of Things: Mitigation Methods and Trust-Based Approaches", IEEE Internet of Things, Vol. 8, No. 6, March, 2021.

[2] Francesca Meneghello, Matteo Calore, Daniel Zucchetto, Michele Polese and Andrea Zanella, "IoT: Internet of Threats? A Survey of Practical Security Vulnerabilities in Real IoT Devices", IEEE Internet of Things Journal, Vol. 6, No. 5, October, 2019.

[3] Kalupahana Liyanage Kushan Sudheera, Dinil Mon Divakaran, Rhishi Pratap Singh and Mohan Gurusamy, "ADEPT: Detection and Identification of Correlated Attack Stages in IoT Networks", IEEE Internet of Things Journal, Vol. 8, No. 8, April, 2021.

[4] Karim Lounis and Mohammad Zulkernine, "Attacks and Defenses in Short-Range Wireless Technologies for IoT", IEEE Access, Vol. 8, May 2020.

[5] Jalal Bhayo, Sufian Hameed and Syed Attique Shah, "An Efficient Counter-Based DDoS Attack Detection Framework Leveraging Software Defined IoT (SD-IoT)", IEEE Access, Vol. 8, December, 2020.

[6] Gulraiz J. Joyia, Rao M. Liaqat, Aftab Farooq and Saad Rehman, "Internet of Medical Things (IOMT): Applications, Benefits and Future Challenges in Healthcare Domain", Journal of Communications, Vol. 12, No. 4, April, 2017.

[7] S. Vishnu, S.R. Jino Ramson and R. Jegan, "Internet of Medical Things (IoMT) – An overview", 5th International Conference on Devices, Circuits and Systems (ICDCS), March, 2020.

[8] Joel J. P. C. Rodrigues, Honggang Wang, Simon James Fong, Nada Y. Philip, and Jia Chen, "Guest Editorial: Internet of Things for In-Home Health Monitoring", IEEE Journal On Selected Areas In Communications, Vol. 39, No. 2, February 2021.

[9] Harsh Gupta and Deepak Kumar, "Security Threats in Cloud Computing", Proceedings of the International Conference on Intelligent Computing and Control Systems (ICICCS), 2019.

[10] Ali Ghubaish, Tara Salman, Maede Zolanvari, Devrim Unal, Abdulla Al-Ali and Raj Jain, "Recent Advances in the Internet-of-Medical-Things (IoMT) Systems Security", IEEE Internet of Things Journal, Vol. 8, No. 11, June, 2021.

[11] P802.15.4y/D2, Oct 2020 – IEEE Draft Standard for Low-Rate Wireless Networks Amendment Defining Support for Advanced Encryption Standard (AES)-256 Encryption and Security Extensions", IEEE Standards, December, 2020.

[12] Noemie Floissac, Yann L'Hyver, "From AES-128 to AES-192 and AES-256, How to Adapt Differential Fault Analysis Attacks on Key Expansion", Workshop on Fault Diagnosis and Tolerance in Cryptography, September, 2011.

[13] Tom Gedeon and H. S. Turner, "Explaining student grades predicted by a neural network", International Conference on Neural Networks (IJCNN-93-Nagoya, Japan), August, 2002.

[14] Wu Wang and Yuan-min Zhang, "Application of Recursive Predict Error Neural Networks in Mechanical Properties Forecasting", International Joint Conference on Artificial Intelligence, April, 2009.

Chapter 9

Secure IoV-enabled systems at Fog Computing

Layout, security, and optimization algorithms and open issues

Anshu Devi, Ramesh Kait, and Virender Ranga

CONTENTS

9.1 INTRODUCTION

Yesteryear's businesses and people are heavily dependent on smart technologies and personal computers to reconcile with routine activities. These smart devices produce data by utilizing a wide range of applications and sensor technologies, and their sophistication is increasing all the time. As a result, businesses continually create and store vast amounts of data. Following the establishment of the Internet of Things, the amount of data created by various sensors has increased. The structure of this chapter is depicted in Figure 9.1.

Big data analytics is currently receiving a great deal of attention due to the rapid growth in the amount of information being generated and the inability of traditional databases to handle the wide range of possible structured and unorganized data. Many service companies, such as [1] Google, IBM, Amazon, and Microsoft, use cloud services. Using Cloud Computing (CC), it is now possible to have multiple issues related to business, software, and education. Cloud data centers are usually geographically dispersed and far from client devices. The cloud data centers suffer from latency and real-time delays, resulting in decreased service quality, network congestion, and round-trip delays. The purpose of Fog in conjunction with IoV is to minimize the quantity of data transported to the cloud for storage,

DOI: 10.1201/9781003269144-9

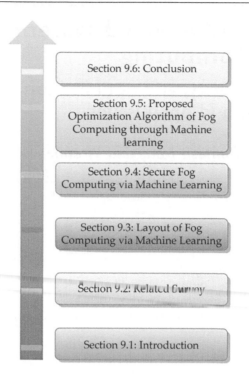

Figure 9.1 Chapter structure.

analysis, processing, and efficiency, while simultaneously increasing performance. In order to reduce latency and network traffic, sensor data is moved to network devices such as network edges for temporary storage and processing rather than being forwarded to the cloud. Together, IoV and Fog Computing have opened up a new market for Fog as a Service, in which multiple fog nodes have been established by the service provider and are operating as an owner to numerous residents from numerous vertical positions all over the world. Each node in the fog is responsible for managing storage, processing, and networking [2]. Unlike CC, which relies on an integrated component, Fog is entirely distributed. CC's latency can be reduced by taking advantage of idle resources on neighboring devices, such as fog. It is despite this fact that the CC is given a large number of responsibilities. Fog Computing services should be improved by enhancing their diversity and transmission efficiency.

This chapter will provide a concise overview of related topics and will analyze current trends in the study field via a literature review, which will contribute to the body of knowledge by summarizing recent work in the field. This second section will provide an overview of securing Fog Computing through Machine Learning from the viewpoint of Fog Computing. Layout of Fog Computing via Machine Learning will be covered in Section 9.3.

Securing Fog Computing via Machine Learning discussed in the fourth section. Section 9.5 elaborated proposed Optimization Algorithm of Fog Computing through Machine learning. Finally, in the concluding section, the findings from Section 9.4 will be summarized and some general observations will be made.

9.2 RELATED SURVEY

The following are the subjects that will be explored in this section of VANET-related research in Table 9.1.

In these investigations, the goal was to improve the intelligence of these devices, for example, by adding smart data processing and networking services to an e-health gateway or a gateway that is capable of doing Machine Learning.

It is also possible to improve coverage and connectivity by employing a neural network model to analyze wireless channel parameters. Thus, the network can be more context aware, make better judgments, and manage local resources.

The second strategy is based on human intellect. The IoV landscape's design is shaped by human users. In IoV networks, humans are the most common data providers. Consequently, their behavior patterns play a key role in educating the network to become more intelligent. Human needs are the focus of numerous academic studies, including managing household appliances and the cognitive IoV-based smart home for improving living quality. Thus, human-driven intelligence helps the network make better decisions. When designing an FC system for an IoV application, device and human intelligence may be considered.

9.3 LAYOUT OF FOG COMPUTING
VIA MACHINE LEARNING

To deliver services and apps, or to improve system operations and network performance, intelligence is added to fog and IoV. Moving certain cloud resources to the network's edge, where IoV devices and human users are typically assumed to be. This indicates that intelligence can be used in two ways in the Fog Computing. Figure 9.2 shows the comparison between secure Fog Computing and Machine Learning.

The first is intelligence that is derived from devices. The addition of sensors makes IoV devices and fog layers smarter, increasing computational power, storage capacity, and communication capabilities, which is depicted in Figure 9.1. The Internet of Things gateways, local servers and access points, and human-carried data aggregation nodes are all instances of such devices.

Table 9.1 Comparison with related survey papers

Related survey	Problem addresses
[3]	Using IoVs with Fog Computing decreases real-time vehicle crashes. Driving under the influence of alcohol or drugs causes most car accidents. Reduce road accidents by constantly monitoring vehicle speed and alcohol intake. IoVs and Fog Computing process data in real time. Machine learning algorithms classify cars as risky or not (non-accident-prone).
[4, 5]	Address the key VANET issues by combining V2V, V2I, and V2B communications with SDN centralized control, maximizing resource efficiency, and lowering latency. Aside from demonstrating the benefits of our proposed architecture, two non-safety use cases (data streaming and lane-change assistance) are described.
[6]	Give a comprehensive study to highlight the Fog computing involves Machine Learning for resource management, accuracy, and security. ML (Machine Learning) is also mentioned in this context. Other ML domain perspectives include application support, technique, and dataset. Finally, research topics and challenges are highlighted.
[7, 8]	Give a comprehensive evaluation of the existing research on the security problems associated with Fog Computing. Various designs that are critical to the security of the fog environment are analyzed using a taxonomy based on numerous security techniques. Machine learning, cryptography, artificial intelligence, and other techniques distinguish this study from earlier evaluations. This study discusses security vulnerabilities in Fog Computing and suggests solutions for both professionals and novices.
[9]	Demonstrate Fog Computing-based industrial cyber-physical system capable of integrating Machine Learning models into factory operations, while conforming to Industry 4.0 design considerations about decentralization, security, privacy, and reliability.
[8, 10]	Addressed numerous difficulties that could occur during the design and implementation of Fog Computing systems. Since Fog Computing-related opportunities and problems can be pursued in this domain, additional research in the field is possible.
[11]	Present a novel distributed and fog (DD-fog) software development platform that combines fog, MEC, and microservices. With this framework, users can migrate microservices between fog structures and elements based on computational and network capabilities. Untethered cars and a tactile internet were also imagined. Two techniques were created to detect the fog migration node and choose load places in the search mechanism for user congestion.
[12]	Presented fundamental building elements and services of the related technology platform and protocol stack, which is the Fog of Everything (FoE). Fourth, They demonstrated the V-FoE prototype's simulated energy delay performance as a proof-of-concept. Then they evaluated the achieved performance to a benchmark technical platform, such V-D2D. Device-to-device linkages are used to establish "ad hoc" communication.

Figure 9.2 Layout of secure Fog Computing via Machine Learning.

Clustering and other unsupervised Machine Learning algorithms have been applied to a variety of IoV applications, including smart farming and traffic management. Machine learning techniques, both unsupervised and supervised, are being applied to enhance the role of Fog Computing at the network's edge [6]. Machine learning techniques were applied on Fog servers to recognize and understand music, as well as to write the score automatically using Machine Learning algorithms.

9.4 SECURE FOG COMPUTING VIA MACHINE LEARNING

It is critical that nodes be installed at diverse locations throughout the system in order for it to function effectively. Many vehicle parameters, such as the car's position and energy use, can be programmed into the system. When a node is sending a packet between two different computers, approximately how much electricity is consumed by the node?

The locations of the beginning point and end destination are determined in the following step. When it comes to the overall functionality of a system, the capacity of a system to successfully transmit data from one point to another is essential. Direct data transmission is suggested if the issue node can be located within its range; otherwise, it is recommended that the route request be broadcast to all nodes in the network to ensure that it is received by everyone.

It will be assigned to the node based on the response provided by the responder node, with the group to which it belongs determined by the number of responses received by the responder node. In exchange for remaining a member of the network, those who choose to do so are required to make a payment to the overall network in the amount of a percentage of their network share, which is calculated on an annual basis.

Using E-Lagrange Interpolation techniques on the respondent-network share, this is accomplished in the following stage and is then completed by the Fog Server in the following phase, which concludes the process. Each car in the network is identified by a single global key, which is retained for the whole network and is used to uniquely identify each vehicle within the network.

In this case, the use of a centralized system is an imperative necessity, as a precaution against the possibility of transmitting the global key to a large number of vehicles at the same time. When a car asks data from a Fog Server or through an RSU, it is feasible that the car may either issue a demand for [1] three shares from any other vehicle on the network or will select two shares at random from a pool of available shares, depending on the circumstances.

That particular share will be one of a total of three that will be assessed in the case of the high-performance vehicle under consideration. It is necessary to employ a Lagrange polynomial in order for the Fog Server to calculate the values displayed in the following table: Calculate the anticipated share in the following step and compare it to the two shares that were previously computed and displayed in the previous step (B1 and B2). When the share falls within a set range, route nodes are added to the network, and route nodes are removed from the network when the share does not fall within a specific range.

If the desired destination has been reached, it is not necessary to select a new responder for the message. Once a specific period of time has passed, it is necessary to select a new respondent and repeat the process until the destination has been reached. As a result, after a long and winding journey, the trail has finally arrived at its destination.

Following that, the parameters that have an impact on the overall quality of the service will be evaluated. In the Fog repository database, it has now been preserved as a parameter that will be used to evaluate the overall quality of the service that was provided.

A total of two layers of authentication are required, according to the design that has been proposed. The FS (Fog Server) and the RSU (Road-Side Unit) are in charge of aggregating the information received from the RSU. To be more exact, both the fog and the RSU have been proven to be effective. In the configuration of a VANET, metrics like throughput, power consumption, and packet delivery ratio are taken into consideration. However, in the creation of a VANET, the Lagrange Polynomial is used to identify nodes that are not trusted by the other nodes in the network.

The Lagrange polynomial [2, 13] $L(X)$ with $degree <= (n-1)$ requires n vehicles with respect to coordinates $x_1, y_1 = f(x_1), x_2, y_2 = f(x_2), :::::: x_m, y_m = f(x_m)$ and is provided by:

$$NS(x) = \sum_{i=1}^{m} PS_i(x)$$

where PS_i (Predicated Share) is provided by:

$$PS_i(x) = y_i \frac{x - x_k}{x_l - x_j}. \text{ where } 1 \geq l, 1 \leq m \text{ and } k! = j$$

9.5 PROPOSED OPTIMIZATION ALGORITHM OF FOG COMPUTING IN MACHINE LEARNING

ALGORITHM FOR PSEUDO-CODE SHARE VERIFICATION NOTATIONS

AODFSV: Authenticating Shares Ordering Demanded by Fog Server from Vehicles

VIC: Vehicle Value's Initial Share is Null

CCV: Contribution for Current Vehicles

DCV: Distribute Critical Values

CDV: Current value of Distributed Vehicle

V_k: Individual kth Vehicle's Number of Shares

SSMCV: Starting Shared Mobility Counter Value

VC: Vehicles' Contribution

VI_{ID}: Value of the Initial Identification

VID_{Num}: Distribute the Vehicle's numerator key

VID_{Deno}: Distribute the Vehicle's denominator key

IVS: Individual lth vehicle will be chosen for sharing

FDVIS: When the first Vehicle Distribution is selected, there will be two leftover Vehicle Shares

CSV: Contribution for the Selected Vehicle, the current share is not the same as the next share selected

LSCV:

Input AS[k],n,k,l,m

Process

1. Initialization

a. $V_k = V_l$;

b. VIC = NULL;

c. AODFSV = n;

d. VID_{Deno} = NULL;

2. If VIC! = NULL;

While V_K = l:n;

3. For SSMCV==l;then

a. VC = VI_{ID};

b. While V_l==l;

c. VC = V_l;

d. VC! = V_l;

e. LSCV = FD_lS;

4. LSCV = LSCV+l;

5. End if

6. End While

7. $VIID_{Deno} = V_i\text{-}(LSCV*V_i\text{-}FD_i\ S;$

8. $VIID_{Num} = LSCV*FD_iS;$

9. $VIC[k] = \dfrac{VIID_{Deno}}{VIID_{Num}};$

10. $DCV = CDV * VIC[k];$

11. End While

Pseudocode communicates [14] via the interpolation order n nodes [15]. In order to determine whether or not the nodes will be selected for data transfer, the final key result, which is established using E-Lagrange's technique, must be determined. One essential generating strategy involves the use of both a numerator and a denominator in order to function properly. In the numerator [16], the network IDs of the vehicles that are still present during the iteration are used to calculate the number of iterations.

9.6 CONCLUSION

This study proposed Authenticating Node, which stands for fog-integrated VANET network. The suggested technique takes into consideration both node-level and network-level security at the same time. The security at the node level helps to develop trust and collaboration with all of the network's neighbors. At the node level, trustworthiness is established to ensure that the entire network delivers packets to the rest of the network system in a timely fashion. The proposed strategy makes advantage of E-Lagrange's interpolation approach to keep foreigners (or outsiders) from accessing the network until they become a part of the home network, hence preventing unauthorized access.

REFERENCES

[1] Sabireen H, and Neelanarayanan V. A review on fog computing: Architecture, fog with IoT, algorithms and research challenges. *ICT Express*, 7(2):162–176, 2021.

[2] Jingyang Lu, Lun Li, Genshe Chen, Dan Shen, Khanh Pham, and Erik Blasch. Machine learning based intelligent cognitive network using Fog Computing. In *Sensors and Systems for Space Applications X*, volume 10196, page 101960G. Anaheim, California, International Society for Optics and Photonics, 2017.

[3] Parveen, Rishipal Singh, and Sushil Kumar. IoV based intelligent vehicle tracker using fog computing with supervised machine learning techniques. *Journal of Discrete Mathematical Sciences and Cryptography*, 24(5):1393–1413, 2021.

[4] Nguyen B Truong, Gyu Myoung Lee, and Yacine Ghamri-Doudane. Software defined networking-based vehicular ad hoc network with Fog Computing. In 2015 IFIP/IEEE International Symposium on Integrated Network Management (IM), pages 1202–1207. IEEE, 2015.

[5] Prathapchandran K, and Janani T. A trust-based security model to detect misbehaving nodes in internet of things (IoT) environment using logistic regression. *Journal of Physics: Conference Series*, 1850:012031, 2021.

[6] Karrar Hameed Abdulkareem, Mazin Abed Mohammed, Saraswathy Shamini Gunasekaran, Mohammed Nasser Al-Mhiqani, Ammar Awad Mutlag, Salama A Mostafa, Nabeel Salih Ali, and Dheyaa Ahmed Ibrahim. A review of fog computing and machine learning: concepts, applications, challenges, and open issues. *IEEE Access*, 7:153123–153140, 2019.

[7] Jimoh Yakubu, Shafi'i Muhammad Abdulhamid, Haruna Atabo Christopher, Haruna Chiroma, and Mohammed Abdullahi. Security challenges in fog-computing environment: A systematic appraisal of current developments. *Journal of Reliable Intelligent Environments*, 5(4):209–233, 2019.

[8] Arun Kumar Sangaiah, Arunkumar Thangavelu, and Venkatesan Meenakshi Sundaram. Cognitive computing for big data systems over IoT. *Gewerbestrasse*, 11:6330, 2018.

[9] Peter O'donovan, Colm Gallagher, Ken Bruton, and Dominic TJ O'Sullivan. A fog computing industrial cyber-physical system for embedded low-latency machine learning industry 4.0 applications. *Manufacturing Letters*, 15:139–142, 2018.

[10] Shanhe Yi, Cheng Li, and Qun Li. A survey of fog computing: concepts, applications and issues. *Proceedings of the 2015 Workshop on Mobile Big Data*, 37–42, 2015.

[11] Volkov Artem, Kovalenko Vadim, Ibrahim A Elgendy, Ammar Muthanna, and Andrey Koucheryavy. Dd-fog: Intelligent distributed dynamic fog computing framework. *Future Internet*, 14(1):13, 2022.

[12] Enzo Baccarelli, Paola G Vinueza Naranjo, Michele Scarpiniti, Mohammad Shojafar, and Jemal H Abawajy. Fog of everything: Energy-efficient networked computing architectures, research challenges, and a case study. *IEEE Access*, 5:9882–9910, 2017.

[13] Samuel Kofi Erskine and Khaled M Elleithy. Secure intelligent vehicular network using Fog Computing. *Electronics*, 8(4):455, 2019.

[14] Samuel Kofi Erskine. Secure Intelligent Vehicular Network Including Real-Time Detection of DoS Attacks in IEEE 802.11 p Using Fog Computing. PhD thesis, University of Bridgeport, 2020.

[15] Jéferson Campos Nobre, Allan M de Souza, Denis Rosário, Cristiano Both, Leandro A Villas, Eduardo Cerqueira, Torsten Braun, and Mario Gerla. Vehicular software-defined networking and Fog Computing: Integration and design principles. *Ad Hoc Networks*, 82:172–181, 2019.

[16] Ashish Rauniyar, Desta Haileselassie Hagos, and Manish Shrestha. A crowd-based intelligence approach for measurable security, privacy, and dependability in internet of automated vehicles with vehicular fog. *Mobile Information Systems*, 2018:1–14, 2018.

Chapter 10

A capability maturity model and value judgment systems for a distributed network of ethical and context aware digital twin agents

Mezzour Ghita, Benhadou Siham,
Medromi Hicham, and Griguer Hafid

CONTENTS

10.1 INTRODUCTION

Recently, with the development and integration of Industrial Internet of Thing, digital engineering and the set of Industry 4.0 evolutions, industrial plants have crossed a new level of intelligence and autonomy that helped several fields to concretize the promulgated vision in 2015 of smart factories proposed by Germany's Platform 4.0 perspective (Gerrikagoitia et al., 2019). Three main pillars can be identified as leading mottos for this vision: intelligence, autonomy, and proprietarily interoperability.

DOI: 10.1201/9781003269144-10

Platform 4.0, in order to achieve interoperability across assets life cycle, has proposed the concept of Asset Administration Shell (AAS) that consists of digital representations of assets that manage all of its life cycle data and knowledge through standardized and domain-oriented sub-models of systems of the real world enabling vertical and horizontal self-synchronization of assets, services, control, and command operations (Birgit Boss (Robert Bosch GmbH) et al., 2020). One of the effective concretizations of AAS was proposed the first time in 2002 by as Digital Twins (DTs) (Kahlen et al., 2016).

According to our previous exploration of concept literature, we define DT as smart agent integrating physical and virtual worlds through a continuous semantic communication and data integration bridge with real twins in order to pursue a set of services and different purposes defined by a group of stakeholders and that are mainly linked to asset life cycles management, human-machine interactions, and assets to assets networks (Ghita et al., 2020). Through their models and digital representations, composite and distributed DT networks can mimic virtually all future, past and present transactions of the real assets across physical environments.

Development efforts have basically focused on technical aspects of the system, and its intended services through the introduction of artificial intelligence modules. However, little interest has been put on the definition of a standard value driven framework for their implementation and permanent evaluation (Qamsane et al., 2020), despite some works that raised the issue through the discussion of business models and views for DTs (Yan et al., 2020), and that defined a structured agent-based approach for DT development in healthcare domain (Croatti et al., 2020). With standardization context beginning to take place mainly through ISO 23247 (Group et al., 2019), Industrial Internet consortium for Industry 4.0 and Platform 4.0 AAS referential (Bradac et al., n.d.), the basic elements constituting a generic DT architecture has been unveiled opening the path for the definition of a formal guided DT development framework that can covers this main element.

A practical tool that can assist this process and provide an end-to-end visibility to DT development and evaluation process across physical and virtual environments is capability maturity model (CMM) (Paulk et al., 2011). CMMs have been known for intensive use in the IT field for cyber security evaluation (U.S. Department of Energy, 2021), companies IT business processes enhancement and project management (PM) (Irfan et al., 2019). CMM defines five maturity evaluation levels for systems under analysis organizational capabilities. Systems capabilities are valuated against a set of characteristics and well-defined requirements and criteria. Criteria are formulated and grouped in a set of domains of concerns. Maturity models aim is threefold, first to provide decision-makers with a benchmarking tool for performances evaluation, a roadmap for DT capabilities development with respect to business concerns and, finally, it represents a gap analysis tool for practitioners in order to detect relevant areas of improvement. The main issues that can hinder the effectiveness of CMM are principally the lack of objectivity for domains evaluation due to the absence, a structured metrics framework or the definition of qualitative scales that error prone to human intervention in the evaluation process.

Taking into consideration these issues, we propose in this chapter a DTCMM with an integrated metrics framework.

Addressing these aspects this chapter pursues three research purposes (RP):

- **RP1:** Identification of maturity domains that can evaluate DT technical and non-technical capabilities through combined macroscopic and microscopic views
- **RP2:** Assessment of company's readiness level for the integration of DT and definition of areas for further improvement
- **RP3:** The integration of both qualitative and quantitative metrics that can help in the objective assessment of maturity levels of each domain of concerns

The remainder of this chapter is organized as follows: Section 10.2 gives an overview of CMMs concept for standards key performance indicators (KPIs) metamodel definition, and explores the different domain of concern for DTs maturity evaluation and levels definition discussed by research communities. Section 10.3 describes the proposed maturity model, its main levels, domains, and metrics and frames it in the context of dedicated value judgment systems through smart autonomous agents. Section 10.4 compares the proposed maturity model to various proposed state of the art DT's maturity models. The last section summarizes this chapter, highlights model's implementation challenges, and opens up on new research directions.

10.2 RESEARCH METHODOLOGY

Our definition of DTCMM is based on the standard structure framed by its various conceptual definitions basically extracted from ISO 23247, IIC and AAS. In order to apprehend the extracted domain of interests, we conducted a state-of-the-art analysis of the existing definition of these categories in the context of smart factories, Industry 4.0 and DTs. The bibliometric analysis concerned two main indexing databases Scopus and Web of science. Through the in-depth analysis of 65 papers on DTs and Industry 4.0 technologies, we were able to extract a set of 93 criteria that we group into nine categories for the definition of DTCMM domains, levels, and attributes for metrics framework. Each domain is represented by a group of concepts of interest that help to describe its requirements with relationship to DT capabilities development. Metrics definition is based on the introduction of KPI and their structuring through ISO 22400 metamodel for enhanced interoperability. The constructed metrics framework and CMM is integrated into the architecture through a policy model and several evaluation grids with the defined KPI, the aim of which is to assist DT agents in pursuing their goals. Details on this part will be presented in future works. A particular focus will be put on ethical aspects considering their importance for extended applications in healthcare domain. Defined metrics and attributes for maturity evaluation were integrated through two intelligent and autonomous cognitive agents within defined DT architecture. The proposed research methodology is presented in Figure 10.1.

10.2.1 DT architectural patterns –
standard perspective

With numerous organization trying to develop their own perception and technologies of DT taking into consideration in their development process, its different structures and applications, and their up-going interest for the integration of the concept for critical application involving artificial intelligence and some major ethical, functional, and quality concerns, a lot of standardization bodies have decided to go through the definition of standard principles and reference conceptual and architectural baseline models and recommendations for DT architecture design and deployment (Jacoby & Usländer, 2020). Through these sections, three propositions are discussed based on our defined dimensions of DT architecture inspired by ISO 42010. ISO 42010 is the reference standards for complex systems architectures development (Júnior et al., 2019). Based on ISO 42010, three dimensions are proposed for DT architecture establishment that involves architecture domains, interactions and common concerns as a reference to architecture framework, stakeholders, and concerns within the standards. This framework is introduced by Figure 10.2.

The first proposition evolves around Industrial Internet Consortium IIC group efforts for DT's architecture development (Industrial Internet Consortium, 2020). The Industrial Internet Consortium (IIC) in the context of their efforts to resorb DT complex structure patterns proposed a generic framework that defines interactions for DT and for each interaction established a set of criteria in order to ensure their efficiency. The discussed criteria are interoperability, administration, Data exchange, information model establishment, synchronization, publish and subscribe as for data and services. These different characteristics are integrated by a set of technologies and serve for different purposes defined as use cases (Industrial et al., 2020). Figure 10.3 introduces the proposed three-dimensional context for DT by the IIC group.

The second proposition was formulated by ISO 23247 standard, and it puts the focus on DT applications dedicated to manufacturing. The standard is formulated through four parts and based on industrial Internet of Things architecture domains with a modified vision taking at the core of the architecture DT platform. The standard defined four main domains that fusion DT core domain with three additional domains that relates to both assets network and users' network that implicitly included other DT as

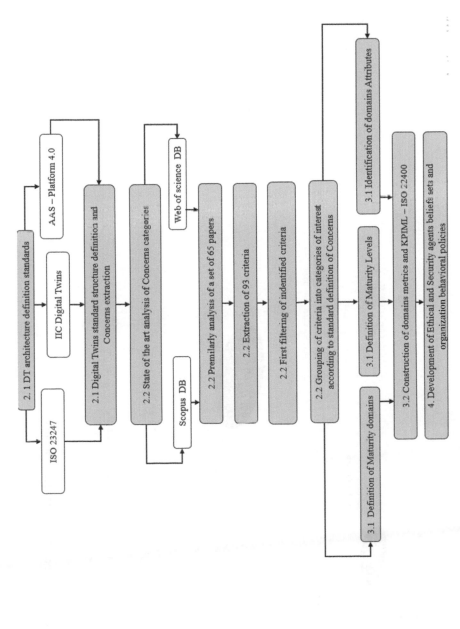

Figure 10.1 Research methodology for DTCMM building.

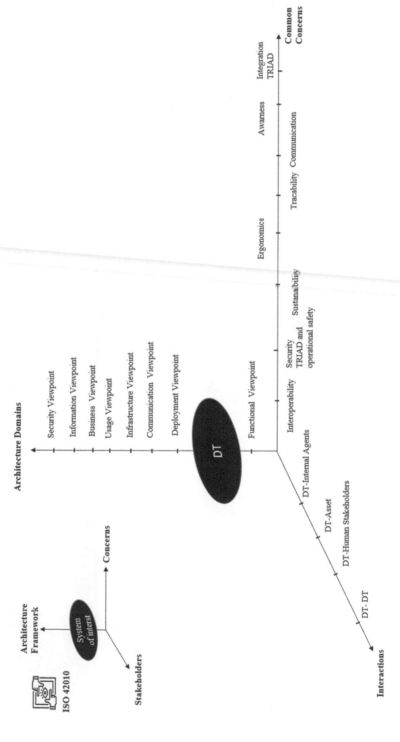

Figure 10.2 Proposed DT architecture framework.

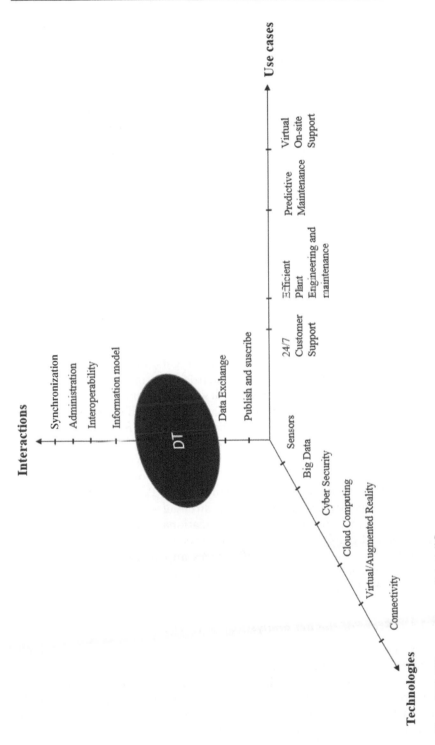

Figure 10.3 DT context according to IIC group.

users of the architecture. Three cross-functioning entities were added to the main architecture of Industrial Internet of things which are security support, interoperability support and data assurance. The proposed implementation of the standard was concretized through a case study that included the STEP framework on DT for machining and collaborative design and engineering (Lu et al., 2020). The group has set up for the development and integration of these interactions through the proposed technologies of Industry 4.0 nine criteria invoking mainly DT architecture constituting modules, element and their internal and external interactions with assets networks, value chain partners and DT network. The proposed framework put the focus on information exchange requirements, digital models building, and synchronization as a major element within industrial internet of things solutions and composite DTs' network.

The last proposition is based on asset administration shell and component 4.0 structures for the deployment of Industry 4.0 under smart factories perspective, AAS was referred to as an implementation scheme for DTs. The proposed structure focused on the analysis of digital representations of Asset through two space dimensions and single time axis that were defined as functional and business views for enterprises horizontal and vertical integration and asset life cycle management for smart end-to-end engineering as represented by RAMI 4.0 reference architecture for Industry 4.0 (Paper & Electrical, 2017). Figure 10.4 represents this perception.

The investigation of these three standards helps in the definition of the main parts that defines DTs process development and technology maturity by technical identification of its main required characteristics. It also gives implicit highlights on two additional elements for capability model development, the first one concerns people within the environment of DTs and the second one organizational areas of DT development project. In our previous works, we defined these aspects as non-contextual requirements for DT development and implementation. People capabilities areas are DT architecture ergonomic for the different stakeholders and ethical concerns for functional safety. For organizational management, dimension standards and regulation management aspects and digital culture establishment are considered. Figure 10.5 gives an overview of the identified categories of concerns, and Table 10.1 presents a synthesis of proposed architectures characteristics.

10.2.1.1 State of the art analysis of concerns

In order to apprehend the different extracted categories of concerns through gray literature, we conducted a bibliometric review that was focused on the definition of these concerns through DT implementations in the last five years from 2016 to 2021. Table 10.2 summarizes the main elements of the bibliometric mapping of the field and describes the implementation process of the mapping. The review included a bibliographical analysis of a total

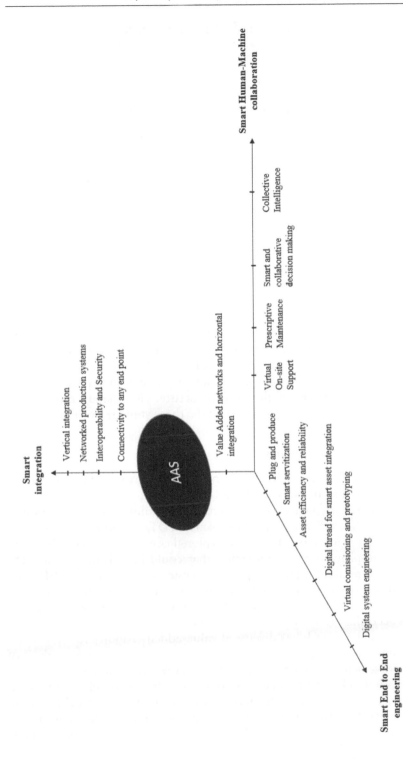

Figure 10.4 AAS context according to RAMI 4.0 and Platform 4.0 perspectives.

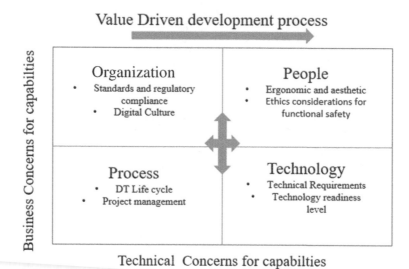

Figure 10.5 Categories of concerns for DT maturity model development.

of 2951 documents extracted basically from academic literature (Scopus and Web of science). We focused on the requirements, standards, and criteria related to the maturity assessment of DT architectures by prioritizing main concepts constituting the three categorizes identified previously and concerns mainly interoperability, infrastructure, data management (DM), communication and security defined by the three standard propositions.

10.2.1.2 Organizational aspects

Intensive research for DT development and implementation analysis has focused on technical aspects of the architecture, implementation technologies and requirements without explicitly detailing their integration at deployment phases. Few research has discussed DTs' organizational aspects, in this sense, research axes that were explored concerned the establishment of generic implementation approaches that could holistically manage DT integration into plant legacy management systems (Zheng et al., 2018) and involve stakeholders views into development process of systems architecture (Brenner & Hummel, 2017). Figure 10.6 summarizes organizational aspects focuses according to the bibliometric review.

Some recent research has discussed value-added visibility for stakeholders through the definition of business views and models, critical analysis of their involvement (Deepu & Ravi, 2021) and the integration of costs analysis through development process by comparing different architectural configurations and protocols, approaches, and deployment plans (Lim et al., 2020). Several organizations with the integration of Industry 4.0 technologies into industrial plants have discussed this aspect citing, for example,

Table 10.1 State of the art maturity models authors and proposed levels

Maturity model	Authors	Maturity levels				
		1	2	3	4	5
Gartner maturity model (GMM)	Gartner	3D mirroring	Real-time (RL) monitoring	Analysis, prediction and optimization	–	–
ETRI DT maturity model	ETRI	Mirroring	Monitoring	Modeling and simulation	Federated	Autonomous
Digital built environment maturity model – DBEM	Individual scholars	Ad hoc data set	DT formation	DT RL automation	DT standard operation	DT intelligence contextualization
Digital twin maturity spectrum (DTMS)	IET and Atkins	Reality capture	2D/3D simulation	Real-time connection to physical asset	Two-way data integration and interaction	Autonomous
Digital twin 8-dimension model (DT8M)	Rainer and Thomas	Static	Dynamic	Ad hoc	Look-ahead perspective	–
Lockheed Martin digital twin maturity model (LMDTMM)	Lockheed and Martin	Virtual DT	PA/DT synchronization	DT/PA validation and verification	DT/PA integration	DT operational ecosystem
DT-GMM (Gemini maturity model)	Research institution	Unaware	Identifiable	Aware	Communicative	Interactive, intelligent and instructive
DTCMM	Our chapter	Initial	Ad hoc	Reactive	Proactive	Autonomous

Table 10.2 State of the art maturity models integrated dimensions

Capability domain		DBEM	GMM	DTMS	DT8M	LMDTM	ETRI-M	DT-GMM
				Maturity models				
Organizational	Regulatory compliance	–	–	–	–	–	–	–
	Digital culture adaptation	–	–	–	–	–	–	✓
	Digital culture integration	–	–	–	✓	–	–	✓
	Standardization	✓	–	–	–	✓	✓	✓
Process	Life cycle management	✓	✓	–	✓	✓	✓	✓
	Project management	–	–	–	✓	✓	–	–
	Process integration	✓	✓	–	✓	✓	✓	✓
People	Cognitive ergonomic	–	–	–	✓	✓	✓	–
	Organizational ergonomic	–	–	–	✓	–	✓	✓
	Ethical compliance	–	–	✓	–	–	–	–
Technology	Security management	–	–	✓	–	–	–	✓
	Data management	✓	✓	✓	✓	✓	✓	✓
	Communication and connectivity	✓	✓	✓	✓	✓	✓	✓
	Hardware adaptability	–	✓	✓	✓	✓	–	✓
	Software quality	–	–	✓	✓	✓	–	✓
	Services management	✓	✓	✓	✓	✓	✓	✓
	Interoperability management	✓	✓	✓	✓	✓	✓	✓

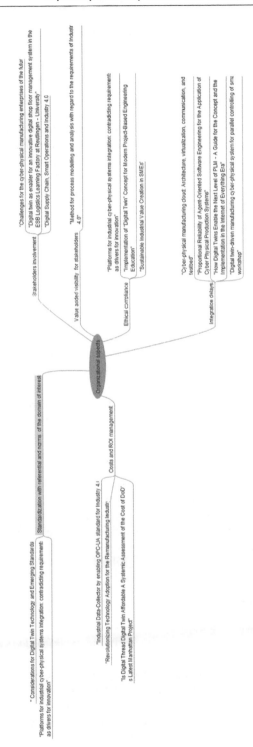

Figure 10.6 Organizational aspects for DT.

NIST for interoperability financial impacts valuation (Tassey et al., 1999), privacy costs for DTs (Voas et al., 2021), and US air force research works that focused on Digital Thread and DT (West & Blackburn, 2017). In this context, general aspects for PM such as quality and delays constraints were also raised by some works (Voell et al., 2018) with relationship with different software development frameworks.

In recent years, some works in the field of healthcare and autonomous vehicles have raised the importance of ethical considerations in DT development and implementation (Braun, 2021). Several frameworks were proposed in order to apprehend ethical concerns in emerging technologies exploiting AI (Siau & Wang, 2020), which can be divided into three main fields: ethics by design, ethics in design, and ethics for design (Leikas et al., 2019). For the purpose of this article and with relationship to DT, the focus is put on the first axis. Ethics by design refers to the integration of ethics within systems enterr (Kieslich et al., 2021). In the last few years, several norms have arisen discussing main guidelines for ethics implementation in the field of AI applications as instance Ethics guidelines for trustworthy AI published in 2019 by EU High Level Expert Group (Cannarsa, 2021), Data Ethics Canvas by the open data institute and Ethics Canvas published by ADAPT enter for digital content technology. IBM and Microsoft cooperate were amongst the first leading companies to shed lights on ethical, legal, and moral concerns in the exploitation of AI particularly for pattern recognition use cases and augmented human intelligence applications (Wu et al., 2020). Feedback experience from these companies and the application of AI and DT in various field has prompted industrial plants to deepen their ethical risks management strategies to encounter consequentialism constraints and hardly deterministic situations that trigger probable threats on human well-being in critical situations thus challenging DT systems cognitive reasoning capacities (Lütge et al., 2021).

Last point that was discussed concerned standardization and regulatory compliance (RC) for an enhanced integration of DT and cyber physical systems into physical twin environment and operational contexts (Heiss et al., 2015). Currently, several standards specific to the field of DTs are under development, suggesting a set of good practices for an efficient integration of DT. Figure 10.7 summarizes these standards.

10.2.1.3 Technology aspects

Technology concerns were broadly discussed during the last few years considering their integrated importance in early life cycles of DTs and for their contribution to DTs conceptual and functional architecture views definition (Fernando et al., 2018). Seven axes constitute this category, security management (SM), data life cycle management, interoperability management (IM), services management (SRM), hardware adaptability (HA), software quality (SQ) management, and finally communication and connectivity management. Figures 10.8 and 10.9 represent, respectively, technical aspects for

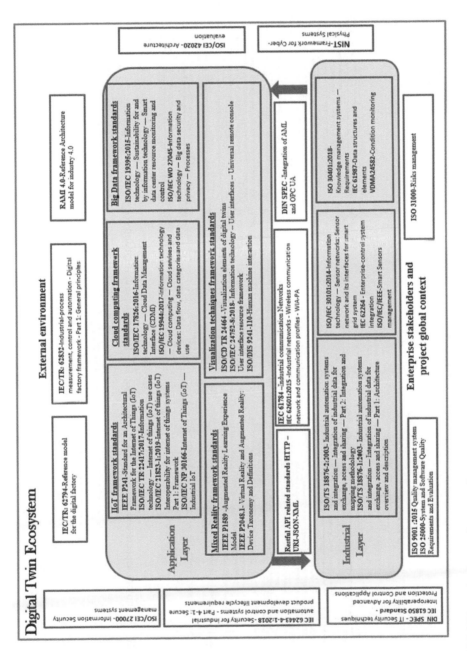

Figure 10.7 DT standardization framework.

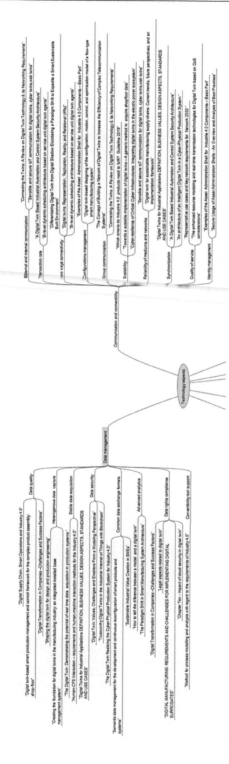

Figure 10.8 Technology aspects and technical requirements for DT data, communication and connectivity management.

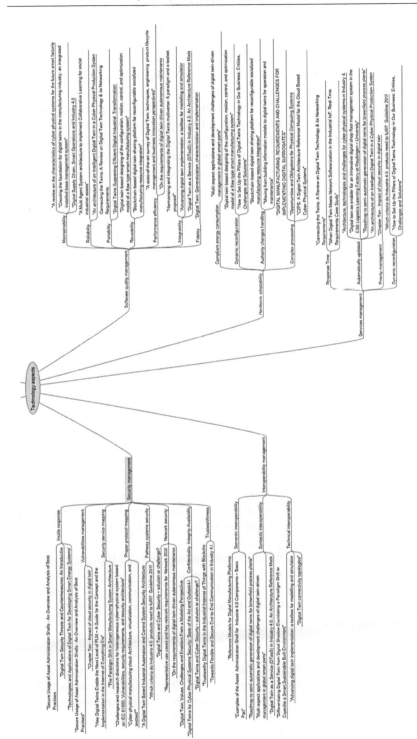

Figure 10.9 Technology aspects for interoperability, services, hardware adaptability, security and software quality management.

DM, communication and connectivity management, and technical requirements for interoperability, services, HA, security and SQ management.

- **Data life cycle management:** Data has been considered as the fuel for DTs across its different representations that were discussed in the literature (Friederich et al., 2022). Different levels of concerns were treated by research works on the subject constituting an entire life cycle framework for data requirements management. This framework extended from stable data acquisition (Uhlemann et al., 2017), heterogenous data capture (Olivotti et al., 2018), data conversion and convertibility tools support, data advanced analytics (Wright & Davidson, 2020), common data exchange formats to more complex aspects that include data quality and SM (Zhuang et al., 2018), and rights compliance that includes conformity to common rules and defined specific laws for industrial contexts and countries (Teller, 2021).

- **Communication and connectivity management:** As defined by Grieves, the communication bridge is one of the main elements of DT foundation structure. The autonomy of DTs has been defined by some recent works through connectivity levels between the two twins, according to Environment (2021); a bidirectional connectivity level is related to higher autonomy of the twin and enhanced performances of its services. Communication and connectivity were apprehended by literature through technical metrics, such as quality of service (Li et al., 2022), transaction rate (Zhang et al., 2021), jitter, scalability (Dittmann et al., 2020) and more complex considerations, mainly synchronization of twins and services (Talkhestani et al., 2019), group communication scheme of DT networks and two-way connectivity managements (Seilov et al., 2021). Some other global concerns included identity and configuration management (Liu et al., 2021), reliability evaluation of communication mediums (Kamble et al., 2022), networks and hardware architecture components, and finally internal and external communication management with both physical and digital users and third tier platforms (Mashaly, 2021).

- **IM:** Platform 4.0 proposition that discussed AAS has put particular focus on interoperability as an enabler for the achievement of Industry 4.0 perspective (Inigo et al., 2020). Interoperability was defined as asset across value chain ability to communicate and exchange seamlessly data and information (Zeid et al., 2019). Interoperability can be apprehended through three axes, semantic, syntactic, and technical. Technical interoperability relates to communication channels and protocols amongst assets, and it defines schemes that ensures the appropriate technical aspects for systems and services linking, including data integration, representation and interfaces specifications (Schroeder et al., 2021). Syntactic interoperability concerns data representations, structures and formats for sharing between different assets networks (Wang et al., 2021). This aspect was detailed through AAS by the focus on the definition of metamodels of assets and their sub-models that are unique and standard-based representations of different domains of concern (Fuchs et al., 2019). Semantic interoperability defines asset's ability to communicate data with unambiguous meanings independent from exchange mediums and platforms. For instance, the structure proposed for AAS aims is to capture this aspect by the introduction at the level of asset domain sub-models, both proprieties and functions (Epple et al., 2017).

- **SRM:** As defined by works on DTs' conceptual structure definition, services are considered as one of the main elements of a DT architecture as the satisfaction of business goals, and users' needs are directly related to this dimension of the architecture, that enables to integrate different heterogenous aspects into shared packages of managed resources (Stief et al., 2018). The introduction of a service perspective into DTs' development process implies different characteristics, mainly dynamic reconfiguration (Liu et al., 2021), automatic updates (Sierla et al., 2021), priority (Susila et al., 2020), and DT functions response time management (Mehdi Kherbache & Eric, 2021).

- **HA management:** As discussed by our previous works and the analyzed literature, DT is constituted by two parts, software and hardware, that are in constant collaboration in order to ensure system's efficient operation (Ghita et al., 2020). Through our analysis to Moroccan context, we were able to identify a set of technical and non-technical requirements of the hardware part. HA requirements include energy awareness (Wang et al., 2021), dynamic reconfiguration, including unit personalization, domain join, basic setting up (Abusohyon et al., 2021), the establishment of a complex processing infrastructure (Alam & Saddik, 2017), and authority changes handling with regards to the different stakeholders involved in DT life cycle phases (Li et al., 2021).

- **SQ management:** Different models exist to represent and evaluate SQ. Quality models can be decomposed into three categories, hierarchical models, meta-model-based models and finally implicit quality models (Wagner, 2013). Hierarchical models discuss quality through a global view and a set of technical factors and metrics defined across product life cycle (Al-Badareen et al., 2011). These approaches give birth in 1991 to ISO/IEC 9126 standard (Birla & Johansson, 2014) and years later to its successor ISO/IEC 25010 (Abran et al., 2008). The two standards evaluate quality athwart three classes, internal, external quality, and quality in use. The basic concept behind meta-model-based models is to create a link between measured metrics and systems quality predefined factors. Some of the popular models within this category are the COQUAMO models which refer to constructive quality model, launched by ESPRIT as a part of the REQUEST project. By this model, ESPRIT aimed to make a quantitative relationship between qualities measured vectors by metrics and quality factors all along the product life cycle (Petersen et al., 1989). The model takes into consideration the fact that stakeholders' needs of measuring and correcting quality deviations from defined plans and requirements are not limited to conception of different steps but expand throughout product life cycle. COQUAMO discusses quality through five attributes which are product, process, personnel, project, and finally organizational attributes. Implicit models are based on prediction studies of software behavior. In order to asset quality factors, across testing phase, proprieties of product, process, personnel, and organization are observed, captured, and taken into analysis to predict quality factors. Some of the most popular models in this category are reliability growth models (Haque & Ahmad, 2021). Metrics defined by these models and standards mainly performance efficiency by time behavior, capacity and resource utilization (Khan et al., 2020), reliability (Bakliwal et al., 2018), maintainability, and portability were implicitly discussed by several resources on DTs (Adrien et al., 2020) Reusability, that is an integrated part of maintainability according to standard definition and concerns asset's ability to integrate in one or more systems without additional development effort, was considered independently by some works that put interests on DT plug and produce and dynamic reconfiguration (Li et al., 2021). Integrability that measures the technical risks and costs related to components unit integration into the system is one of the main steps of a software architecture development process: in Cimino et al. (2021), authors in order to apprehend this axis have proposed a new approach based on a harmonization of data and models interpretations for DT through a digital multiverse. Several research dealt with this point and its effective evaluation through different existing methods developed for models' verification and validation and their consistency to address DT complex structure (VanDerHorn & Mahadevan, 2021). Despite the interests raised for the definition of metrics for DTs' quality evaluation, to our knowledge existing works on DT haven't discussed practical implementation of a structured quality evaluation model.

• **SM:** Through literature, SM was considered in a microscopic and macroscopic view. In the macroscopic view, confidentiality, integrity, and availability of CIA triad were considered. According to Holmes et al. (2021), from a DT perspective confidentiality consists on providing authorized access to data and information of both physical and DT, this can be achieved according to the authors by ensuring proper configurations for DT systems and establishing a strong security architecture that can handle threats coming from cyber and physical spaces. Availability concerns DT just in time operation, as raised by the authors' failures on the twin can mutually affect system maintainability, thus contradicting the main purpose it was conceived for. Integrity consists of ensuring DT models, configurations and information from and to the physical twin are consistent and reliable and represents accurately system behavior. The microscopic view takes a detailed approach to security that deal with different concerns impacting all DT blocks and elements, such mainly proper protocol mapping (Feng et al., 2021) and pathway systems security for bidirectional communication bridge management (Gehrmann & Gunnarsson, 2020), incidence response and vulnerabilities management in the context of AAS (Feng et al., 2021), security service mapping, network security (Khan et al., 2020), and more recently trustworthiness management for heterogenous data exchange between physical and digital entities constituting the operational context of DT (Suhail et al., 2021). In some recent works, more integrated approaches were proposed in order to apprehend this aspect citing, for example, commonly used methods for the evaluation of research and development projects evolution such as technology readiness level method (TRL) (Straub, 2015).

10.2.1.4 Process aspects

Recently, process aspects mastering has been taking increasing interests amongst DT practitioners due to their contribution to efficient development of the twin and its practical implementation within constrained physical environments governed by various rules and different views and business concerns. From the bibliographic review, two approaches can be distinguished agile approaches that define flexible, collaborative, and generative perspectives integrating holistic methods as instance model-based systems engineering and traditional approaches based, for example, on a V cycle and an iterative development process. Works on both approaches discussed metamodels, versions and configurations management concerns as they constitute main elements for a sustainable development process and it also helps to address traceability issues. Threats management and prevention were briefly discussed through cyber security and risks resulting from some business implications on DT integration process across plants management architecture business and functional layers. A set of best practices were proposed in order to monitor these risks, reduce their criticality and evaluate their impacts on DT development operations. Figure 10.10 presents process aspects for DT.

10.2.1.5 People aspects

Some works highlighted the relevant contribution of human factors for the deployment of DTs into industrial plants. These factors can be apprehended by the analysis of the mutual ergonomic considerations between the twin and its categories of physical stakeholders. Interactions of users with

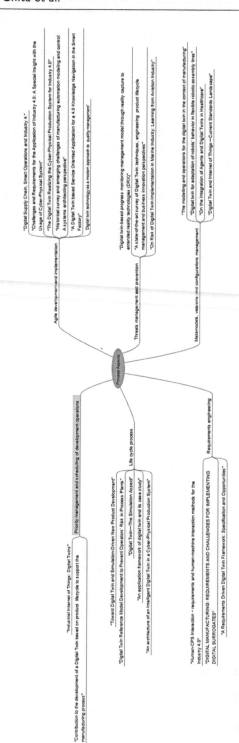

Figure 10.10 Process aspects for DT.

the DT raise several cognitive and organizational ergonomic (OE) implications. Cognitive ergonomics (CEs) of the twin were mainly approached with the analysis of DT graphical users interfaces aesthetics through 3D visualizations and models explain ability, consistent mapping of DT blocks and services, system status visibility according to users' views and interests, situation and context awareness, and error prevention for enhanced autonomy and assistance for users. OE concerns the establishment of a digital culture within the implementation environment of the twin. It focuses on the establishment of both specific communication patterns among DT different stakeholders during deployment and development phases of the twin and the development of a dedicated support for multidisciplinary documents management for collaborative integration of the twin. It also involves ensuring assistance and tutoring for efficient integration of the digital culture that could assist in the large-scale deployment of the concept into the industrial tissue of the hosting environment. The pillars for this digital culture will be discussed further through the presented proof of concept. Figure 10.11 introduces people aspects for DT.

10.3 DTCMM – DIGITAL TWIN CAPABILITY MATURITY MODEL

10.3.1 DTCMM maturity levels, capability domains, and metrics

The proposed maturity model is based on the insights concluded from the previously presented bibliometric review and the standards analysis of proposed best practices for DT development and deployment. DTCMM's main purpose is to support and help managers in their DT development journey through guidance on their main capabilities' strengths and weaknesses and different potential areas of technical and non-technical improvements to their current digital culture, IT infrastructure, and operational environment. The model consists of four domains and five maturity levels. The five maturity levels define different degrees of autonomy of the DT and the contribution of the defined aspects to this autonomy globally, and specifically, it's intended to give an overview on the progression of DT implementation across the hosting environment from a holistic perspective. The four defined domains and their attributes summarize the discussed points from our analysis and constitute inputs for the development of DT policy model and value judgment system particularly focusing for this part on technology and process aspects.

10.3.1.1 DTCMM maturity levels

The five maturity levels are initial, ad hoc, reactive, proactive, and autonomous. Maturity level definition is common to all domains, and the achievement of a maturity level for DT depends on ML of all defined domains.

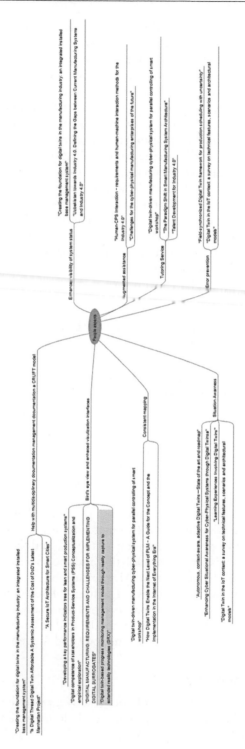

Figure 10.11 People aspects for DT.

Maturity levels are assigned in an increasing order; for instance in order to reach a maturity level of 3, the twin in all domains must reach a maturity level of 3, which also implies that all domains meet the criteria defined to meet maturity levels 1 and 2.

- **ML0 (Initial):** At this level, the organization has only an initial elementary vision of the DT and its requirements, basic concepts are defined and known by the collaborators, and a first perspective is put in place on the expectations of the stakeholders toward DTs value added to the company but the process for its development and implementation are not defined. No ethical concerns have been defined by the company.
- **ML1 (Adhoc):** Elementary knowledge of best practices and standards constituting DT process are communicated to the involved stakeholders in the project, and technology requirements for the company are defined. Ethics principles for the context are defined.
- **ML2 (Reactive):** At this stage, a first prototype of the twin is developed based on static and dynamic data from the physical twin and its physical environment. DT is considered the unique source of truth for process, systems and core business understating. Process for DT monitoring is clearly defined through elaborated procedures across the organization. Collaborators have clear understanding of DT value, and its elements and a communication platform for DT management among different users is developed and managed. A digital culture is taking place and different standards for its control have been developed for large-scale deployment. Ethics deviations are identified by the twin and communicated to concerned stakeholders.
- **ML3 (Proactive):** At this stage, the developed DT mimics faithfully its physical twin and is proactive to its changes and to environment dynamics and interacts with it continuously. Process for DT monitoring is completely deployed, which complies to adopt standards. Collaborators participate in the monitoring of the twin and its improvement, and the twin is proactive to ethical concerns. Ethical decisions are provided by the twin and communicated to concerned users.
- **ML4 (Autonomous):** At this level, the twin is autonomous, and it can adapt to predictable and unpredictable situations. Collaborators interact dynamically with the twin, and active communication bridge is developed between its stakeholders. Smart contracts are developed to manage internal and external interactions of the twin, and a dedicated security agent is integrated to ensure the autonomy of this process. Process for DT monitoring is mastered and controlled, and continuous improvement actions are put in place for its enhancement. The DT has developed a value judgment system and a learning block in order to decide about ethics and generate ethical rules for its different services.

10.3.1.2 DTCMM capability domains

The four defined capability domains are organization, process, people, and technology. As defined through the previous parts, these four aspects are relevant to evaluate DT integration and to support its development and deployment cycles. Figure 10.12 introduces DTCMM scheme.

Features of these domains are described in this part:

1. **RC:** This domain put the interest on twins' compliance and alignment with basic standards, policies, and laws on the physical environment of the physical twin and in the context of emerging technologies deployment and development. The analysis concerns all the regulations imposed by state, federal or international government and company regulatory context; it includes technological, domain-based and legal aspects. Insights can be deduced from deployed emerging technologies, for instance, internet of things and cloud computing within the country in critical domains, such as healthcare and public administration management. Concerning domain-based standards and company policies deployed methods for new product and software product integration can be adopted, legal aspects for DT according to best practices review from AAS and IIC can be integrated within specific audits conducted in this context by company regulatory board members. Cooperate compliance that defines conformity to internal policies and procedures are not considered at this level and will be detailed further through process aspects.

2. **Digital culture integration and adaptation (DCI-A):** The multidisciplinary nature of DT gave birth to a set of interactions that the twin develops throughout its life cycle with internal and external users and business partners. This point focuses on environment adaptation for DT integration through the culture of the company, its leadership and strategic components. Seven features can define digital culture adaptation across the company from an organizational perspective, innovation, customer centricity, flexibility and agility, collaboration, digital-first mindset, openness, and data-driven decision-making. These features contribute independently and collectively to DT practical integration as their maturity level evolve.

3. **Standardization (S):** This point concerns standards practices implemented in order to support the integration of DT into company's policies and strategies. It concerns all the aspects and defined criteria that help in making the twin a part of company's systems and daily management diagnosis actions established in order to achieve this goal and control the involvements of related stakeholders in this process.

4. **CE:** As defined by the state-of-the-art analysis, this point evaluates the cognitive features of the twin and twins' interactions with its users and how it can provide clear guidance to users in order to

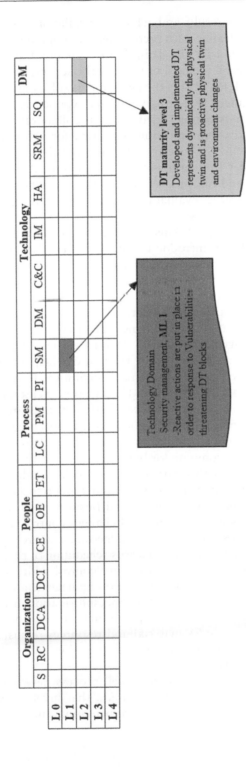

Figure 10.12 DTCMM domains and levels.

interpret analysis results and achieve for collaborative an augmented intelligence for dealing with predictable and unpredictable events and situations. Criteria for the definition of this point are inspired by a set of standards on the field of Graphical User Interfaces ergonomics mainly ISA 101 for HMI efficiency and Jakob Nielsen's 10 general principles for interaction design and user experience.

5. **OE:** This point is apprehended through collaborative development and established communication platforms for DT integration process management. It concerns structure, policies and processes put in place in order to monitor social interactions of the twin, including assistance and tutoring services and documents management for traceability concerns. Evaluation is based on social capabilities of the twin as discussed below.

6. **Ethical compliance (EC):** This point is focused on EC degrees of DT. It is approached by the introduction of smart ethical agents that according to predefined functional safety, accountability, data privacy principles try to evaluate DT networks behaviors and actions before their effective communication to PT. Utilitarian theory is applied to measure the ethical satisfaction of actions. Authors can refer to for more details on different moral and ethical theories.

7. **Life cycle management (LC):** As detailed earlier, this axis concerns the definition of a LC specific for DT that can help for potential plug and produce. It concerns requirements definition, testing procedures, modeling rules and validation and verification cycles that can help in accelerating development processes. Different tools are developed to automate the process depending on selected conceptual architecture.

8. **PM:** This point concerns PM dimensions. Defined areas for this point are intended to be common for both agile and traditional approaches. Five areas constitute this part, scope, cost delay quality (CDQ) triad, communication management, risks and procurement management. Scope criteria concerns technical and business requirements definition, deliverables management, and changes control. Costs management involves costs estimation, budgeting, resource planning and control, delays management concerns scheduling of project tasks and its activities management, and quality control addresses assurance, control, and planning. Communication management concerns interaction channels control, issues tracking, information distribution, and reporting means. The last two points involve risk and procurement management; it includes material and resources requisition, licenses and contract management, risks identification and estimation, and response plans development.

9. **Process integration (PI):** At this level, process development cycle is evaluated according to a set of criteria that involves plan development, execution management, documentation and traceability, and changes control.

10. **SM:** As defined by the state of the art, SM addresses aspects that relates to overall DT architecture layers and components security concerns. Main references for this point are ISO 27002, AAS Security criteria and NIST cyber security framework. Additionally, to CIA Triad apprehended by ISO 27002, particular concerns are evaluated, such as incidence management and vulnerability control.

11. **DM:** As described in previous parts, this point involves all the aspects that relates to data control, acquisition, quality, rights, and life cycle management. Maturity evaluation considers different areas of DLC from data collection and acquisition to dissemination and disposal. Data quality is regarded throughout four main metrics accuracy, consistency, timeliness, completeness, validity, and uniqueness inspired by ISO/IEC 25012:2008.

12. **Communication and connectivity (C&C):** As defined by the three conceptual propositions, DT develops a set of interactions with digital and physical users. The assessment of the efficiency of these interactions can be apprehended by both qualitative and quantitative metrics that constitute means of control for connectivity evaluation. Three main metrics are considered quality of service, jitter, scalability, and connectivity index. Protocol, interfaces, and network performance assessment are considered in the context of technical interoperability. Technical interoperability is assessed through used technologies, defined networking architecture, and data publication and exchange mediums.

13. **IM:** At this level, two areas of interoperability are considered semantic and syntactic. As described by previous parts, semantic interoperability concerns defined data structures meaning for collaborative exchange of information among assets. Its maturity is evaluated by data meta structure definition and control, linked data development, data discovery capacities and taxonomies deployed for various domains of interests. Syntactic interoperability maturity concerns data structure assessment and control for dynamic exchange of information. AAS requirements are considered for maturity evaluation of compliant interoperable data structures.

14. **HA:** At this level, adaptability of hardware components is defined as mainly considered axes are authority changes handling, configuration dynamic management, energy consumption and complex processing capacities. Criteria for this different areas' evaluation are formulated based on experience feedback for smart technologies implementation within industrial plant, targeted goals, and environmental constraints for DT by its different users.

15. **SRM:** This category includes SRM capabilities and criteria to ensure optimized response of DT and autonomous handling of its main functions. It includes response time and priority management degrees, dynamic reconfiguration capacity, hardware and software

components changes handling and automatic updates establishment for all provided services of DT.

16. **SQ:** This last point concerns software components quality management metrics. It includes the three types: ISO 21050 standard is used as a roadmap to assess all software components quality aspects. The focus is put particularly on portability, maintainability and efficiency as main elements for DT in the context of smart factories.

10.3.2 Metrics framework toward security and ethical agents

The apprehension of these aspects across literature was mainly based on the definition of qualitative assessment models that can evaluate conformity with a set of formulated requirements incorporating a part of the discussed domains and attributes for each aspect. Qualitative models for capabilities maturity assessment help to orient decision makers' and managers' interests toward areas of potential disfunction with regards to best practices and recommended actions by experts and practitioners, whereas quantitative models establish a structured and formulated relationship between these practices and company strategy and goals. Quantitative models were only considered for SM concerns through the exploitation of some commonly known methods such as Fuzzy Analytical Hierarchy, Bayesian Networks and Check list-based analysis. In this context, the proposed framework is based on the combination of both qualitative and quantitative metrics that can integrate all aspects and evaluate their impacts on DT architecture by the establishment of a policy model for runtime behavioral mapping and verification of DTs. Proposed quantitative metrics framework is based on a set of defined KPIs encapsulated in a standard-based format and integrated into maturity assessment grid through interactive dashboards and runtime environment of the DT by two autonomous agents. The main purpose of introducing these agents into DT architecture is to learn on the basis of experience and agents' interaction with the real environment, a set of practical rules that can be used in further implementation of a value judgment system for DTs. Figure 10.13 presents proposed conceptual model for DT agents.

Evaluation of defined aspects of DTCMM is based on a grid communicated to project stakeholders; the results of the evaluation of the different points are communicated to the teams involved by interactive dashboards of the different KPIs defined and registered for further processing and for the definition of ethical and security agent case bases. In addition to these two agents, this feedback will help for potential implementation of an authorized agent that can automatically manage all the aspects and introduce a set of reorganization rules for DT networks efficient runtime execution.

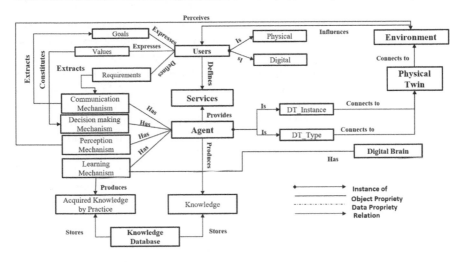

Figure 10.13 DT Agents conceptual model.

10.4 STATE-OF-THE-ART MATURITY MODELS DEVELOPMENT EFFORTS

Recently, several models were proposed in order to support the development of DT across industrial tissues, it is ranged from global to more specific models. Specific models were dedicated to application in particular domains, especially in the construction field with the integration of BIM (Business Information Models). Table 10.1 presents seven proposed maturity models in the literature. These models share a main purpose to support DT implementation and to develop a common framework and road map for the development of generic and standard DT architectures. In general, two aspects were discussed and analyzed by the model DT behavioral and structural aspects. Structural aspect is concerned with DT mirroring of Physical Twins components and systems geometric features, assemblies' characteristics and static representations. Behavioral aspect analysis developed DT systems monitoring capabilities it includes simulation dimension, communication and connectivity aspects, data and information modeling for dynamic mirroring of physical twins' interactions, and operation within physical environments. For most of the proposed models, the evaluation of structural aspects is included in their preliminary maturity levels, for instance, for Gartner and IET and Atkins models levels 1 and 2 and for ETRI model on level 3. Authors in that analysis of DT maturity from a BIM perspective focused on data and information modeling aspects; thus, DT is evaluated by its information modeling capabilities through five levels. In this context of BIM Gemini proposed generic model was defined by three main dimension purpose, trust, and functions and six levels that mainly assesses DT awareness. In addition to data and information concerns, the model integrates organization and security aspects and gives a theoretical and structured framework for qualitative assessment of the different proposed categories and defined criteria for each dimension. It is used as a benchmarking tool and a strategic methodology for DT development projects. Human interactions were only considered implicitly by Lockheed Martin model and directly by Rainer and Thomas 8-dimensional model that contrary to most of the model analysis both DT context and environment and proposes for each dimension different maturity levels. As represented by Table 10.2, DT8M covers main aspects of DT technology and process as it details major factors for DT development at a large scale.

LMDTMM, similar to DT8M, tries to integrate aspects of the environment in its assessment process and extend it to digital environment by the introduction of operational ecosystem that includes both of them. Main Pros of this model is their focus on technical aspects by a two-way analysis that covers dynamic and static representations of physical assets and provides guidelines for their practical assessment by visualized and some quantitative views. Cons of some models is their limitation to these aspects without taking into consideration human in the loop in their evaluation process as well as environment awareness that are both crucial for DT implementation and usage and operation life cycle phase. Our proposed model tries to cover these limitations by the integration of human in the loop dimension into people category, and defined subcategories are concerned with different interactions that can result from this integration in both long- and short-term considering DT actions and environments states by the introduction of ethics and moral principles.

10.5 CONCLUSION

DTs' application in different domains has given birth to an increasing concern for the development of a standardization framework as well as development of road maps to support companies in their journey for DT practical integration into their processes and management architecture. This chapter has been apprehended by the proposition of various maturity models which aims to define main areas for DT development and deployment that could be applied within different physical environments and contexts. Four aspects were considered, organization, people, technology, and process. These aspects were detailed independently by several sources, and structure capability dimension were identified by our bibliometric review describing all relevant criteria for its assessment. The bibliometric review as well as the analysis of different propositions for conceptual structure of DT resulted in our proposition of a DTCMM with 5 maturity levels and capability defined by the four deducted aspects. In order to facilitate model, short- and long-term implementation and validation both qualitative and quantitative metrics and criteria were defined. Criteria are used for maturity levels identification, and metrics are maintained for continuous control and long-term improvement of the model and DT. Testing of the model and its implementation can result in the development of a solid case base of actions and situations that are used for the conception of two autonomous agents integrated into the architecture to support DT and to offer improvement opportunities for DT stakeholders. Security and ethical agents interact with DT agents constantly and PT in order to help it decide on appropriate and ethical actions and ensure dynamically that rules are respected by operating DT agents. Our future works will be based on the structure proposed for these two agents, and it will be concentered mainly on their further development in the context of organization-based multiagent engineering systems OMASE approach.

REFERENCES

Abran, A., Al-Qutaish, R. E., Desharnais, J.-M., & Habra, N. (2008). Measuring Software Product Quality: The ISO 25000 Series and CMMI European SEPG Dave Zubrow. *Software Quality Measurement – Concepts and Approaches*, 61–96.

Abusohyon, I. A. S., Crupi, A., Bagheri, F., & Tonelli, F. (2021). How to set up the pillars of digital twins technology in our business: Entities, challenges and solutions. *Processes*, 9(8), 1–19. https://doi.org/10.3390/pr9081307

Adrien, B., Maia, E., Feeken, L., Borchers, P., & Praça, I. (2020). *A New Concept of Digital Twin Supporting Optimization and Resilience of Factories of the Future*. May 2017.

Al-Badareen, A. B., Selamat, M. H., Jabar, M. A., Din, J., & Turaev, S. (2011). Software quality models: A comparative study. *Communications in Computer and Information Science*, 179 CCIS(PART 1), 46–55. https://doi.org/10.1007/978-3-642-22170-5_4

Alam, K. M., & Saddik, A. E. L. (2017). C2PS: A digital twin architecture reference model for the cloud-based cyber-physical systems. *IEEE Access*, 5, 2050–2062. https://doi.org/10.1109/ACCESS.2017.2657006

Bakliwal, K., Dhada, M. H., Palau, A. S., Parlikad, A. K., & Lad, B. K. (2018). A multi-agent system architecture to implement collaborative learning for social industrial assets. *IFAC-PapersOnLine*, 51(11), 1237–1242. https://doi.org/10.1016/j.ifacol.2018.08.421

Birgit Boss (Robert Bosch GmbH), Somayeh Malakuti (ABB C. R. C., Germany), Shi-Wan Lin (Yo-i), Thomas Usländer (Fraunhofer IOSB), Erich Clauer (SAP), Michael Hoffmeister (Festo SE & Co. KG), Ljiljana Stojanovic (Fraunhofer IOSB). (2020). *Digital Twin and Asset Administration Shell Concepts and Application in the Industrial Internet and Industrie 4.0*. https://www.platt-form-i40.de/PI40/Redaktion/EN/Downloads/Publikation/Digital-Twin-and-Asset-Administration-Shell-Concepts.pdf?__blob=publicationFile&v=9

Birla, S., & Johansson, M. (2014). Quality Requirements for Software-dependent Safety-critical Systems History, current status, and future needs. *Proceedings of the 38th Meeting in the Series of Enlarged Halden Programme Group Meetings*, 1.

Bradac, Z., Marcon, P., Zezulka, F., Arm, J., & Benesl, T. (n.d.). *Digital Twin and AAS in the Industry 4.0 Framework.* https://doi.org/10.1088/1757-899X/618/1/012001

Braun, M. (2021). Represent me: Please! Towards an ethics of digital twins in medicine. *Journal of Medical Ethics, 47*(6), 394–400. https://doi.org/10.1136/medethics-2020-106134

Brenner, B., & Hummel, V. (2017). Digital twin as enabler for an innovative digital shopfloor management system in the ESB logistics learning factory at Reutlingen – University. *Procedia Manufacturing, 9,* 198–205. https://doi.org/10.1016/j.promfg.2017.04.039

Cannarsa, M. (2021). Ethics Guidelines for Trustworthy AI. *The Cambridge Handbook of Lawyering in the Digital Age,* 283–297. https://doi.org/10.1017/9781108936040.022

Cimino, C., Ferretti, G., & Leva, A. (2021). Harmonising and integrating the digital twins multiverse: A paradigm and a toolset proposal. *Computers in Industry, 132,* 103501. https://doi.org/10.1016/j.compind.2021.103501

Croatti, A., Gabellini, M., Montagna, S., & Ricci, A. (2020). On the integration of agents and digital twins in healthcare. *Journal of Medical Systems, 44,* 1–8. https://link.springer.com/article/10.1007/s10916-020-01623-5

Deepu, T. S., & Ravi, V. (2021). Exploring critical success factors influencing adoption of digital twin and physical internet in electronics industry using grey-DEMATEL approach. *Digital Business, 1*(2), 100009. https://doi.org/10.1016/j.digbus.2021.100009

Digital Twins for Industrial Applications (2020). https://www.iiconsortium.org/pdf/IIC_Digital_Twins_Industrial_Apps_White_Paper_2020-02-18.pdf

Dittmann, S., Zhang, P., Glodde, A., & Dietrich, F. (2020). Towards a scalable implementation of digital twins – A generic method to acquire shopfloor data. *Procedia CIRP, 96,* 157–162. https://doi.org/10.1016/j.procir.2021.01.069

Environment, S. B. (2021). Differentiating digital twin from digital shadow: elucidating a paradigm shift to expedite a smart. *Buildings, 11*(4), 1–16. https://doi.org/10.3390/buildings11040151.

Epple, U., Mertens, M., Palm, F., & Azarmipour, M. (2017). Using properties as a semantic base for interoperability. *IEEE Transactions on Industrial Informatics, 13*(6), 3411–3419. https://doi.org/10.1109/TII.2017.2741339

Feng, H., Chen, D., & Lv, H. (2021). Sensible and secure IoT communication for digital twins, cyber twins, web twins. *Internet of Things and Cyber-Physical Systems, 1*(November), 34–44. https://doi.org/10.1016/j.iotcps.2021.12.003

Fernando, L., Dur, C. S., Haag, S., Anderl, R., Sch, K., & Zancul, E. (2018). Digital Twin Requirements in the Context of Industry 4.0.1, 204–214. https://doi.org/10.1007/978-3-030-01614-2

Friederich, J., Francis, D. P., Lazarova-Molnar, S., & Mohamed, N. (2022). A framework for data-driven digital twins for smart manufacturing. *Computers in Industry, 136,* 103586. https://doi.org/10.1016/j.compind.2021.103586

Fuchs, J., Schmidt, J., Franke, J., Rehman, K., Sauer, M., & Karnouskos, S. (2019). I4.0-Compliant Integration of Assets Utilizing the Asset Administration Shell. *IEEE International Conference on Emerging Technologies and Factory Automation, ETFA, 2019-Septe,* 1243–1247. https://doi.org/10.1109/ETFA.2019.8869255

Gehrmann, C., & Gunnarsson, M. (2020). Control system security architecture. *IEEE Transactions on Industrial Informatics*, 16(1), 669–680.

Gerrikagoitia, J. K., Unamuno, G., Urkia, E., & Serna, A. (2019). Digital manufacturing platforms in the Industry 4.0 from private and public perspectives. *Applied Sciences (Switzerland)*, 9(14). https://doi.org/10.3390/app9142934

Ghita, M., Siham, B., Hicham, M., Abdelhafid, A., & Laurent, D. (2020). Digital twins: Development and implementation challenges within Moroccan context. *SN Applied Sciences*, 2(5), 1–14. https://doi.org/10.1007/s42452-020-2691-6

Haque, M. A., & Ahmad, N. (2021). An effective software reliability growth model. *Safety and Reliability*, 1–12. https://doi.org/10.1080/09617353.2021.1921547

Heiss, M., Oertl, A., Sturm, M., Palensky, P., Vielguth, S., & Nadler, F. (2015). Platforms for industrial cyber-physical systems integration: contradicting requirements as drivers for innovation. *Procedia CIRP*. https://doi.org/10.1109/MSCPES.2015.7115405

Holmes, D., Papathanasaki, M., Maglaras, L., Ferrag, M. A., Nepal, S., & Janicke, H. (2021). *Digital Twins and Cyber Security – Solution or Challenge?* 1–8. https://doi.org/10.1109/SEEDA-CECNSM53056.2021.9566277

Inigo, M. A., Porto, A., Kremer, B., Perez, A., Larrinaga, F., & Cuenca, J. (2020). Towards an Asset Administration Shell Scenario: A Use Case for Interoperability and Standardization in Industry 4.0. *Proceedings of IEEE/IFIP Network Operations and Management Symposium 2020: Management in the Age of Softwarization and Artificial Intelligence, NOMS 2020*. https://doi.org/10.1109/NOMS47738.2020.9110410

Irfan, M., Hassan, M., & Hassan, N. (2019). The effect of project management capabilities on project success in Pakistan: An empirical investigation. *IEEE Access*, 7(April), 39417–39431. https://doi.org/10.1109/ACCESS.2019.2906851

ISO/TC 184. (2019) https://www.ththry.org/activities/2020/AdHocGroup_Digital Twin_V1R8.pdf

Jacoby, M., & Usländer, T. (2020). Digital twin and internet of things – Current standards landscape. *Applied Sciences (Switzerland)*, 10(18). https://doi.org/10.3390/APP10186519

Júnior, A. A. C., Misra, S., & Soares, M. S. (2019). A systematic mapping study on software architectures description based on ISO/IEC/IEEE 42010:2011. *Lecture Notes in Computer Science (Including Subseries Lecture Notes in Artificial Intelligence and Lecture Notes in Bioinformatics)*, 11623 LNCS, 17–30. https://doi.org/10.1007/978-3-030-24308-1_2

Kahlen, F. J., Flumerfelt, S., & Alves, A. (2016). Transdisciplinary perspectives on complex systems: New findings and approaches. *Transdisciplinary Perspectives on Complex Systems: New Findings and Approaches* (Issue March). https://doi.org/10.1007/978-3-319-38756-7

Kamble, S. S., Gunasekaran, A., Parekh, H., Mani, V., Belhadi, A., & Sharma, R. (2022). Digital twin for sustainable manufacturing supply chains: Current trends, future perspectives, and an implementation framework. *Technological Forecasting and Social Change*, 176(December 2021), 121448. https://doi.org/10.1016/j.techfore.2021.121448

Khan, S., Farnsworth, M., Mcwilliam, R., & Erkoyuncu, J. (2020). On the requirements of digital twin-driven autonomous maintenance. *Annual Reviews in Control, June*. https://doi.org/10.1016/j.arcontrol.2020.08.003

Kieslich, K., Keller, B., & Starke, C. (2021). *AI-Ethics by Design. Evaluating Public Perception on the Importance of Ethical Design Principles of AI.* http://arxiv.org/abs/2106.00326

Leikas, J., Koivisto, R., & Gotcheva, N. (2019). Ethical framework for designing autonomous intelligent systems. *Journal of Open Innovation: Technology, Market, and Complexity,* 5(1). https://doi.org/10.3390/joitmc5010018

Li, J., Zhang, Y., & Qian, C. (2022). The enhanced resource modeling and real-time transmission technologies for Digital Twin based on QoS considerations. *Robotics and Computer-Integrated Manufacturing,* 75(January 2021), 102284. https://doi.org/10.1016/j.rcim.2021.102284

Li, M., Li, Z., Huang, X., & Qu, T. (2021). Blockchain-based digital twin sharing platform for reconfigurable socialized manufacturing resource integration. *International Journal of Production Economics,* 240(May), 108223. https://doi.org/10.1016/j.ijpe.2021.108223

Lim, K. Y. H., Zheng, P., & Chen, C. H. (2020). A state-of-the-art survey of Digital Twin: Techniques, engineering product lifecycle management and business innovation perspectives. *Journal of Intelligent Manufacturing,* 31(6), 1313–1337. https://doi.org/10.1007/s10845-019-01512-w

Liu, Q., Leng, J., Yan, D., Zhang, D., Wei, L., Yu, A., Zhao, R., Zhang, H., & Chen, X. (2021). Digital twin-based designing of the configuration, motion, control, and optimization model of a flow-type smart manufacturing system. *Journal of Manufacturing Systems,* 58(April), 52–64. https://doi.org/10.1016/j.jmsy.2020.04.012

Lu, Y., Liu, C., Wang, K. I. K., Huang, H., & Xu, X. (2020). Digital Twin-driven smart manufacturing: Connotation, reference model, applications and research issues. *Robotics and Computer-Integrated Manufacturing,* 61(July 2019), 101837. https://doi.org/10.1016/j.rcim.2019.101837

Lütge, C., Poszler, F., Acosta, A. J., Danks, D., Gottehrer, G., Mihet-Popa, L., & Naseer, A. (2021). AI4people: Ethical guidelines for the automotive sector-fundamental requirements and practical recommendations. *International Journal of Technoethics,* 12(1), 101–125. https://doi.org/10.4018/IJT.20210101.oa2

Mashaly, M. (2021). Connecting the twins: A review on digital twin technology & its networking requirements. *Procedia Computer Science,* 184(June), 299–305. https://doi.org/10.1016/j.procs.2021.03.039

Mehdi Kherbache, M. M. & Eric R. (2021). When Digital Twin Meets Network Softwarization in the Industrial IoT: Real-Time Requirements Case Study. *Sensors,* 21(4), 1–17. https://doi.org/10.3390/s21248194

Olivotti, D., Dreyer, S., Lebek, B., & Breitner, M. H. (2018). Creating the foundation for digital twins in the manufacturing industry: An integrated installed base management system. *Information Systems and E-Business Management,* 0123456789. https://doi.org/10.1007/s10257-018-0376-0

Paper, W., & Electrical, G. (2017). *Examples of the Asset Administration Shell for Basic Part.* April.

Paulk, M. C., Curtis, B., Chrissis, M. B., & Weber, C. V. (2011). Capability Maturity Model, Version 1.1. *Software Process Improvement,* 79–88. https://doi.org/10.1109/9781118156667.ch2

Petersen, P. G., Andersen, O., Heilesen, J. H., Klim, S., & Schmidt, J. (1989). Software quality drivers and indicators. *Proceedings of the Hawaii International Conference on System Science*, 2, 210–218. https://doi.org/10.1109/hicss.1989.47994

Qamsane, Y., Balta, E., Kovalenko, I., & Faris, J. (2020). *A Requirements Driven Digital Twin Framework: Specification and Opportunities*. June. https://doi.org/10.1109/ACCESS.2020.3000437

Schroeder, G. N., Steinmetz, C., Rodrigues, R. N., Rettberg, A., & Pereira, C. E. (2021). Digital Twin connectivity topologies. *IFAC-PapersOnLine*, *54*(1), 737–742. https://doi.org/10.1016/j.ifacol.2021.08.086

Seilov, S. Z., Kuzbayev, A. T., Seilov, A. A., Shyngisov, D. S., Goikhman, V. Y., Levakov, A. K., Sokolov, N. A., & Zhursinbek, Y. S. (2021). The concept of building a network of digital twins to increase the efficiency of complex telecommunication systems. *Complexity*, *2021*. https://doi.org/10.1155/2021/9480235

Siau, K., & Wang, W. (2020). Artificial intelligence (AI) ethics: Ethics of AI and ethical AI. *Journal of Database Management*, *31*(2), 74–87. https://doi.org/10.4018/JDM.2020040105

Sierla, S., Azangoo, M., Rainio, K., Papakonstantinou, N., Fay, A., Honkamaa, P., & Vyatkin, V. (2021). Roadmap to semi-automatic generation of digital twins for brownfield process plants. *Journal of Industrial Information Integration*, August, 100282. https://doi.org/10.1016/j.jii.2021.100282

Stief, P., Dantan, J., Etienne, A., & Siadat, A. (2018). Digital twin service towards smart manufacturing. *Procedia CIRP*, *72*(June), 237–242. https://doi.org/10.1016/j.procir.2018.03.103

Straub, J. (2015). In search of technology readiness level (TRL) 10. *Aerospace Science and Technology*, *46*, 312–320. https://doi.org/10.1016/j.ast.2015.07.007

Suhail, S., Hussain, R., Jurdak, R., & Hong, C. S. (2021). Trustworthy digital twins in the industrial Internet of Things with blockchain. *IEEE Internet Computing*, *1*, 1–7. https://doi.org/10.1109/MIC.2021.3059320

Susila, N., Sruthi, A., & Usha, S. (2020). Impact of cloud security in digital twin. In *Advances in Computers* (1st ed., Vol. 117, Issue 1). Elsevier Inc. https://doi.org/10.1016/bs.adcom.2019.09.005

Talkhestani, B. A., Jung, T., Lindemann, B., Sahlab, N., Jazdi, N., & Architektur, E. (2019). An architecture of an intelligent digital twin in a cyber-physical production system. *at – Automatisierungstechnik*, *67*(9), 762–782.

Tassey, G., Ph, D., & Martin, S. A. (1999). Interoperability cost analysis of the U. S. Automotive Supply Chain Interoperability Cost Analysis of the U.S. Automotive Supply Chain. *Environmental Research*, 7007. http://www.rti.org/publications/abstract.cfm?pub=1390

Teller, M. (2021). Legal aspects related to digital twin. *Philosophical Transactions of the Royal Society A: Mathematical, Physical and Engineering Sciences*, *379*(2207). https://doi.org/10.1098/rsta.2021.0023

Uhlemann, T. H. J., Schock, C., Lehmann, C., Freiberger, S., & Steinhilper, R. (2017). The digital twin: Demonstrating the potential of real time data acquisition in production systems. *Procedia Manufacturing*, *9*, 113–120. https://doi.org/10.1016/j.promfg.2017.04.043

U.S. Department of Energy (2021). *Cybersecurity Capability Maturity Model (C2M2), Version 2.0.* July. https://www.energy.gov/sites/default/files/2021-07/C2M2%20Version%202.0%20July%202021_508.pdf

VanDerHorn, E., & Mahadevan, S. (2021). Digital twin: Generalization, characterization and implementation. *Decision Support Systems, 145*(June 2020), 113524. https://doi.org/10.1016/j.dss.2021.113524

Voas, J. M., Mell, P. M., & Piroumian, V. (2021). *Considerations for Digital Twin Technology and Emerging Standards – Draft NISTIR 8356.* 1–34. https://doi.org/10.6028/NIST.IR.8356-draft

Voell, C., Chatterjee, P., & Rauch, A. (2018). *How Digital Twins Enable the Next Level of PLM – A Guide for the Concept and the Implementation in the Internet of Everything Era.* Springer International Publishing. https://doi.org/10.1007/978-3-030-01614-2

Wagner, S. (2013). Software product quality control. In *Software Product Quality Control.* https://doi.org/10.1007/978-3-642-38571-1

Wang, K., Hu, Q., Zhou, M., Zun, Z., & Qian, X. (2021). Multi-aspect applications and development challenges of digital twin-driven management in global smart ports. *Case Studies on Transport Policy, 9*(3), 1298–1312. https://doi.org/10.1016/j.cstp.2021.06.014

West, T. D., & Blackburn, M. (2017). Is digital thread/digital twin affordable? A systemic assessment of the cost of DoD's latest Manhattan project. *Procedia Computer Science, 114*, 47–56. https://doi.org/10.1016/j.procs.2017.09.003

Wright, L., & Davidson, S. (2020). How to tell the difference between a model and a digital twin. *Advanced Modeling and Simulation in Engineering Sciences, 7*(1). https://doi.org/10.1186/s40323-020-00147-4

Wu, W., Huang, T., & Gong, K. (2020). Ethical principles and governance technology development of AI in China. *Engineering, 6*(3), 302–309. https://doi.org/10.1016/j.eng.2019.12.015

Yan, K., Lim, H., Zheng, P., & Chen, C. (2020). *A State-of-the-Art Survey of Digital Twin: Techniques, Engineering Product Lifecycle Management and Business Innovation Perspectives.* August. https://doi.org/10.1007/s10845-019-01512-w

Zeid, A., Sundaram, S., Moghaddam, M., Kamarthi, S., & Marion, T. (2019). Interoperability in smart manufacturing: Research challenges. *Machines, 7*(2), 1–17. https://doi.org/10.3390/machines7020021

Zhang, J., Deng, T., Jiang, H., Chen, H., Qin, S., & Ding, G. (2021). Bi-level dynamic scheduling architecture based on service unit digital twin agents. *Journal of Manufacturing Systems, 60*(February), 59–79. https://doi.org/10.1016/j.jmsy.2021.05.007

Zheng, Y., Yang, S., & Cheng, H. (2018). An application framework of digital twin and its case study. *Journal of Ambient Intelligence and Humanized Computing.* https://doi.org/10.1007/s12652-018-0911-3

Zhuang, C., Liu, J., & Xiong, H. (2018). *Digital Twin-Based Smart Production Management and Control Framework for the Complex Product Assembly Shop-Floor.* https://link.springer.com/article/10.1007/s00170-018-1617-6

Chapter 11

A detailed cram on artificial intelligence industrial systems 4.0

P. Dharanyadevi, R. Sri Saipriya, T. C. Adityaa,
B. Senthilnayaki, M. Julie Therese, A. Devi,
and K. Venkatalakshmi

CONTENTS

DOI: 10.1201/9781003269144-11

11.1 INTRODUCTION

11.1.1 What is artificial intelligence?

Artificial intelligence (AI) could be considered the ability of a machine using programming techniques to mimic the intelligence of humans and also the ability to perform tasks that require learning and reasoning. The need for AI has found a profound increase in everyday life. It is also the reason for the quick leap in technical and business fields. Even a simple request by man will depend solely on computers and AI just like the weather temperature could be given by Siri or Galaxy [1].

11.1.2 What is Industry 4.0?

Industry 4.0, otherwise called the fourth industrial revolution, refers to the current trend of digitization, exchange and automation of data in the mechanized process. Big data, cyber-physical systems (CPS), autonomous robots, the Internet of Things (IoT), additive manufacturing cloud computing and cognitive computing form an integral part of Industry 4.0. Industry 4.0 harnesses the advanced communication technology to create "smart factories." CPS play an important part in monitoring the physical processes in smart factories. They also generate a virtual replica of the physical environment and are capable of communicating and cooperating with each other and with humans. They are also capable of making decisions in a decentralized manner. Some essential Industry 4.0 design principles include decentralization, virtualization, modularity, service orientation, interoperability and real-time capability. These design principles aid companies in recognizing and enforcing Industry 4.0 technologies.

11.2 INDUSTRIAL REVOLUTIONS

Over the years, there have been distinct transitional changes that have caused shifts in the speed, quality and organization of production. Each transition had its unique contribution to the contemporary world we live in today. Each era of the industrial revolution had its own technological impact that transformed society with the creation of new jobs and better living conditions.

11.2.1 First industrial revolution (1784)

The late 18th and early 19th centuries were characterized by industrialization. Use of water and steam to mechanize production evolved. Cort's puddling and rolling process was initiated in the making of iron. Samuel Crompton invented the spinning mule for cotton, which revolutionized textile production. Another noteworthy invention was the Watt steam engine. These inventions augmented productivity. Chemicals, such as concrete, sulfuric acid, bleaching powder, hydrochloric acid, sodium sulfate, alkali and sodium carbonate, were produced on a large scale. These chemicals were used in making textile, glass, fertilizers, soap etc. The first industrial revolution shifted the production from a previously labor-intensive to a more capital-intensive market [2]. It witnessed the mechanized, industrial system.

11.2.2 Second industrial revolution (1870)

The second industrial revolution started with the use of electricity for mass production. Inventions such as electricity, internal combustion engine, telegraphy, telephony and radio were the major breakthroughs. Advancements in the mass production of petroleum, paper and steel were made. Developments in economy, business, transportation and communication were also made. Edward Alfred Cowper invented the Cowper stove in 1857, which led to an efficient blast process in the making of steel. It employed a regenerative heater system for producing high heat enabling very high throughput of blast furnaces. Generally, the second industrial revolution can be broadly characterized by the expansion of industries and electricity-dependent assembly-line production based on division of labor [3].

11.2.3 Third industrial revolution (1969)

The third industrial revolution took a paradigm shift from mechanical processes and from analog technology toward digitization. The blend of electronics with information and communications technology (ICT) revolutionized the automation of industrial sector. Introduction of ICT, Internet and computers revolutionized industries. This period was one of the rapid technological advancements linked with the evolution of information technology. It is in this era that electronic and information technology was used to further advance automation [4].

11.3 TRANSITION FROM INDUSTRY 3.0 TO INDUSTRY 4.0 AND A COMPARISON OF THE TWO REVOLUTIONS

The third industrial revolution started with the advent of computer technology during the 1970s. This period, consequently, saw a boom in the IT industry and the electronics industry. Several new technologies like computers and the Internet made possible many management processes such as shipping logistics, tracking and inventory management. Programmable logic controllers and robots were used on a large scale and were getting cheaper. Computers made designing, control, data handling, processing and transfer more convenient. As a result, productivity and quality were boosted, and human errors minimized. Manufacturing processes were also getting streamlined. Advancements in computer numerical control machines enabled mass production and the elimination of the need for prototypes. They also made manufacturing more precise and efficiency was increased. While Industry 2.0 relied on assembly lines with a lot of human intervention, robots of Industry 3.0 made such processes more efficient and faster. Work processes were also made safer and faster. However, in the fourth industrial revolution, the degree of human intervention decreased dramatically.

As the manufacturing industry became more consumer-centric, development periods needed to be reduced, flexibility needed to be increased and resource efficiency had to be increased [5]. As a result, new innovations like smart sensors and embedded systems were brought about, starting a new era of industrial revolution. The fourth industrial revolution saw leaps in technologies like 3D printing, Big Data and AI. The introduction of new technologies like IoT and cloud computing have enabled connected devices and smarter manufacturing. Digital systems could record and monitor data almost fully by themselves. Predictive maintenance has reduced the possibility of errors, and hence costs incurred during manufacturing. Another latest technology is the 3D printing. It has simplified the design process, made mass manufacturing easier and is also environmentally friendly. Some revolutions in data like big data analytics and edge computing have made data storage more efficient and faster. Hence, the innovations in machines that can store data, process information and perform tasks collaboratively with other machines, and independent of humans, has resulted in industrial outputs being consumer driven and of higher quality. Table 11.1 explains the comparison between Industry 3.0 and 4.0.

Based on a survey conducted by Deloitte with executives worldwide, technologies such as Big Data, IoT, cloud and AI are expected to make

Table 11.1 Comparison between Industry 3.0 and 4.0

Characteristics	Industry 3.0	Industry 4.0
Industrial process	Automation using PLC, robots and computer technology combined with manual processes for data analysis [6]	High degree of automation with enabling technologies such as AI, IoT, CPS and data analytics in smart factories [6]
Robotics	Industrial robots for manufacturing	Smarter "robots" to join forces with humans and to execute repetitive tasks such as inspection in factories
Process complexity	Basic and less complex	More complex with advanced technologies
Base for revenue model	Selling products	Servitized business model
Decision-making	Days to months [6]	Minutes to hours, based on real-time data and predictive analytics [6]
Data collection and analysis	Manual	Automated
Challenges	Errors may arise due to human intervention	Cyber security issues

a profound impact in Industry 4.0, which is depicted in Figure 11.1. As depicted in Figure 11.1, AI is estimated to play a pivotal role in various sectors of Industry 4.0.

11.4 IMPACT OF AI IN INDUSTRY 4.0 IN VARIOUS SECTORS

11.4.1 Impact of AI in Industry 4.0 in the manufacturing sector

Figure 11.2 illustrates some Industry 4.0 applications. The foreword of new-fangled technologies like AI and machine learning to Industry 4.0 led

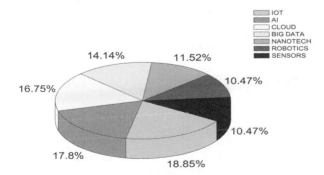

Figure 11.1 Expected impact percentages of various technologies in Industry 4.0.

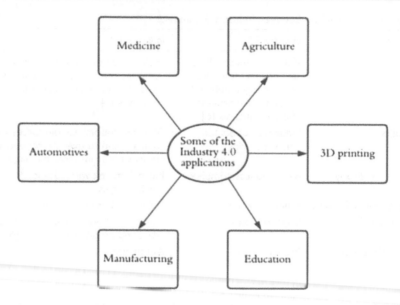

Figure 11.2 Some Industry 4.0 applications.

to significant advancements in manufacturing industries. These innovations can open up new ventures in industrial sectors and these results in advantages like, but not limited to, improvements in efficiency.

Some of the important causes for most industries to shift toward Industry 4.0 and automate manufacturing include:

- Increased productivity
- Minimized human/manual errors
- Optimization of production costs
- Focused human efforts on non-repetitive tasks to improve productivity

The five main areas where AI's impact on manufacturing are:

1. Predictive Quality and Yield
2. Human-robot collaboration
3. Predictive maintenance
4. Market adaptation/supply chain
5. Generative design

11.4.1.1 Predictive quality and yield

With the growing population and increased availability of a variety of products, it becomes imminent for the manufacturers to reduce their manufacturing losses and improve their yield.

Predictive quality and yield uses industrial AI to identify the core causes of many of the day-to-day production losses that occur in many industries. This is accomplished by continuous, multivariate analysis that makes use of machine learning algorithms that have been carefully trained to comprehend each distinct manufacturing process. Supervised machine learning training algorithms are practiced here to recognize the trend and the pattern of the data.

11.4.1.2 Predictive maintenance

Predictive maintenance makes use of technologies like AI and machine learning for the prediction of possible damages and the possible component or system failure and also alerts the maintenance personnel to carry out the maintenance procedures to prevent the possible occurrence of failure. The benefits are numerous that include significant cost reduction and the reduced need for system maintenance.

11.4.1.3 Human-robot collaboration

The reports obtained from International Federation of Robotics (IFR) indicate an estimate of 1.64 million industrial robots to be in operation globally, as of the year 2020.

With the application of robotics in the manufacturing sector expanding day by day, AI will perform an increasingly important role in protecting human workers while also empowering robots to work collaboratively with human beings in a shared manner. Furthermore, the manufacturing process could also be improved by the precise and quick decisions made by the robots based on the collected data in real time.

11.4.1.4 Generative design

AI aids manufacturers in generating designs and testing them out in the design sector. Design-generating software generates various possible design solutions based on the input given by the design engineer. The testing phase gives an idea about the various design options available and an optimum design solution can be chosen by the design engineer to meet his needs. There is also a feasibility to augment any improvements required so as to arrive at an optimal solution.

11.4.1.5 Market adaptation/supply chain

AI algorithms can be used to improve manufacturing operations' supply chains and help better respond to and anticipate market changes. Algorithms can use demand patterns classified by location, socioeconomic attributes, macroeconomic behavior, availability of goods and resources and other factors to create market demand estimates.

Intelligent manufacturing optimizes the manufacturing process by incorporating real-time data analysis, AI and machine learning. It can be used in various industries such as healthcare, paint, agriculture, education and in some emerging fields of Industry 4.0, which are discussed in the forthcoming sections.

11.4.2 Impact of AI in Industry 4.0 in the healthcare industry

Automated technology provides promising solutions in the field of healthcare, attributable to its quickness and accuracy.

It paves a way for better care for the patients by assisting the doctors in providing a quick and reliable diagnosis. It also plays a pivotal role in accurate medical imaging and smart wearable medical devices. Telemedicine is yet another area where the importance of automated technology is realized to reduce the cumbersome commuting of patients and, particularly, the disabled in this crucial pandemic period, Figure 11.3 illustrates the healthcare applications of AI in Industry 4.0. Currently the improvement within the automatic technology extends its skills to enhance the simple, repetitive obligations into greater complicated operations that have previously relied closely on human input.

11.4.2.1 Artificial intelligence, predictive analytics to accelerate healthcare

In labor-intensive medical fields like radiology, it becomes challenging to do diagnosis, prognosis and treatment with reasonable levels of accuracy.

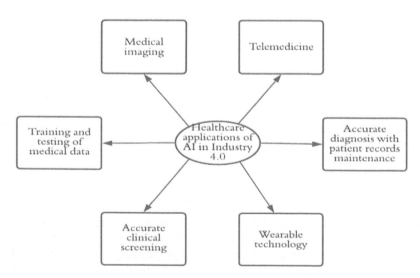

Figure 11.3 Healthcare applications of AI in Industry 4.0.

AI can lessen the quantity of labor and help in better maintenance of patient records. Predictive analytics provides a promising solution to better patient monitoring and deciding the effective treatment technique, thereby reducing the adverse effects.

11.4.2.2 Healthcare 4.0: the digital revolution in healthcare industry

In healthcare-related applications, the main purpose of AI and Healthcare 4.0 is to analyze the relationship between treatment methodologies and patient results. AI programs are applied to practices such as process deviation, plan design treatment, drug development, personalized medicine and monitoring and nursing. AI-assisted tools aid the doctors in better analysis of symptoms, diagnosing the causes and providing better healthcare.

11.4.3 Impact of AI on Industry 4.0 in the paint industry

Industry 4.0 is mainly applied in paint mixing rooms, where a particular quantity of different liquids with different colors is to be mixed in the appropriate proportions. Paint mixing is a vital step in the industrial finishing process. If it is not carried out properly, it can lead to paint shear, repetitive flushing and other issues that directly affect the production chain.

Factory paint lines can gain more efficiency and better results by implementing the technologies of Industry 4.0 to closely monitor paint quality and equipment performance. A smart factory increases production performance and efficiency and is fully autonomous.

11.4.4 Impact of AI in Industry 4.0 in the agriculture sector

Weather data acquired in real time by weather stations or various sensors provides information regarding humidity, rainfall, temperature and so on. If weather conditions are unfavorable, alerts are also sent as a warning for precaution. Machine learning algorithms could be utilized to provide smart information regarding climatic changes to the farmers, crop consultants and retailers.

It allows farmers to make better planning and take better decisions regarding the spacing of seeds, crops that can be grown and harvested. In addition, the appropriate amount of fertilizers for the crops is measured and applied in real time based on the amount of light reflected back to the optical crop sensors, preventing excess chemicals from draining neighboring water bodies.

Optical sensors, drones and satellite photos can also be used to assess the health of various crops. Using mobile phones and tablets, any pest population or weed activity on the farm may be verified, and the efficacy of pest- and disease-control strategies can then be evaluated. The Normalized Difference Vegetation Index (NDVI) is one of the most frequent approaches in vegetation monitoring and in determining the type of land. It detects agricultural variability and different crop stages using infrared (IR) and visible light wavelength.

11.4.4.1 In the agricultural sector, Industry 4.0 is being implemented

i. **Remote Access:** By strengthening security surrounding barns and pastures and allowing remote access to animals from anywhere, IoT-based systems can obtain information about the whereabouts and health of cattle.

ii. **Communication:** RFID, GPS and biometrics can all be used to automatically identify and deliver critical data on animals. Figure 11.4 illustrates the agricultural applications of AI in industry.

iii. **Data management (using software and platforms):** Data analysis clubbed with powerful AI tools helps in better crop monitoring, harvesting schedule and following better farming practices using the collected data on temperature, humidity and weather conditions. Obtained data can also be used to make informed decisions and reduce uncertainty when predicting the future.

iv. **Precision farming:** Livestock monitoring, irrigation monitoring, database gathering, as well as telematics, are all examples of precision

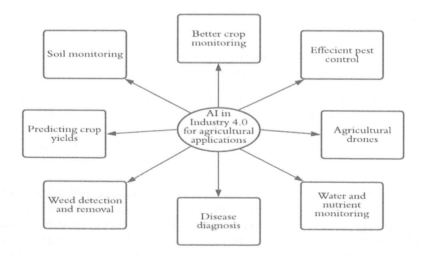

Figure 11.4 Agricultural applications of AI in industry.

smart farming applications that are becoming increasingly popular and efficient. Detectors can now generate data that can then be evaluated to make informed and timely decisions. Sensors may be used to analyze soil characteristics, moisture and nutrient levels, and IoT can be used to monitor all of these in real time. These IoT-based systems aid in improving farming's operational efficiency.

v. **Smart greenhouse:** Smart greenhouses are more efficient than traditional farming because they produce insecticide- and pesticide-free crops and provide an environment conducive to plant growth. Furthermore, anyone with no prior knowledge of farming can install this system in their home (rooftop greenhouse). This regulated environment can be used to grow a wide variety of crops. In addition, all significant variables, such as humidity, soil moisture or visible light are factored in the flowering plants. The users may adapt many of the detectors' features to aid the growth of various species and plant kinds [7].

vi. **Agricultural drones:** Latest technologies have changed the agricultural operations where the recent disruption is agricultural drones. Agricultural drones can be used for planting and spraying crops, monitoring health assessments and also making field analysis more efficient and safer. Drone technology has aided farmers in enhancing their farming operations, which has had a favorable influence on the agricultural industry. Drones can collect data on plant diseases, soil characteristics and soil conditions and can help improve crop yield.

11.4.5 Impact of AI in education sector

With the introduction of the latest technologies in the education sector, there has been a paradigm shift toward smart learning. Education 4.0 focuses on innovation-based education.

Infiltration of technology in Education 4.0: Tablets and smartphones, supportive classrooms, online assessments are some of the tools applied in the education sector. These technologies transform the future of education using advanced technology and automation. Education 4.0 has its base in creativity and in a smart learning environment.

Trends in Education 4.0 are:

1. **More personalized learning:** Personalized teaching with the help of AI and cloud computing
2. **More remote learning opportunities:** Learning available everywhere through Active Blended Learning (ABL) Concept
3. **The education tools, plethora:** Students can choose their educational tools
4. **Data at fingertips:** Statistical analysis of students' performance

5. **Easy and accurate assessment:** Both online and offline assessments possible
6. **Project-based learning:** Incorporates fun and curiosity

The role of teachers is that of facilitators. Education institutions can be prepared for Education 4.0 by remodeling their curriculum, improving digital skills, tweaking the course delivery and with the help of technology-built classrooms.

Paradigm shifts in education include demand led, competency based, lifelong learning with modular degree and emphasis of emotional quotient (EQ), which focuses on mindfulness and incorporating technologies and skill sets.

AI helps in bringing the easy and effective education with smart content and better outreach involving simplified administrative tasks.

Some differences between previous education revolutions with Education 4.0 include the student becoming an active recipient, technology being a part of training, a learning based system rather than an exam-based system, focus on quality rather than quantity, faster and smarter interaction [8]. It helps the teachers in profiling and predicting results, retention and dropout, to make decisions on admissions, academic achievement, student models and scheduling the courses by incorporating intelligent tutoring systems [9]. Figure 11.5 illustrates the applications of AI Industry 4.0 for education sector.

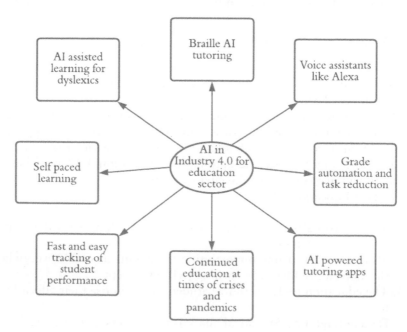

Figure 11.5 Applications of AI Industry 4.0 for education sector.

11.4.6 Impact of AI in financial services and banking

It includes:

- Online payments
- Digital loans
- Plastic money
- Cryptocurrency etc.

Finance 4.0 will help the emerging economies grow by over 6%, which accounts for $3.7 trillion by 2021, as predicted by McKinsey Global Institute.

Impact includes fastest financial transactions, decrease in thrift institutes' running costs, removal of middleman, effective marketing, reduced risk factors, financial deepening of underprivileged and deprived people, reduced number of fraud and burglary.

With a real-time analysis of payment data, AI-based businesses have an advantage. AI adds a layer of protection for businesses and consumers.

The Banking 4.0 characteristics are as follows:

- Transiting product-based operations to service-based roles
- Increased customer-centric approach to banking
- Shift toward digitization
- Collaborating with fintech companies to create co-branded products

The assured result of Industry 4.0 and digital economy is the appearance of blockchain technologies and cryptocurrencies [10].

With the help of AI, banks adopt customer support and help a desk that ultimately gives a personalized banking; they increase efficiency. Using AI chatbots, financial advice can be sought. Rural households can be benefitted. Furthermore, it provides security from fraudulent actions in banking [11].

11.4.7 Some emerging technologies in Industry 4.0

Digitalization, or IoT, is a new technology that allows interconnected devices to communicate with one another. Though IoT was first proposed in 1982, it has recently found a home in a variety of applications [12, 13]. Smart assistants are able to connect to other devices. This has made homes smart. Environmental factors like light, temperature and air can be changed according to human behavior using ambient technology [14]. Optimal usage of water in a household can also be calculated by using IoT technology [15]. This helps reduce water wastage. IoT devices also reduce costs and energy usage. RFIDs, an important part of IoT, act as electronic barcodes for automatic identification. They are also extensively used in logistics for tracking goods. In cold chain logistics, wireless sensor networks are used to monitor the status of goods. IoT is also applied in healthcare. Parameters of patients can be sent to doctors if they exceed a certain value. The user's facial expressions, sounds they made and their posture are also used to check patients [16]. This helps doctors monitor their patients better.

Augmented reality (AR) is an emerging technology in which digital elements are superimposed on the real world. AR and AR-related technologies are used in manufacturing to make better 3D models. With AR models of the workplace, robots can be calibrated better and can have better perspectives of the workplace [17]. Optimization of factory layouts and visualization and measurement of floor plans can be made easier with AR [18]. It is also used in healthcare. As it can give an internal view of the patient, it reduces the need for invasive procedures. It can also be used in healthcare education as it provides students with a more explorative and personalized learning experience. It is also used to reduce the pain of amputees [19]. AR contact lenses for the blind are being developed by several companies. AR is also being used by some militaries to train. AR also has also introduced new teaching techniques. It can develop spatial concepts, creativity, and can stimulate interest. It creates a fun learning environment for children.

Autonomous robots: Autonomous robots are machines that can handle tasks intelligently without the need for human intervention. Autonomous and semi-autonomous robots are being used in search and rescue operations in some locations. They are also being designed to aid in space exploration. The Mars rovers Spirit and Opportunity could navigate their own routes to the destination. They are also used extensively in factories. They can sense the environment, navigate and do tasks on their own. They can work for prolonged periods without human intervention.

They are also used in construction tasks such as building, surveillance and earthmoving. They are used in food processing and manufacturing industries and can perform tasks like picking, packaging and placing items. Furthermore, they are also used to inspect the quality of food [20].

11.5 ADVANTAGES OF AI IN INDUSTRY 4.0

11.5.1 Direct automation

Industrial Internet of Things (IIoT) links all IoT-enabled devices to the factory floor, allowing them to be integrated with PLCs and also augmenting production processes using Big Data. Data can now be collected, recorded and evaluated for all parts of the production process, from temperature to item selecting and packaging, thanks to the expanded usage of precise sensory equipment. AI-enabled programmable logic controllers with deep learning capabilities can therefore respond automatically to the continuously generated data and implement the modifications without the need for human intervention. AI-processed big data analytics is also important for improving a manufacturer's performance. Figure 11.6 illustrates the expected percentage of automation in various sectors over the years.

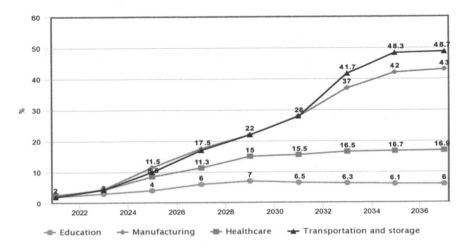

Figure 11.6 Expected percentage of automation in various sectors over the years.

11.5.2 Higher productivity

This appears to be the case with each industrial revolution, with each period's throughput increasing 50 times to the one before; its proficiency is anticipated to increase by 5–8% over the next 5–10 years because of growth in automation.

11.5.3 Faster decisions

When IIoT is combined with AR and cloud computing, companies may share simulations, confer on industrial activities and communicate vital or relevant information in real time, independent of their geographical location. Consumer behavior is determined using data from sensors and beacons, allowing firms to predict future demands and make rapid production decisions, as well as speeding up communication between manufacturers throughout the manufacturing process and being managed remotely. This enables faster decision-making.

11.6 DISADVANTAGES OF AI IN INDUSTRY 4.0

AI-based systems require huge installation costs with more complexities. It also poses potential risks in Industry 4.0 with respect to security and ethical issues due to connected technology. Furthermore, in some areas, robots can never replace the human presence.

The challenges and complexities involved in AI Industry 4.0 are machine-to-machine interaction, data quality and cyber security. The explanations are as follows.

11.6.1 Machine-to-machine interaction

AI is very sensitive to small changes in input, such as machine-to-machine interaction. Personal approaches and strategies must be ensured that AI solutions do not hamper the operation of other systems.

11.6.2 Data quality

AI techniques entail reasonably large and neat data sets that can deviate only a little from the expected data. If the data sets are incorrect and inadequate, it results in wrong learning, leading to deficient downstream results.

11.6.3 Cyber security

Because of the growing usage of interconnected technologies in smart manufacturing systems, there is a risk of cyber assaults. The magnitude of this exposure is generally underestimated, and the sector is not yet prepared to confront and overcome the security dangers that exist [21].

11.7 FUTURE OF INDUSTRY 4.0: INDUSTRY 5.0

The successive phase of industrialization involves the collaborative working of robots, smart machines and the people. With the digital revolution, such as Big Data and IoT, robots assist humans in working more efficiently. Industry 5.0 boosts collaborative performance productivity. Industry 5.0 aims at mass customization involving human-machine interaction for which the groundwork is laid by Industry 4.0. It harnesses the robotic perception skills blended with the creativity fostered by man to arrive at a unique solution. Mixed reality also plays a prominent role in Industry 5.0 where the physical world and digital world are integrated to leap a mile forward in innovative technology [22].

Visualization, process designing, tracking systems will improve material wastage reduction, preventing theft, and management of assets prevention when IoT and machine learning are combined. Virtual training, smart sensing, employs many tasks paving a way for an era with advanced technological practices.

Humans and computerized machinery bring another level of speed and perfection. The relationship among computers, robots and human workers will be mutually rewarding to mark a footprint in bringing out new advancements in the digital world. The smaller, affordable and feasible robots can be employed in small businesses. Industrial 5.0 brings mass personalization by putting forward humans at the center of industrial production. The benefits of IR 5.0 include cost optimization, greener solution, personalization and creativity. Furthermore, trained personnel and the right technology are the key factors in Industry 5.0 [23].

Industry 5.0 does indeed have two main aims:

1. Direct human-robot interaction
2. Bioeconomy [21]

IR 5.0 focuses on sustainability by obtaining electrical power through renewable resources. It involves technologies such as:

- Sustainable agricultural practices
- Bionic technology
- Renewable resources
- Collaborative robots for human-robot coordination [24]

11.8 CONCLUSION

For a large number of businesses around the world, Industry 4.0 is already a reality. Nevertheless, it is worth noting all of the changes required to fully participate in this industrial revolution for reaping the profits that it may bring will not occur overnight. This is a continued process that is constantly improving, just like digital transformation and automation.

AI is a critical component of this revolution and also, the use of AI in Industry 4.0 comes with its own advantages and disadvantages. The future prospects seem brighter and can be considered advantageous for a smarter and a more connected society.

REFERENCES

1. Alsedrah, M. K. Artificial Intelligence: Advanced Analysis and Design: CNIT 380. *International Journal of Science and Research*, 5, 1–12, 2018.
2. Mohajan, H. The First Industrial Revolution: Creation of a New Global Human Era. *Journal of Social Sciences and Humanities*, 5(4), 377–387, 2019.
3. Mohajan, H. The Second Industrial Revolution has Brought Modern Social and Economic Developments. *Journal of Social Sciences and Humanities*, 6(1), 1–14, 2019.
4. Brian. R. The Third Industrial Revolution: Implications for Planning Cities and Regions. *Urban Frontiers*, 1(1), 1–22, 2015.
5. Lasi, H., Fettke, P., Kemper, H. G., Feld, T., & Hoffmann, M. Industry 4.0. *Business and Information Systems Engineering*, 6(4), 239–242, 2014.
6. Torn, I. A. R., & Vaneker, T. H. J. Mass Personalization with Industry 4.0 by SMEs: A Concept for Collaborative Networks. *Procedia Manufacturing*, 28, 135–141, 2019.
7. Muthupavithran, S., Akash, S., & Ranjithkumar, P. Greenhouse Monitoring Using Internet of Things. *International Journal of Innovative Research in Computer Science and Engineering (IJIRCSE)*, 2, 13–19, 2016.

8. Dr, P. M. G., Kumar, P., Johri, P., Srivastava, S. K., & Suhag, S. A Comparative Study of Industry 4.0 with Education 4.0. *SSRN Electronic Journal*, 2020. https://doi.org/10.2139/ssrn.3553215.

9. Zawacki-Richter, O., Marín, V. I., Bond, M., & Gouverneur, F. Systematic Review of Research on Artificial Intelligence Applications in Higher Education – Where Are the Educators? *International Journal of Educational Technology in Higher Education*, 2019. https://doi.org/10.1186/s41239-019-0171-0.

10. Mekinjić, B. The Impact of Industry 4.0 on the Transformation of the Banking Sector. *Journal of Contemporary Economics*, 1(1), 1–23, 2019.

11. Mhlanga, D. Industry 4.0 in Finance: The Impact of Artificial Intelligence (AI) on Digital Financial Inclusion. *International Journal of Financial Studies*, 8(3), 1–14, 2020.

12. Dharanyadevi, P., Therese, M. J., & Venkatalakshmi, K. Internet of Things-Based Service Discovery for the 5G-VANET Milieu. In *Cloud and IoT-Based Vehicular Ad Hoc Networks* (pp. 31–45), 2021.

13. Therese, M. J., Dharanyadevi, P., & Harshithaa, K. Integrating IoT and Cloud Computing for Wireless Sensor Network Applications. In *Cloud and IoT-Based Vehicular Ad Hoc Networks* (pp. 125–143), 2021.

14. Kelly, S. D. T., Suryadevara, N. K,, & Mukhopadhyay, S. C. Towards the Implementation of IoT for Environmental Condition Monitoring in Homes. *IEEE Sensors Journal*, 13(10), 3846–3853, 2013.

15. Lynggaard, P., & Skouby, K. E. Complex IoT Systems as Enablers for Smart Homes in a Smart City Vision. *Sensors (Switzerland)*, 16(11), 1–14, 2016.

16. Asghari, P., Rahmani, A. M., & Javadi, H. H. S. Internet of Things Applications: A Systematic Review. *Computer Networks*, 148, 241–261, 2019.

17. Novak-Marcincin, J., Barna, J., Janak, M., & Novakova-Marcincinova, L. Augmented Reality Aided Manufacturing. *Procedia Computer Science*, 25, 23–31, 2013. ScienceDirect 2013 International Conference on Virtual and Augmented Reality in Education.

18. Doil, F., Schreiber, W., Alt, T., & Patron, C. *Augmented Reality for Manufacturing Planning* (pp. 71–76). Association for Computing Machinery (ACM), 2003.

19. Ortiz-Catalan, M., Sander, N., Kristoffersen, M. B., Håkansson, B., & Brånemark, R. Treatment of Phantom Limb Pain (PLP) Based On Augmented Reality and Gaming Controlled by Myoelectric Pattern Recognition: A Case Study of a Chronic PLP Patient. *Frontiers in Neuroscience*, 8, 1–7, 2014.

20. Iqbal, J., Khan, Z. H., & Khalid, A. Prospects of Robotics in Food Industry. *Food Science and Technology*, 37(2), 159–1652, 2017.

21. Lee, J., Davari, H., Singh, J., & Pandhare, V. Industrial Artificial Intelligence for Industry 4.0-based Manufacturing Systems. *Manufacturing Letters*, 18, 20–23, 2018.

22. Özdemir, V., & Hekim, N. Birth of Industry 5.0: Making Sense of Big Data with Artificial Intelligence, "The Internet of Things" and Next-Generation Technology Policy. *OMICS A Journal of Integrative Biology*, 22(1), 65–76, 2018.

23. Demir, K. A., Döven, G., & Sezen, B. Industry 5.0 and Human-Robot Co-working. *Procedia Computer Science*, 158, 688–695, 2019.

24. Demir, K. A., & Cicibaş, H. The Next Industrial Revolution: Industry 5.0 and Discussions on Industry 4.0. In *Industry 4.0 from the MIS Perspective* (pp. 247–260), 2019.

Chapter 12

Ensuring liveliness property in safety-critical systems

Ankur Maurya, Sharad Nigam, and Divya Kumar

CONTENTS

12.1 INTRODUCTION

Safety-critical systems are those systems, the malfunctioning or failure of which can create serious issues such as death or critical injury, economical loss or environmental damage [1]. The examples of safety-critical systems are blowout preventer [2], nuclear power plants [3, 4], airbag systems [5], and railway systems [6]. A safety-critical system requires high reliability, safety, and performance demand. Reliability is an important parameter because if a system does not fail, it means there is less chance to produce a functional error. Indian Railways are one of the most complex critical systems in the world. It is divided into various sections, i.e., signaling section, power section, mechanical section, and customer relations sections. These sections are interrelated and interfere with each other. In the signaling system, if an error occurs the probability of an accident is high.

DOI: 10.1201/9781003269144-12

Table 12.1 Accident record from 2009 to 2015

Accidents types	Number of three warnings accidents
Collisions	38
Accidents in Level Crossing	349
Derailments of Train	373
Fire in trains	29
Misc. Accidents	14

The most critical part of a railway system is crossing. Railway crossings are of two types: level crossing and diamond crossing. In the level crossing, track and road are at the same level and intersect each other. Before the train passes, the road is separated from the gates. The diamond crossing is a special type of crossing, where two different types of tracks meet each other perpendicularly. For example, in India, Nagpur diamond crossing is a double-track crossing, where the eastern line comes from Gondia, the northern line comes from New Delhi, the Western line comes from Mumbai and the Southern line comes from Kazipet. There are two types of railway paths: single track and multi-track. In the single track, at a time, the train travels in a single direction. While in multi-tracks, the train can travel in both the directions at the same time. In the Indian context, the railways are now facing big challenges, which are: competitive transport markets, the need for effective and efficient use of resources, training of personnel for railways and train maintenance, operation and control, dynamic customer requirements, service reliability, and availability. Automation of the railways is required because most of the accidents are due to human error. Statistics of different types of failures are given in Table 12.1.

This chapter proposes a working model for level crossing and double diamond crossing in railways, which is based on railway traffic lights.

A report from Indian railways shows that there are 803 accidents occurred in duration of six years from 2009 to 2015. In these accidents, most of the accidents are due to train derailments and level crossing accidents. The statistics of accidents are given in Table 12.2.

The structures of this chapter are as follows, Section 12.2 studies the related work in this field. Section 12.3 describes the preliminaries and petri net model. Section 12.4 contains working of petri net model. Lastly, the conclusion and future scope are given in Section 12.5.

12.2 RELATED WORK

A fuzzy knowledge-based system for railway traffic control is studied by Alexander et al. [6]. He has implemented a system based on fuzzy logic with Petri net. This chapter is based on a flexible design and modular structure

Table 12.2 Train accidents in India

Date	Accident type	No. of death	No. of injuries	Description
08/05/2020	Medium	15	0	Train accident at Aurangabad Maharashtra
03/02/2019	Large	7	29	11 Seemanchal Express derailed in Sahadai
24/07/2018	Medium	5	4	Train accident at St. Thomas Mount Chennai
24/11/2017	Medium	3	9	The derailment of Vasco Da Gama-Patna Express Chitrakoot, UP
23/08/2017	Medium	0	100	Kaifiyat Express (12225) derailed, Patna
17/08/2017	Large	23	97	Puri-Haridwar Kalinga Utkal Express derailed in Khatauli, Uttar Pradesh
21/01/2017	Large	41	68	Near Kuneru Vizianagaram Jagdalpur-Bhubaneswar Express derailed
6/12/2016	Medium	2	6	Rajendra Nagar-Guwahati Express Derailed
19/10/2018	Large	59	100	The train moved into the crowd who were standing on the tracks
10/10/2018	Medium	7	12	Coaches Derail Racbareli, UP
23/07/2014	Large	23	0	The passenger train and a school bus collision at a level crossing
30/07/2012	Large	47	25	Fire caught in Tamil Nadu Express caught Nellore, Andhra Pradesh
10/07/2011	Large	70	300	Derailed Kalka Mail near Fatehpur, UP

for fuzzy rules that are based on "IF-THEN" statement. The limitation of this chapter is that they consider a pre-defined structure in which insertion of a new train is difficult. So, the train may get stuck in starvation. Swarup et al. [7] presented a paper based on FMEA and FTA for the railways. In this chapter, they used fault tree method to determine the possibility of failure of the railroad crossing. The limitation of this chapter is that they have not provided decentralized control. Cheng et al. [8] discussed fuzzy-based Petri approach on the Taiwan railway system. They cover CTC failure, locomotive failure, and ATP failure but the main limitation of this method is sometime trained can go into starve state. In [9] p-time Petri net was presented for modeling and performance evaluation of the railway system. This chapter covered single and double track rail transportation but the limitation of this system is that they do not cover crossings and other stoppages. D. Wu [10] used colored Petri nets. The hazardous state is automatically identified in this chapter. Xiaoli et al. [11] worked on Colored Petri Net (CPN) techniques. The advantage of using CPN is that it can be used to verify that a system is in a safe state or not. The advantage of this chapter is the capability to find hazardous states. Evaluating fault tree using CPN to analyze the railway system is studied by Haifeng Song [12]. In this chapter, hazard analysis is done. This chapter mostly focuses on finding a logical relationship between failure and its causes.

12.3 PRELIMINARIES

There are various methods to analyze safety in the critical systems; some of the most important methods used in literature are:

- Failure Mode and Effects Analysis (FMEA) [13],
- Fault Tree Analysis (FTA) [14],
- Markov Chain Modeling [15], and
- Petri Nets (PN) [16].

12.3.1 Failure mode and effect analysis

This technique is used to guarantee quality. A step-by-step approach to identifying all possible failures is done by this method. This is used to find the danger in model by analyzing all the effects. It is used in quality function deployment, analyzing failure of an existing process. FMEA is utilized for dissecting the individual dangers of a framework. Further investigation of components, fault tree examination is more fitting.

12.3.2 Fault tree analysis

FTA is used to analyze the reliability, maintainability, probability of failure and safety in a system. It is a bottom-up approach used to find the possible combination of software and hardware errors. The failure of the system is represented at the root of the diagram. It uses the deductive technique to find an error in the root. FTA combines different situations by using two gates (AND, OR). It finds the probability of failure by an analytical or statistical approach. The fault tee analysis of the railway system is given in Figure 12.1.

12.3.3 Markov process

It is a memory less loosely coupled architecture model. It involves a random process with property that future events are independent of past events. It is a similar to mealy machine where previous transition and current states predict future state.

12.3.4 Petri net

Petri nets are an acronym of place transition nets. It is a mathematical model that is based on distributed systems. Petri nets are represented by five tuples:

- $PN = (P, T, I, O, M_0)$. Where,
- P stands for a set of places or states, they are finite and represented by a circle.

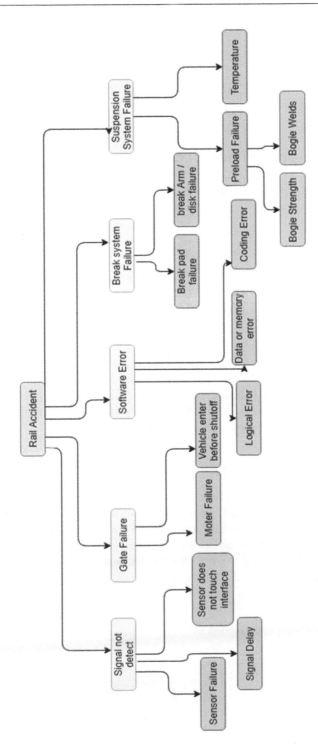

Figure 12.1 FTA.

- T stands for transitions, they are also finite and represented by rectangular.
- I stands for a matrix P*T, where an arc comes from place Pi to transition Tj.
- O stands for a matrix P*T, where an arc comes from transition Tj to place Pi.

12.4 PROPOSED METHODOLOGY

The proposed framework for the reliability analysis of train derailment is as follows. The proposed methodology is shown in Figure 12.2.

12.4.1 Requirement analysis

In this phase, all the requirements of the system are analyzed. The requirements of the system are captured through the events that happened in the past. The necessary information is gathered by documentation of Indian railway.

12.4.2 Validity

In this phase, the required model will be verified in order to capture all the requirement of the system, if any of the requirement is found unaddressed, then the process is repeated from the initial phase.

12.4.3 Petri net analysis

We are considering a double line track with a diamond crossing and two level crossings. In this model, we are mainly working by train traffic light signal. There are three types of signals in the train: red, yellow, and green. The red signal means the track is not clear and the train has to stop immediately. The yellow signal means that the second train is occupied by the crossing, so there is a need to slow down the speed of the train and then proceed according to the next signal. A green signal means the track is clear

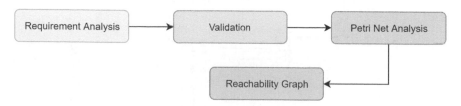

Figure 12.2 Proposed methodology.

Table 12.3 Possibilities of signals

3rd signal	2nd signal	1st signal	Taken action
Green	Green	Green	Train can cross diamond crossing
Red	Green	Green	Stop the train
Yellow	Red	Green	Move train in moderate speed and check 3rd signal again
Green	Yellow	Red	Stop immediately
Green	Green	Yellow	Move train in moderate speed
Other combinations			Invalid

so the train can proceed at its maximum speed. Possibilities of signals are shown in Table 12.3. The accidents percentage due to different causes are shown in Table 12.4.

- If the 3rd, 2nd, and 1st signals are green, then that means the diamond crossing is free and the train can cross it with the full speed.
- If 3rd signal is red and other signals are green, it means that another train is coming from vertical tracks, so the train will have to stop.
- If the 3rd signal is yellow, 2nd signal is red and 1st signal is green, then the train can move in moderate speed and then it will again check the 3rd signal.
- If the 3rd signal is green, 2nd signal is yellow and 1st signal is red, the 2nd train is on the diamond crossing.
- If 3rd signal is also green and 1st signal is yellow, then it means another train has just crossed diamond crossing. So, the train can move forward at a moderate speed.
- All other combinations apart from these combinations are not valid. Example, let us say if the combination is (yellow, green, and red), then 1st signal implies that there is a train but 2nd signal implies that the track is free, which leads to conflict (may be due to signal problem). So, the train will stop and wait for a clear signal.

Table 12.4 Accidents percentage in different scenario

Causes of accidents	Percentages of failure (%)
Human (by staff)	40.70
Human mishandling (by others)	45.70
Component failure	2.20
Sabotage	5.50
Some Incidental Factors	3.40
Unknown causes	0.7
Accidents under inspection	1.80

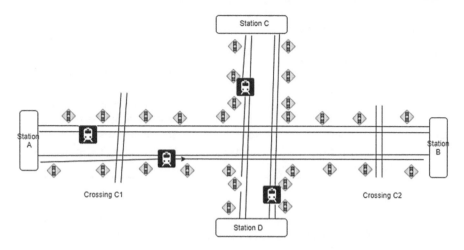

Figure 12.3 Scenarios of diamond crossing.

Figure 12.3 shows the real-time scenario of diamond crossing. It contains four station (A, B, C and D), two level crossing (C1 and C2), and a diamond crossing. We assume that the train can move in single track, i.e., the train is either going or coming.

- Station A is shown by place P_0 and station D is represented by place P_{22}. If there is a yellow signal in place P_0, then the train can move in moderate speed and reach to the place P_1, after that it can move with maximum speed.
- When train gets signal before the level crossing, i.e., place P_3 and if signal is red, it will go into stop place P_5 and checks signal again. If signal is yellow, then it will go to place P_4, which is a moderate speed place and it will check the signal again.
- If signal is green, it means level crossing is closed so train can cross with maximum speed. Before diamond crossing, it checks the 3rd signal at place P_8, if it is red, then transition will go in place P_{10}, which is a stop state, if it gets yellow signal, then the train will go to place P_9 in moderate speed.
- For previous two transitions, 3rd signal again will be checked again. If we get green signal, the transition will go to place P_{13} and checks the signal of 1st signal pole, if it is a red, then train go in place P_{18}, which is a stop state. If it gets a yellow signal, then it will go to place P_{17} in moderate speed.
- After these two transitions, we check 1st signal again if we get green signal, the transition will be at place P_{19}, which means the train has crossed diamond signal. The real-time simulation of the proposed framework using a Time net tool [17] is shown in Figure 12.4.

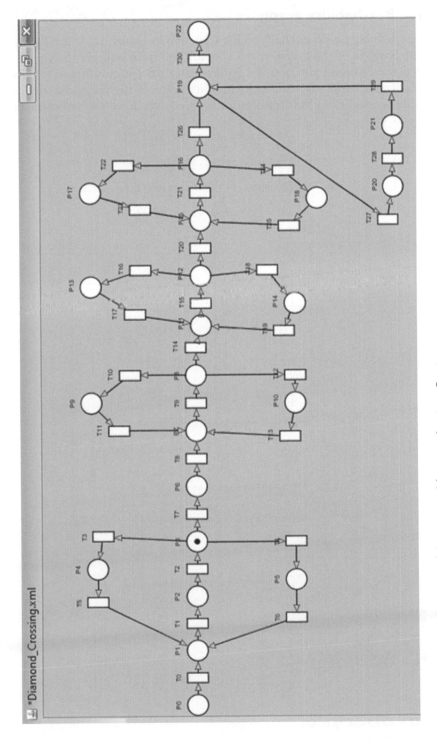

Figure 12.4 Real-time simulation of the proposed framework using a Petri net.

12.4.4 Reachability graph

The reachability graph of the Petri net is shown in Figure 12.5. It tells the current position of the token in the system. The train will get the chance to cross the diamond junction if it is having a sufficient number of tokens in the corresponding place. The reachability graph of the proposed framework shows that the given framework is free from deadlock as no token

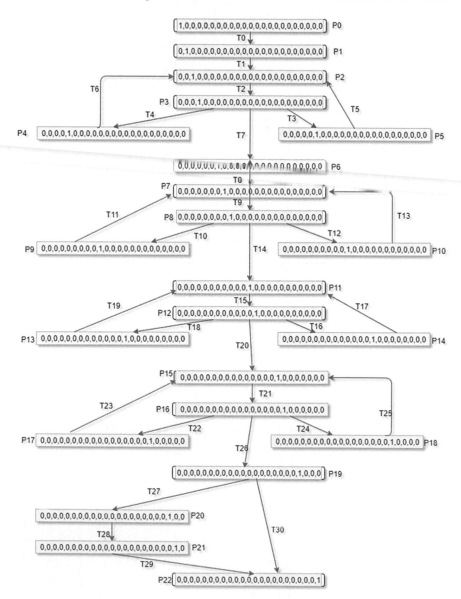

Figure 12.5 Reachability graph.

stuck in a loop and holds liveliness property because every state is reachable from starting state.

12.5 CONCLUSION

The failure and bad handling of safety-critical systems are dangerous and can be life threatening. Our proposed framework is safe and can be used for real-life scenarios since it has no deadlock and holds liveliness property. It also provides an accident-free crossing with less human intervention. This model is based on simple railway signals.

REFERENCES

[1] Ankur Maurya and Divya Kumar. Reliability of safety-critical systems. A state-of-the-art review. *Quality and Reliability Engineering International*, 36(7):2547–2568, 2020.

[2] Javed Akbar Khan, Sonny Irawan, Ahgheelan Seela Thurai, and Baoping Cai. Quantitative analysis of blowout preventer flat time for well control operation: Value added data aimed at performance enhancement. *Engineering Failure Analysis*, 120:104982, 2021.

[3] Vinay Kumar, Lalit Kumar Singh, Pooja Singh, Karm Veer Singh, Ashish Kumar Maurya, and Anil Kumar Tripathi. Parameter estimation for quantitative dependability analysis of safety-critical and control systems of NPP. *IEEE Transactions on Nuclear Science*, 65(5):1080–1090, 2018.

[4] Mohan Rao Mamdikar, Vinay Kumar, Pooja Singh, and Lalit Singh. Reliability and performance analysis of safety-critical system using transformation of UML into state space models. *Annals of Nuclear Energy*, 146:107628, 2020.

[5] Ankur Maurya and Divya Kumar. Translation of SysML diagram into mathematical petri net model for quantitative reliability analysis of airbag system. *International Journal of Vehicle Design (In Press)*, 18–36, 2021.

[6] Alexander Fay. A fuzzy knowledge-based system for railway traffic control. *Engineering Applications of Artificial Intelligence*, 13(6):719–729, 2000.

[7] Ben Swarup Medikonda, P. Seetha Ramaiah, and Anu A Gokhale. Fmea and fault tree based software safety analysis of a railroad crossing critical system. *Global Journal of Computer Science and Technology*, 2011.

[8] Yung-Hsiang Cheng and Li-An Yang. A fuzzy petri nets approach for railway traffic control in case of abnormality: Evidence from Taiwan railway system. *Expert Systems with Applications*, 36(4):8040–8048, 2009.

[9] Wenzheng Jia, Baohua Mao, Tinkin Ho, Haidong Liu, and Bo Yang. Bottlenecks detection of track allocation schemes at rail stations by petri nets. *Journal of Transportation Systems Engineering and Information Technology*, 9(6):136–141, 2009.

[10] Daohua Wu and Jintao Liu. An approach to safety analysis of train control systems with coloured petri nets. In *2021 40th Chinese Control Conference (CCC)*, pages 4744–4750. IEEE, 2021.

[11] Xiaoli She and Jian Yang. Petri net based functional safety verification framework on rail control system. *Metallurgical and Mining Industry*, (2):78–84, 2016.

[12] Haifeng Song and Eckehard Schnieder. Evaluating fault tree by means of colored petri nets to analyze the railway system dependability. *Safety Science*, 110:313–323, 2018.

[13] Jia Huang, Jian-Xin You, Hu-Chen Liu, and Ming-Shun Song. Failure mode and effect analysis improvement: A systematic literature review and future research agenda. *Reliability Engineering & System Safety*, 199:106885, 2020.

[14] Iram Akhtar and Sheeraz Kirmani. An application of fuzzy fault tree analysis for reliability evaluation of wind energy system. *IETE Journal of Research*, 1–14, 2020.

[15] Frej Sundqvist. Developing Markov chain models for train delay evolution in winter climate, Master's thesis in Engineering Physics at Umeå University, 2021.

[16] Daohua Wu, Debiao Lu, and Tao Tang. Qualitative and quantitative safety evaluation of train control systems (CTCS) with stochastic colored petri nets. *IEEE Transactions on Intelligent Transportation Systems*, 23(8):10223–10238, 2021.

[17] Armin Zimmermann. Modelling and performance evaluation with TimeNET 4.4. In *International Conference on Quantitative Evaluation of Systems*, pages 300–303. Springer, 2017.

Chapter 13

Machine learning for intelligent analytics

*Jyoti Pokhariya, Pankaj Kumar Mishra,
and Jyoti Kandpal*

CONTENTS

13.1 INTRODUCTION

Artificial intelligence (AI) is a collection of technologies that extract patterns and valuable insights from massive datasets, making forecasts dependent on that data. AI exists today that can assist you with getting more value out of the information you have, bind together that data, and make forecasts about customer behaviors based on it [1]. The adoption of AI has been driven not just by increased computational power and new algorithms yet additionally by the growth of data now accessible. For intelligence analysts, that multiplication of data implies reliable data overburden. Human analysts essentially can't adapt to that much information. They need assistance. Intelligence leaders realize that AI can assist in adapting to this data downpour, yet they may likewise consider how AI will have on their work

DOI: 10.1201/9781003269144-13

and staff. For example, Twitter utilizes machine learning (ML) and AI to assess tweets in real time and score them using different measurements to show tweets that can drive the most engagement. AI plays a significant part in assisting organizations with handling data without forfeiting accuracy or speed. ML is a subset of AI, a considerably more extensive field of research. AI focuses on using various ways to make machines intelligent, whereas ML focuses on a single approach to creating robots that can learn to execute jobs. Expert systems development is an example of an AI technique that isn't dependent on learning. Despite the difficulty of describing intelligence, it seems clear that ML is a branch of AI. Unfortunately, due to a dominant perception that ML is the only possible strategy for attaining AI's goals, the vast majority of people believe AI and ML are synonymous.

The domain of AI has been established for more than six decades, and it has gone through several hypes and subsequent crashes throughout that time [2]. However, ML methodologies are on the rise to solve real-world problems in people's everyday lives.

ML is a specific mechanism that enables the program to improve its accuracy in projecting results independently without having to be expressly and explicitly coded. ML is predicated on establishing algorithms that could take in data and apply statistical analysis to anticipate a conclusion while altering conclusions as current information becomes accessible. Machine learning is introduced in various areas, from outsourcing ordinary chores to providing insightful additional insight, and companies across the board are attempting to capture the benefits [3]. For example, my applications available on our mobile phones have intelligent assistance like Siri and Bixby, which saves our time and makes our lives easy. Due to the rising production of the vast amount of data available on the web, machines can design and construct predictive systems that can explore and interpret enormous volumes of information to uncover significant clarity and generate improved appropriate solutions; top-tier firms use a lot of data to create machine learning tools that help them find good possibilities and avoid future risks. We want a method for structuring, analyzing, and extracting relevant insights from data due to the uncontrolled transition of information. ML utilizes information to overcome concerns and discover a resolution to the many complex challenges businesses challenges. If all the challenges are eliminated, it is easy for firms to make better decisions for a profitable future business [4].

The digital world has a wealth of information; ML applications and algorithms can be used to build real-world applications that can reduce human workload. However, AI expertise, specifically ML, must intelligently analyze these data and construct the associated innovative and automatic applications. AI and ML frameworks exist that utilize analytics data to assist you with foreseeing results and influential blueprints. AI-empowered frameworks can analyze information from many sources and deliver forecasts about what works and what doesn't. It can likewise deeply jump into details about your customers and offer predictions about buyer inclinations, marketing and sales channels, and product development strategies. AI/ML advances empower companies across various industries to harness value from customer information with no trouble [5]. For instance, AI data integration solutions empower all business users to map information between multiple fields to simplify the data into a unified database. Since non-technical users can effortlessly utilize these arrangements, IT people need not assume full responsibility. However, this leaves IT to zero in on other vital tasks. These solutions use ML algorithms to provide data predictions, which can also quicken the data transformation process. Since the decisions are taken utilizing algorithms, the chance of mistakes like missing qualities, deceptions, errors, and so on reduce. Hence, companies can use AI/ML tools to change how they deliver customer value. They can plan and integrate data and keep up data integrity, improving decision-making and boosting growth [6].

The advantages of AI and ML, notwithstanding, can go a long way beyond time savings. Intelligence work is a never-ending process; there is consistently another difficulty that demands attention [9, 10]. Therefore, saving time with AI won't decrease the staff or trim intelligence budgets. Or maybe, the more substantial value of AI comes from what may be named an "automation dividend": the better ways experts can utilize their time after these advances reduce their workload. Figure 13.1 represents the relationship/difference among AI, ML, and deep learning.

ML is a computational science domain that addresses methodologies and strategies for automating difficult-to-solve challenges that conventional programming can't resolve [7].

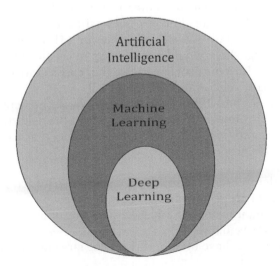

Figure 13.1 Relationship among AI, ML, and deep learning.

In the classical programming paradigm, there are two essential stages: the first step is to create a complete programmed design, which is a collection of processes or guidelines for addressing the reasons based on a programmed specification (i.e., what the programmed is supposed to accomplish, not how it is going to do it). The precise design is then incorporated into a computer program in the second stage. Unfortunately, this approach is challenging to apply to many real-world issues where, despite a precise specification, generating a comprehensive design can be complex. ML is indeed an area of study that concentrates upon two interconnected questions: how could someone implement software systems that focus on improving individuals over time apparently? Which are the core statistics, computational, as well as information-theoretic principles that regulate most learning methods, involving computers, humans, and sometimes even organizations? ML research is necessary for tackling these basic underlying scientific and technological challenges, as well as the effective and efficient software applications it has generated and deployed inside a wide range of applications.

ML would also have evolved a long way in over last 2 decades, through a laboratory curiosity into a fundamental tool in widespread usage for business purposes [8]. ML would also have arisen considered a subset of AI that certainly benefit from software for controlling robots, computer vision, identification of speech, natural language processing, and many other applications. The first building model premised upon the dataset and afterward implemented that modeling to anticipate a peripheral device data point; ML algorithms take a roundabout approach to solving a problem. Supervised ML is the name given to this approach. ML technologies are more efficient than human-created algorithms because they assess all data points in a dataset without any human bias based on prior knowledge. However, even if ML algorithms are successful, it is still unclear how a problem is resolved. This is especially true for ML algorithms based on neural networking. This would be referred to as the probability-based constraint model. In some problem areas, the representativeness of an ML algorithm is equally crucial and helpful [9–12].

Through till the mid-2000s, ML research made moderate but steady gains in handling complicated issues, after which the field surged dramatically [13–15]. The following are some of the factors that have contributed to this remarkable progress:

   i. Due to the internet, enormous datasets of photographs and other types of data are readily available on the web.
   ii. Massive computing power and large amounts of memory and processing space are available.
   iii. Algorithms that have been optimized for large amounts of data have been enhanced.

13.2 MAJOR CATEGORIES OF MACHINE LEARNING

ML technology is frequently characterized by how the algorithm optimizes its forecasting accuracy. The discipline of ML is commonly divided into the following branches:

1. Supervised learning
2. Unsupervised learning
3. Reinforcement learning

13.2.1 Supervised learning

The most common aspect and well category of ML involves supervised learning. This is probably considered the most fundamental technique of ML. This is identical to teaching with flashcards for a toddler to distinguish items. Algorithms are trained to distinguish the given data as a kid. Take, for example, the preceding information as samples using labeling. As a result, in supervised learning, techniques were given various example labeled combinations one after the other, enabling them to anticipate the future title for each instance.

Every individual that provides the algorithms with various sample labels makes recommendations on each and every assumption, whether it was really accurate or not. Every process usually repeated till the algorithms are able to accurately forecast the nature of the association between both the samples and associated labels. Never-seen-before connection would be observed by the supervised learning algorithm model and expect a good title when fully trained. Because it is necessary to repeat a task countless times until it is completely accurate, supervised learning can sometimes be characterized as task-oriented. Figure 13.2 represents the classification of supervised learning.

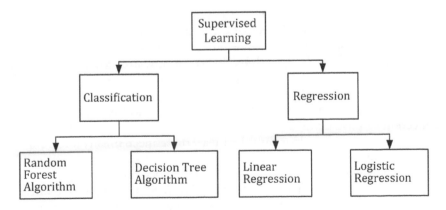

Figure 13.2 Classification of supervised learning.

There is the following application that is discussed below:

i. **Popularity of the commercial:** Choosing a commercial that will frequently grab much popularity used to determine supervised learning. We see ads even though some learning could be accomplished simultaneously browsing the net algorithms projected that they'd earn a decent amount of recognition and click ability. We frequently come across advertisements on a specialized platform or a particular website as well as type in a search term. According to a trained algorithm, combining particular advertisement and positioning would be beneficial.

ii. **Types of spam:** Spam emails have been considerable pressure on consumers. However users, on the other hand, are hardly longer bothered by them. Spam filters are available in current email servers such as Gmail. The spam scanner is basically more than a framework for supervised learning. Email samples as well as labels (spam mail/not a spam mail) are presented, as well as they are programmed to distinguish between these. Such supervised learning techniques understand to segregate unwanted spam and harmful emails before they receive. Most of these tools also have the functionality to provide users with new labels to understand user requirements.

iii. **Face recognition:** Facebook is capable of analyzing faces and proposing that users tag them. What makes it feasible? Our faces are most often possibly utilized in a supervised learning system that has been designed for scanning our faces. A supervised method can recognize faces in a photograph and recommend that we tag them. This supervised approach is also used by Google Photos. If you've used it, you'll recall the programmed that allowed you to share your photo with others.

13.2.2 Unsupervised learning

Unsupervised ML is a type of method, in which the algorithms answer anonymous as well as unlabeled data. Unsupervised techniques are used by data scientists commonly for exploring variations when working with new sets of data. Clustering algorithms, like K-means, are extensively used in unsupervised ML approach. Unsupervised learning method is the exactly opposite of supervised learning. There are no labels used during unsupervised learning. In unsupervised learning, the method is explained a vast collection of unstructured data and the capabilities to determine the database's attributes. The algorithm then uses these mechanisms for grouping the data, clustering, and organizing the given data so that the final result, i.e., the newly acquired data, can be better understood by any programmers and a human. Unsupervised learning is a very challenging and intriguing area because of its potential to arrange huge amounts of disorganized and unlabeled data. This is because the vast bulk of unlabeled set of data exists all around us. If we could somehow extract some useful information from this data, it will be really advantageous. It is made achievable by unsupervised learning algorithms, which generate substantial benefits. We can call unsupervised learning data-driven because it is dependent on data and its characteristics. The results of unsupervised learning tasks are driven by the data and how it is formatted. The following are some illustrations of unsupervised learning application areas:

Some applications of unsupervised learning are:

i. **Recommender systems:** Unsupervised learning has been used discreetly when binge-watching shows on Netflix as well as other OTT sites. When we use these platforms to watch and wish list our favorite episodes, we are providing data to the learning algorithm. A video suggestion technology is implemented on several platforms. Here the mechanism of unsupervised learning considers unorganized material from user browsing record, show genres, timeframes, and categorizes this information. Then it compares the results to others that kind of as shows currently offered and provides a recommendation of shows that a user might just prefer. This type of unsupervised training system is likewise used by YouTube.

ii. **Online buying:** We're practically more used to shopping online, and each one of us possesses our own buying preferences. Many folks enjoy shopping on a certain website. We keep a wish list and keep track of our purchases. This is all information. It's feasible that all of our purchasing patterns are stored in a database that was being regularly exchanged as you read this. Unsupervised algorithms organize clients into comparable purchase segments based on their shopping behavior in the past. Companies use this to advertise certain products to meet people's needs elements.

iii. **Grouping logs of customer:** Users' logs and concerns could also be grouped using unsupervised learning. Unsupervised learning isn't as user-friendly as supervised learning, but it's really beneficial. Organizations have used this to determine the core element of challenges that their customers are experiencing and afterward seek to tackle those concerns. It can also be utilized to design a product and prepare FAQs. Whenever one reports a problem or a bug, it is possible that you may have supplied the information to unsupervised learning algorithm that clusters it with other similar problems.

13.2.3 Reinforcement learning

It varies from supervised and unsupervised learning in a number of different aspects. Mostly on foundation of labeled and unlabeled occurrences, we may also distinguish supervised and unsupervised learning and reinforcement learning, on the other hand, doesn't even involve these kind labels. The correlation with reinforcement learning seems a little hazier. Some

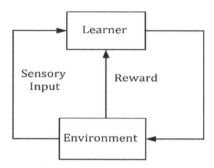

Figure 13.3 Process of reinforcement.

experts try to attach it up in knots by trying to refer to it as an aspect of learning that uses a time-dependent sequence of labels. The correlation with reinforcement learning seems a little hazier. Some experts try to attach it up in knots by trying to refer it as a sort of learning that uses a time-dependent series of labels. Reinforcement learning is behavior-driven learning. It is influenced by the disciplines of psychology and neuroscience. Researchers learn regarding Pavlov's dog in psychology class. We get the notion of reinforcing a particular agent from it. As more than just a result, we might think of reinforcement learning as the process of learning from one's own failures. Whenever a reinforcement technique has been used in the certain domain, it produces a huge amount of errors outcomes in the beginning. It improves the moment when the algorithm receives a signal associating good behavior with something like a positive indicator and destructive behavior with a negative one is delivered. It tends to commit fewer errors with practice. Figure 13.3 represents the process of reinforcement.

13.3 APPLICATIONS OF REINFORCEMENT LEARNING

    i. **Video games:** Video games are among the foremost prominent venues involving reinforcement learning. AlphaZero, a Google reinforcement learning tool, and AlphaGo, which learned how to play Go, are two such examples. An excellent illustration of a reinforcement learning application seems to be Mario's game. The individual understands techniques in the game, and the game seems to be the environment. The agent undertakes a series of challenges. Each of the latest game frame functions as the current progress, and there shall be button states. Our rewarding indication is the modification in the scoring. As far as we maintain interconnecting all of these pieces, a reinforcement learning scenarios would emerge.

   ii. **Industrial simulation:** In businesses wherein robots are designed to undertake numerous activities, it is essential to guarantee that they are worthy of successfully completing their assignments without supervision. It is a less expensive option and more efficient alternative, and more than that, it diminishes the chances of error. Moreover, the machines can be programmed to consume less electricity and reduce costs.

iii. **Management of resource:** Google's information hubs incorporate reinforcement learning method that can help to maintain balance such a need to fulfill customer's power consumption needs while doing it as effectively as possible and saving money. What impact does this have on the normal individual as well as on us? We can save money on information storage and also have a lower footprint on the environment that all inhabit.

These three methods of ML strive to help instruct computer algorithms that are increasingly efficient at doing jobs.

13.3.1 Constraints of machine learning

ML is utilized to find characteristics and tendencies in massive datasets. In addition, it's frequently intended to create models that learn from current information to predict or anticipate events or behavior. Following are a few examples involving ML problems:

i. **Classification:** The classification system divides things into several or even more subcategories (classes). They are identifying whether or not a particular email contains spam, for example. So, for example, distinguishing images of an animal as a dog, cat, or even another animal.

ii. **Clustering:** Clustering is generally the method of grouping a significant quantity of data points into just a few clusters that share some characteristics. Unlike categorization, the number of clusters might not be anticipated ahead of time.

iii. **Prediction:** Models depending upon previous data can anticipate future values. Consider the demand for a particular product throughout the Christmas season.

13.4 APPLICATIONS OF MACHINE LEARNING ALGORITHM

a. **Recognition of image:** Image recognition is the most popular and common application of ML algorithm. It's being used to recognize pictures of people, locations, and digital photographs. Automatic buddy tagging recommendation is a common application case for recognition of image and face identification. Automatic friend tagging recommendations are accessible on Facebook. As a result, anytime we share a photograph with our Facebook peers, we are presented with such a tagging recommendation that comprises a username. Face detection and identification algorithms based on ML are at the heart of this technology. It is premised upon the "Deep Face" Facebook venture, which is responsible for handling face recognition and individual identification part in photographs.

b. **Speech recognition:** When customers use Google, users have the opportunity to "Search by voice" that falls under the umbrella of speech recognition as well as being a prominent ML technique.

Speech recognition often referred to as "Speech to text" or "Computer speech recognition." It is the process of turning spoken requests into written text. ML algorithms now are prominently used in a variety of fields of speech recognition applications. For example, Alexa, Siri, Cortana, and Google home assistant implement speech recognition algorithms for following speech instructions.

c. **Traffic monitoring:** Whenever someone wishes to travel to new place, we are now using Google Maps that offers user the fastest route with the lowest distance and anticipates traffic conditions.

It includes two approaches to anticipate traffic situations, like whether traffic is empty, sluggish moving, or cluttered:

i.   Vehicles position in real time through Google Maps plus sensors.
ii. The average duration of time has been determined over the previous few days at the same time.

Everyone whoever uses Google Map contributes to the app's enhancement. It collects input from users and feeds it directly to its own database in order to boost its efficiency and effectiveness.

d. **Product advertisements:** Due to ML, numerous multimedia organizations and e-commerce, including prime, Netflix, and many other OTT platforms, incorporate ML that helps in making item recommendations for viewers. For example, when we search for an item on Amazon, we are bombarded with adverts for comparable products whenever browsing the web on an identical browser. Applying several ML methods, Google tries to deduce the user's preferences and suggests different types of items based on their preferences. Similarly, we get several suggestions for entertainment series, films, and other things whenever we access Netflix. ML is also used to accomplish this.

e. **Self-driving cars:** ML is being used with some of the greatest innovative ways. ML serves a vital role in self-driving cars. Tesla, one of the most well-known car company, is working on a self-driving vehicle. It trains automobile models to recognize faces as well as things even during driving using an unsupervised learning technique.

f. **Email spam and malware filtering:** Every time when we acquire a new email, it is immediately categorized as an essential routine. ML provides the technologies that allow necessary messages mostly with the necessary flag in our inbox and spam emails in our spam box; the essential spam detectors are used by Gmail:

i. Filtering post
ii. Filtering header
iii. General blocklist filters
iv. Rules-based filters
v. Permission filters

For email spam monitoring and antivirus identification, machine learning ML techniques such as multi-layer perception, decision tree, and naive Bayes classifier are used.

g. **Virtual personal assistant:** We have Google Assistant, Alexa, Cortana, and Siri, among other virtual assistants. They help us in finding data with the help of our speech commands, as the name suggests. Such assistants can help users in numerous ways by simply following our voice instructions, like playing songs, making a phone call, reading an email, appointment scheduling, and many more task. ML techniques are an important component of these virtual assistants.

h. **Identification of internet fraud:** By identifying illegal transactions, ML maintains our digital transactions safe and protected. Whenever users engage with online marketing, there seem to be several different ways that a bogus transaction could occur, including the use of phony usernames, fake identities, as well as the theft of funds within the process of a purchase. To recognize fraud, a Feed Forward Neural Network aids us all by analyzing whether transaction is authentic or fraudulent. The outcome of each valid transaction is translated into some hash functions, which are then used as the entry for the next round. For each fraudulent source of funds, a consistent pattern is updated for every genuine marketing. As a result, it monitors it as well as strengthens the security of our online transactions.

i. **Trading in the stock market:** Throughout stock market trading, ML is commonly used. Because there is constantly the risk of stock market ups and downs, this ML's extendable short-term neural memory network is applied to forecast stock market patterns.

j. **Healthcare diagnosis:** ML is being used to determine disorders in medical science. As a result, medical science is rapidly progressing and could indeed now create three-dimensional simulations that can estimate the precise location of tumors in the nervous system.

Along with determining brain tumors, various other brain-related diseases, as well as other body-part-related diseases, like heart diseases, can be determined quickly with the help of ML algorithm.

k. **Automatic language conversion:** Nowadays, visiting a new place but not knowing the local tongue is not even an issue; ML can assist us with this by simply transforming the words into our native languages. This tool is available via Google's GNMT (Google Neural Machine

Translation), which is a cognitive machine learning that automatically converts the word into our native language.

The series to the sequence learning approach, which itself is used with image identification and converts words from one dialect to the other, has been at the heart of the machine translation method.

13.5 INTELLIGENT ANALYTICS

Intelligent analytics (IA) scientific research and technology accumulates, integrates, and analyzes big data to determine and visualize behaviors. The ML algorithm can assist with intelligent analytics to enhance overall business productivity. AI and ML algorithms usually utilize big data analytics to lend a hand to determine outcomes and generate successful layouts accurately. Intelligent analytics is a new revolution in the age of ample data information. We still live in a time when IA is considered the norm, but with the help of new emerging ML algorithms and applications, it is possible to believe in these unexpected predictions. AI and ML advancements have made it possible for organizations across diverse enterprises to harvest money using customer information efficiently. AI-based assimilation approaches, for example, say, allow all enterprise funders to correlate necessarily critical data across many fields to make data collaboration into a unified platform simpler. These settings are simple enough for non-technical people to utilize, so IT professionals don't have to undertake full ownership.

Intelligent analytics can be classified into intelligent, diagnostic, predictive, and knowledge, information, big data, insight, and wisdom all benefit from predictive data analysis.

Intelligent big data analytics has made remarkable achievements, thanks to the dramatic development of big data as well as big data analytics. However, intelligent information analytics, intelligent knowledge analytics, and intelligent wisdom analytics have not yet drawn significant attention in academia and industry. We still indulge in the age of big data and ignore the dawning age of important information, big knowledge, considerable data intelligence, and immense wisdom. Big data is a foundation of great details, broad knowledge, and big intelligence or understanding. Therefore, we are still at the foundational stage of the emerging age of important information, broad knowledge, immense intelligence, and considerable wisdom.

13.5.1 Intelligent analytics application

13.5.1.1 Business intelligence

The different methodologies and techniques adopted by different organizations both for database evaluation as well as management of organizational valuable data are classified as business intelligence (BI). Reporting, web analytics, analytics, information extraction, process mining, massively parallel processing, analytics, and prescriptive analytics are all preferred attributes of BI techniques.

13.6 THE SIGNIFICANCE OF BUSINESS INTELLIGENCE

BI systems let people make conclusions premised upon information from the past, present, and beyond.

- **Descriptive analytics:** Dashboards, business reporting, information warehouse management, and balanced scorecard are all using analytics to showcase whatever has actually occurred or is going to occur in future. When handled appropriately, you'll have such a greater real understanding of your company's problems and also be able to identify areas for modification.
- **Predictive analytics:** It integrates data gathering, predictive modeling, and ML to anticipate upcoming occurrences and evaluate the possibility of future occurrence.
- **Prescriptive analytics:** Prescriptive analytics provides the opportunity for improvement, simulation, and decision modeling, as well as providing the most accurate analysis for corporate operations and decisions.

13.7 ADVANTAGES OF USING BUSINESS INTELLIGENCE

- Advanced dynamic dashboards with simplified user interactions allow you to visualize data in a graphical style to have a better understanding of it.
- To allow extensive reporting and analysis, various systems enable user scalability. Dashboards and statistics are therefore available to a wide range of consumers, not just the organization's data analysts and executives.
- BI can certainly help you understand exactly what services or goods you're missing and make the required modifications to boost client satisfaction. Information available helps in the understanding of client behavior, the development of user personas, and the utilization of real-time data on customer reviews to make corrections and optimize customer service and, to result in, customer satisfaction.
- BI aids businesses in getting a competitive advantage by assisting businesses in trying to identify emerging opportunities and implementing wiser approaches. Use the information to spot market trends and maximize the firm's revenue gross margin. Statistics based on

monitoring specified KPIs keep the company on track to meet or surpass its objectives.

- Because it has significant exposure to worldwide data, BI can undertake quicker reporting, analyzing, and planning. Because of the system's analysis skills, it is able to respond fast to market or other scenarios quickly.
- BI software can be used both online and on mobile devices. Tools strengthen system productivity, allowing businesses to transmit additional knowledge to targeted people more quickly. These solutions give exceptional query performance in multi-terabyte information warehouses.

13.7.1 Some real-world applications of business intelligence

1. **BI in supermarkets:** SAP's HANA is a kind of cloud-based technology that big companies generally are using to navigate repositories of data they've accumulated. Wolmart is one such example of a large corporation that typically uses HANA to tackle a massive range of transactional entries in a matter of seconds.
2. **BI in social networking sites:** Domo's artificial intelligence also for organization yield insight into individual consumers, revenues, and commodity stocks; the dashboard expands mostly with the magnitude of an enterprise and acquires statistical information from apps, including Square, Facebook, as well as many others.
3. **Competitive intelligence (CI):** It is basically the approach and procedure for acquiring material regarding the competitive surroundings in addition to strengthening organizational productivity. It entails comprehensive data assembling as well as interpretation from such a diversity of inputs, along with well-coordinated competitive intelligence (CI) programmers. It is the process of essentially trying to identify, accumulate, and test intelligence about products and services, consumers, competitors, and any other required component of the environment that is required to assist leaders and representatives in formulating strategic decisions for a business.

13.7.2 Some real-world applications of competitive intelligence

1. **Tourism industry:** The tourism sector is an excellent demonstration of how CI could be implemented in the realistic world. Travel businesses adjust cost of the tickets mostly on a fairly regular basis depending on a number of external factors. For example, if many of the companies raise their tariffs for a particular destination, a transportation operator will rapidly accompany suit in order to achieve huge margins.

Furthermore, client data is continuously often utilized to make pricing modifications. Tourism enterprises can see whenever a potential consumer is continually browsing for similar ticket information and raise the costs during the time because they know that the consumer would truly want to travel on all these days by monitoring certain individuals.

2. **Job postings sites**: Through more and more database analysis, one may estimate their competitor's purpose and strategy based on whichever resources they recruit. It empowers you to make your own planned countermove. When your competition is seeking for a digital marketer, for instance, it is indeed evident that they're attempting to upgrade their advertising game; therefore, your marketing organization needs to do the same. If they're seeking for a position as a java developer, they want to boost their programming abilities and get work. As a result, make sure your coding teams are ready. Ensuring they're receiving monthly updates and quick notifications so that they do not, however, miss out on any of the critical information

REFERENCES

[1] McCartney, A., Whelan, B., & Ancev, T. (2005). "Future directions of precision agriculture". *Precision Agriculture*, 6: 7–23.

[2] Borne, Kirk D. (12 May 2010). "Astroinformatics: data-oriented astronomy research and education". *Earth Science Informatics*, 3 (1–2): 5–17.

[3] Nikolay Kirov. (2010). The fifth SEEDI International Conference Digitization of cultural and scientific heritage, May 19–20, 2010, Sarajevo.

[4] "Computer-Aided Diagnosis: The Tipping Point for Digital Pathology". Digital Pathology Association. 27 April 2017.

[5] Hinton, Geoffrey, & Sejnowski, Terrence. (1999). *Unsupervised Learning: Foundations of Neural Computation*. MIT Press. ISBN 978-0262581684.

[6] Hayes, Joseph. (2007), "Analytic Culture in the U.S. Intelligence Community. Chapter One. Working Definitions", *History Staff, Center for the Study of Intelligence, Central Intelligence Agency*, retrieved 2016-05-24.

[7] Gopinath, Rebala, Ravi, Ajay & Chriwala, Sanjay. (2019). *An Introduction to Machine Learning*. Germany: Springer Science and Business Media LLC.

[8] Marston, Richard C., & Turnovsky, Stephen J. (1985). "Macroeconomic stabilization through taxation and indexation: The use of firm-specific information". *Journal of Monetary Economics*. 16(3):375–395. ISSN 0304-3932, https://doi.org/10.1016/0304-3932(85)90042-X.

[9] Prakash, Ashish, & Gagan Deep Meena. (2022). "Observed design for apex height and vertical velocity of single-leg hopping during stance phase". *Robotica* 40(6):1868–1879. doi:10.1017/S0263574721001429

[10] Radrigo Fernandes de Mello Moacir Antonelli Ponti. (2018). *Machine Leaning: A Practical Approach on the Statistical Learning Theory*. (1st. ed.). Springer Publishing Company, Incorporated.

[11] Brynjolfsson, Erik, & Mitchell, Tom. (2017). "What can machine learning do? Workforce implications". *Science*. pp. 1530–1534. https://doi.org/10.1126/science.aap8062.

[12] Dedić, N., & Stanier C. (2016). "Measuring the success of changes to existing business intelligence solutions to improve business intelligence reporting". Measuring the Success of Changes to Existing Business Intelligence Solutions to Improve Business Intelligence Reporting. Lecture Notes in Business Information Processing. Lecture Notes in Business Information Processing. 268. Springer International Publishing. pp. 225–236. https://doi.org/10.1007/978-3-319-49944-4_17.

[13] Madureira, L., Popovic, A., & Castelli, M. (2021). Competitive intelligence: a unified view and modular definition. *Technological Forecasting and Social Change*. 173: 121086. https://doi.org/10.1016/j.techfore.2021.121086.

[14] Singh, Arjan (2019) https://www.lifescienceleader.com/doc/collecting-competitive-intelligence-at- conferences-0001

[15] Learn Computer Science (2020). www.learncomputerscienceonline.com

Chapter 14

Secure 3D route optimization of combat vehicles in war field using IoV

Alok Nath Pandey, Piyush Agarwal, and Sachin Sharma

CONTENTS

14.1 INTRODUCTION

In terms of both breadth and size, the Internet of Things (IoT) is rapidly increasing. From smartphones and watches to home management systems, autos, and entire infrastructures, manufacturers have extended and enhanced the communication and interconnection of different forms of technology. Every industry is affected by today's technological revolution. Autonomous technologies account for a sizable portion of the IoT market. Sensors, software, and technologies make up the Internet of Vehicles (IoV), which evolved from VANET. Vehicles and infrastructure may interact using IoV, which aids in the creation of smart systems such as intelligent traffic management systems and other smart city systems. In IoV, the objects in the network are always moving, making them transient and unstable, and so the nodes or things in the network are constantly changing. Today's automobile-inventive and prescient management system manages traffic

DOI: 10.1201/9781003269144-14

more efficiently, with fewer delays and pollution, resulting in a greater level of passenger comfort. For better results, features of cloud computing can also be used with IoV, to enable the vehicles to share different resources and can access the variety of information that will help in making useful decisions [1]. For the secure transmission of the data between the vehicle in IoV, blockchain can be used [2]. Furthermore, when it comes to security application sectors, a combat vehicle (CV) is even more critical to safeguarding the lives of our personnel. The research area still has airless, naval, and land motors. Artificial intelligence is transforming this research field into an opportunity. Our autonomous CV concept [3] is oriented for structures that are empty, low-cost, and technologically advanced. It is vital to modernize the fighting vehicle in order to protect many lives at the border. An unmanned vehicle poses a potential threat since it may perceive our friendly soldiers as adversaries. Route optimization is the process of determining the most cost-effective route. It's more difficult than it appears to find the shortest path between two places. It should include all important details, such as the location and number of required stops along the route, as well as delivery time frames. It's more concerned with cutting down on total travel time when making many stops. In route optimization, algorithms are frequently utilized. The reason for this is that humans are unable to calculate all of the many parameters required to determine an optimized route due to the intricacies of route optimization. Many distinct varieties are explored later in this work, especially in a short length of time.

14.2 LITERATURE REVIEW

The goal of route optimization is to make the most of available resources. It is the process of constructing a mathematical model of a real-world physical problem and attempting to solve the problem using these tools. In today's industrial production, cooperative methods are commonly used. A single automobile may contain over 20,000 different key components sourced from numerous cities and nations. This situation puts a lot of strain on areas like real-time automobile mobility on designated routes using various route optimization techniques, which improves the ability of vehicles to move from one point to another quickly and effectively using essential components and connected tech that runs on various algorithms and techniques. Furthermore, after more analysis, it became obvious that taking into account only distance isn't producing the desired effects for CVs for timely deployments in the furthest locations. Real maps generally include the source of data required to build high-quality routes for the movement of vehicles from point one to another. McGinty et al. [4] state in order to give a more comprehensive solution, two new measures (path quality and user happiness) were developed for the routing obstacle. The primary goal of the vehicle routing problem (VRP) is to discover a way through a cluster of locations that minimizes the lengths of all interconnected cities' paths. R. K. Kedia et al. [5] presented techniques for optimizing the vehicle's route, operation, and efficiency. In mobility, navigation, transportation, and a variety of other industries, path-finding is an issue that must be solved. The key to solving this challenge is to figure out how to locate the shortest route. So to solve this problem A-star, Dijkstra, and other conventional algorithms were used to solve the above-said problem. The studies of Wang et al. [6] on the contrary showed the inefficiency of typical algorithms in generating optimal paths in the presence of dynamic and evolving variables.

To enable this using a mathematical model, Cheng et al. [7] designed an equation that updated the A-star algorithms to improve the effectiveness and precision of searching. In the coming years, the ubiquity of intelligent systems are man-made intelligent systems for advanced routing techniques, so Ovaska et al. [8] proposed a fusion of SC and HC that have the capacity to solve problems that neither methodology can solve satisfactorily on its own. With the use of their integral algorithms based on genetic algorithms, Ferdous et al. [9] proposed in VANETs the ant colony optimization (ACO) technique that was employed to optimize vehicle paths. They proposed a system that might give a better platform for considering traffic flow and congestion patterns in order to avoid traffic jams.

14.3 FEATURES OF COMBAT VEHICLES

As self-driving vehicles move from science fiction to reality over the next decade, automakers are likely to make significant advances in this area. In automated driving, cameras, LiDAR, Sonar, ultrasonic, GPS, lasers, and other sensors can be utilized to assist vehicles in traveling autonomously. Sensors allow a vehicle to examine its surroundings and for an advanced system to make judgments based on that observation in order to guide the vehicle (Figure 14.1). To move, autonomous vehicles need to be given a source and a destination location. The car will communicate with other vehicles in its vicinity to determine the shortest way to the destination, allowing the traveler to arrive in the shortest time possible. This autonomous vehicle capability can be employed in CVs or any other emergency vehicle to transport people to their destinations. CVs are military vehicles loaded with weapons and are used for the combat operations. On the basis of operating mechanism, CVs can be divided into five categories.

- Level 0 – No automation: Not operating automatically: requiring human labor to operate: non-automated and automated process non-automated machines.
- Level 1 – Driver assistance: Advanced driver-assistance systems (ADAS) are technologies that automate, enhance, or customize part

or all of the duties involved in operating a vehicle to make motor vehicle travel safer.

- **Level 2 – Partial automation:** Longitudinal and lateral controls are taken up by the system in partial automation; however, the driver must keep a close eye on the system and be ready to take control at any time.
- **Level 3 – Conditional automation:** The third level of automation in driving is conditional automation. Approximately 75% of the work is automated at this stage. The level 3 car conducts safety-critical functions like acceleration, deceleration, and steering via conditional automation.
- **Level 4 – High automation:** Longitudinal and lateral controls are taken up by the system and it is no longer necessary for the driver to keep an eye on the system on a continuous basis. When a take-over request is sent, the driver must take control of the vehicle with a particular period of buffer time.
- **Level 5 – Full automation:** No or extremely limited driver control is defined as full automation. Such automation would be achieved via cars on the roads, a combination of sensor, computer, and communications systems.

No Automation

Driver Assistance

Full Automation

COMBAT

VEHICLES

Partial Automation

High automation

Conditional Automation

Figure 14.1 Varied types of combat vehicles under different conditional usages.

The conditions are regulated by an IoT module [10] from a remote server in planned level 3. This level provides safer driving. Obstacle detection is performed at level 4 and updated to the IoT module if any are discovered; this is still in the development stage as a fully autonomous CV.

Here's our concept for CVs using artificial intelligence and digital design. It appears to be a CV. But there's a lot more to it. To replace the present tank fleet, the Indian Army is looking for a cutting-edge Main Combat Tank called the Future Ready Combat Vehicle (FRCV) [11]. Across the entire spectrum of warfare, it would be necessary to work in urban, semi-desert, and desert environments, including at high altitudes, and will be a highly advanced futuristic tank capability of satisfying present and future operating needs over and above 2050. As the pioneer, the Main Combat Tank – FRCV will open the path for a range of supplementary units based on some kind of modular architecture and standardizing of the base platform.

In November 2019, the RFI (the request for information) for 198 wheeled armored fighting vehicles (AFVs) was issued. All these RFIs, issued so far for big-ticket procurement, support the realization of "Atmanirbhar Bharat." The RFI looks for three versions, 55% gun, 20% command, and 25% command and surveillance, with design modularity, enabling the development of a family of supporting AFVs in varying roles.

14.4 OVERVIEW OF ROUTE OPTIMIZATION TECHNIQUES IN COMBAT VEHICLES

The route is a path or track that can be traversed between the initial point and a target [12]. From the start to the finish, as well as from the starting point to the ending point, between the two nodes or places, the route is an established or feasible path. If a path connects two points (origin and destination) but does not facilitate movement between them (regardless of how fast that path appears to be), it is not a valid path therefore not really a route.

One of the most important aspects of logistics and industrial automation is intelligent vehicles, of which route optimization is one of the most important technologies. Several algorithms are used here and hence, as a result, they can compute the fastest route more quickly than using generic graphs (graph edges and lengths). These are broadly classified into two main parts that are summarized here:

14.4.1 Hard computing techniques

Hard computing is best for solving mathematical problems that don't solve the problems of the real world. Some related algorithms include:

- **Dijkstra's algorithm:** Dijkstra's algorithm is a method for determining and selecting the shortest routes between nodes in the network, which might be used to depict transportation networks.

- **A* search algorithm:** Intellectual ability knowledge is what that we have used is the human species' greatest asset to enrich our lives. Hence, we came up with the idea of artificial intelligence to help people learn more and civilizations will be able to thrive and prosper in ways they have never been able to before.
- **Arc-flags algorithm:** Arc-flags are really a Dijkstra algorithm enhancement that is used to avoid investigating unneeded routes when determining the shortest route. We believed that the issue of the shortest way must be addressed periodically for different node pairs for the same input graph and ensure that only the regions that have been identified to be of interest are visited.

14.4.2 Soft computing techniques

Soft computing is better used in solving real-world problems as it is stochastic in nature, i.e., it is a randomly defined process that can be analyzed statistically but not with precision. Some related algorithms include:

- **Fuzzy logic:** The concept "fuzzy" refers to something that is unclear or ambiguous. In the actual world, we frequently encounter situations in which we are unable to tell whether a condition is true or untrue; their fuzzy theory provides extremely significant reasoning flexibility. In this approach, we can account for any situation's inaccuracies and uncertainties.
- **Ant colony algorithm:** The ant colony algorithm is a method for calculating the size of an ant colony and is an inhabitants-based meta-heuristic algorithm that can be applied to challenging optimization problems to obtain approximate solutions. Artificial ants are software agents that hunt for workable solutions to optimize problems in ACO.
- **Particle swarm optimization algorithm:** Particle swarm optimization algorithm (PSO) is a society-based stochastic optimization algorithm that is influenced by cognitive and collective behavior of some creatures such as bird flocks or fish schools. It has undergone numerous improvements since it was first introduced in 1995.

14.5 REQUIREMENT OF ROUTE OPTIMIZATION TECHNIQUES

The military ground vehicle route optimization in a hazardous battleground is a unique type of difficulty with route planning, where military vehicles are subjected to a huge number of randomly launched strikes. Due to the large number of possible scenarios resulting from the mix of uncertainty, CVs in the conflict will be diverted from their default paths to some faster and more optimal routes. In order to accomplish their operational objectives during conflict, CVs must generally travel a complicated route network and get out of their secret bases or hidden spots (origins), and they arrive at predetermined locations (end). CVs are vulnerable to man-made attacks when moving through the road network because there is a lack of supply of fortification and camouflage materials. On the battlefield, such attacks, which are caused primarily by ground assaults and air raids, are almost certain to occur on a regular basis. According to the South Asia Terrorism Portal (SATP) and the data given between 2008 and 2014, there were 309 attacks against NATO supply convoys in Pakistan, according to the Global Security Organization (GSO) [13, 14]. As a consequence, effectively designing CV routes on battlefield road networks can be unpredictable to limit the chance of being attacked and is an essential military topic worth investigating.

14.6 BENEFITS AND CHALLENGES

Troop movement involves the transportation of military personnel and CV from one location to another using available means. In wartime, rapid and efficient troop movement offers many benefits and challenges in battle.

14.6.1 Benefits

- **Efficiency:** Efficient troop movement saves time and resources, which can be used for combat preparation and future operations. To win a battle, the commander must concentrate on combat power at the opportune place and time to achieve a relative advantage over the enemy [15].
- **Fuel efficient:** Your drivers will spend less time driving if your routes are well planned; lesser distance means lower carbon emission and pollution. This saves money on gas and increases the amount of time a driver can spend on-site and the number of stops he makes in a day.
- **Exactness:** It reduces human errors that mean investing less but getting a greater return on it (greater ROI – Return on Investment).
- **Route optimization:** It is a process in which a solution loads and distributes routes and stops to achieve the lowest number of miles driven and can substantially minimize fuel consumption, vehicle wear and tear, and exposure risk, all of which have an impact on deployment timeliness.
- **Maintenance costs:** Fleet maintenance costs can be reduced with effective route planning. Vehicles are driven for fewer hours and waste less mileage. As a result, there is less wear and tear on the vehicle, as well as cheaper fuel expenses.
- **Safer driving:** Because left turns and U-turns are more dangerous than driving straight or making right turns, the route planning software can be set to employ less of them. If you plan your path ahead of time, the driver can concentrate on the road rather than deciding where to stop next or which path to take to get to your destination.

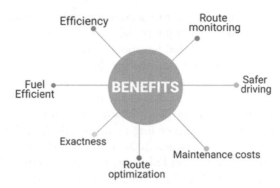

Figure 14.2 Benefits of route optimization for combat vehicles.

- **Route monitoring:** Fleet management may keep a real-time eye on the deployment of CV, responding to commandant questions and overseeing operations and drivers.
- **Transportation:** The procedure for tactical troop movement in wartime consists of the reconnaissance troops patrolling the area where the units and equipment will be transported because of enemy threats (Figure 14.2).

14.6.2 Challenges

- **Enemy threats:** Such as an ambush or surprise attack, the reconnaissance troops are deployed to protect the vehicle movement undertaken by the transportation unit during an operation.
- **Varied locations:** Executing different routes, especially in the densely packed suburbs and cities, is one of the main challenges for the last-mile deployment of CVs.
- **Untimely deployment:** One of the most typical issues for last-mile delivery services is late and untimely deployment. There are various variables that could cause a delivery delay and cause your timetable to be disrupted.
- **Management:** Apart from the safety concerns, managing CVs for a quick movement time, even in rural areas, is a common challenge that armed forces face.
- **Operational cost:** The fleet size, capacity utilization, and route length are major cost drivers to manage operational costs. The challenge is to reduce the cost involved for every trip through optimized delivery planning.
- **Lack of transparency:** It is important to remove inefficiencies in this process and needs optimization across a fleet of vehicles, delivery personnel, input costs such as fuel, route changes due to emergencies, and many more (Figure 14.3).

Transportation

Lack of
transparency

Enemy
threats

CHALLENGES

Operational
cost

Varied locations

Untimely
deployment

Management

Figure 14.3 Challenges of route optimization for combat vehicles

14.7 RESEARCH METHODOLOGY

There are several impediments [16] and motions in the natural environment. CVs must be able to adjust to changing conditions. This research
looks into how cars avoid obstacles in an unfamiliar area. Throughout the
movement operation, the obstacle's route, as well as its speed and direction,
are constantly analyzed. The experiment demonstrates that the algorithm
is effective in dealing with barriers of varying sizes and speeds, as well
as having a broader application. The purpose of 3D route optimization
is to discover an optimal and collision-free path while taking kinematic
limitations into account (including geometric, physical, and temporal constraints). Unlike motion planning, which takes into account dynamics, the
purpose of 3D route optimization is to find a kinematically optimal path
in the lowest amount of time while accurately describing the surroundings.
The foundations of the most effective CV, 3D path planning algorithms,
have been built in recent years, with a focus on generally applicable algorithms for CV. 3D route optimization can be used in various fields, such as
CVs and a variety of additional uses. One of the most prominent obstacles
within field optimization is 3D route planning that is beneficial to CVs to
travel from the starting point to the objective location (war zone) while
avoiding obstacles and attaining the shortest path with the least amount
of energy and the quickest time. CV path planning can be categorized
into two categories: (i) global path planning or static motion planning and
(ii) local path planning [16].

- Static motion planning is another name for the global path planning
  approach [12, 16] because it computes the CV's trajectory before it
  starts moving. When the terrain is stable and also the environment
  is well known, the CV's trajectory is created. (There are no dynamic
  constraints.) Even though this type of motion planning ensures that

the target point will be obtained or even that the target point will be unreachable, it also assists in determining if the goal point will be reached.

- The other type, known as local path planning [17], is a sort of dynamic route planning method for which the CV's course is generated online based on the most recent data received by the CV's onboard smart sensors and is also called dynamic path planning. Because of its fast responses to the changing shapes and obstacle locations in a challenging environment, this motion planning system is termed a more robust and scalable method than that of the previous type.

A number of practical applications (sensors) have emerged in recent years, needing periodic and detailed inspections to check for potential structural changes. As a result, the original study's key contribution is the advancement of a methodology for analyzing obstructions and road projects utilizing a novel algorithm based on point cloud data. We can stimulate CVs in real time to navigate them to their respective conflict zone sites for timely deployments using this 3D route optimization approach.

14.8 COMPARATIVE STUDY AND DISCUSSION

A comparison of some of the research work done in recent years on the same domain is shown in Table 14.1

14.9 CONCLUSION AND FUTURE WORK

It can efficiently boost the Army's present operations with 3D route optimization-integrated structure and sensor capabilities. When this is paired with machine learning, we may be able to gain important battlefield insights in near real time, allowing officers to change their plans of action on the battlefield and carry them out effectively during operations. IoV can help the military with a range of duties, such as tactical warfare, snooping and monitoring an enemy base or terrorist hideaway, search and rescue, surveillance, and intelligence gathering. There are various other improvements that might be made to this work to make it a more complete model. Image processing techniques such as edge detection and lane detection could be used to improve the feature's mobility. To avoid collisions, the machine learning technique might be used to recognize friendly forces in the surroundings of the autonomous vehicle, as well as compute the distance between two nodes. Obstacle detection, which can be broadened to include object detection and recognition, as well as determining the type of object or vehicle, are all part of our work.

Table 14.1 Comparative examination of various algorithms and strategies

Authors	Method type	Techniques	Shortcomings	Advantages
Noto et al. [18]	Dijkstra's algorithm	Non-intelligent (hard computing)	Time complexity is high and not suitable for real-life problems	Simple to implement in a variety of settings
Wang et al. [6]	A*		Time is a major constraint. Non-smoothness	Ability to search quickly, allowing for online implementation
Kalpana et al. [19]	Arc-flags algorithm		Very long pre-processing times	Fast and easy to understand
AbuSalim et al. [20]	BFA		Slower than Dijkstra	Able to detect negative cycles
Johnson et al. [19]	Johnson's algorithm		Works best with sparse (fewer edges) graphs	Eliminates any negative edges and calculate the shortest paths
Shi et al. [20]	Fuzzy logic, GA, ANN	Intelligent (soft computing)	A lot of testing for validation and verification Too much time-consuming The duration of the network is unknown	It resembles human reasoning where ambiguous inputs are available and take decisions accordingly Influenced by nature and its elements and can improve over time It is like a human neural system and fault-tolerant
Ferdous et al. [9]	ACO		High time complexity	Capable of dealing with difficulties involving several objectives and continual planning
Kennedy et al [21]	PSO		Premature convergence Parameter sensitive	It works faster than GA and can handle a smaller number of individual issues

REFERENCES

1. Sachin Sharma and Seshadri Mohan. "Cloud-Based Secured VANET with Advanced Resource Management and IoV Applications." In *Connected Vehicles in the Internet of Things*, pp. 309–325. Springer, Cham, 2020.
2. Sachin Sharma, Kamal Kumar Ghanshala, and Seshadri Mohan. "Blockchain-Based Internet of Vehicles (IoV): An Efficient Secure Ad Hoc Vehicular Networking Architecture." In *2019 IEEE 2nd 5G World Forum (5GWF)*, pp. 452–457. IEEE, 2019.
3. R. Abhishek, S. Caroline and A. D. Jose Raju, "IoT driven defence vehicle system," 2019 International Conference on Recent Advances in Energy-efficient Computing and Communication (ICRAECC), 2019, pp. 1–4, doi: 10.1109/ICRAECC43874.2019.8995073.
4. Lorraine McGinty and Barry Smyth. "Personalised Route Planning: A Case-Based Approach." In *European Workshop on Advances in Case-Based Reasoning*, pp. 431–443. Springer, Berlin; Heidelberg, 2000.
5. R. K. Kedia and B. K. Naick, "Review of vehicle route optimisation," 2017 2nd IEEE International Conference on Intelligent Transportation Engineering (ICITE), 2017, pp. 57–61, doi: 10.1109/ICITE.2017.8056881.
6. Wang, Haifeng, Jiawei Zhou, Guifeng Zheng, and Yun Liang. "HAS: Hierarchical A-Star algorithm for big map navigation in special areas." In 2014 5th International Conference on Digital Home, pp. 222–225. IEEE, 2014
7. L. Cheng, C. Liu and B. Yan, "Improved hierarchical A-star algorithm for optimal parking path planning of the large parking lot." In 2014 IEEE International Conference on Information and Automation (ICIA), 2014, pp. 695–698, doi: 10.1109/ICInfA.2014.6932742.
8. Ovaska, S. J., H. F. VanLandingham, and A. Kamiya, "Fusion of soft computing and hard computing in industrial applications: an overview." In IEEE Transactions on Systems, Man, and Cybernetics, Part C (Applications and Reviews), vol. 32, no. 2, pp. 72–79, May 2002, doi: 10.1109/TSMCC.2002.801354.
9. Ferdous Fahim and Mohammad Sultan Mahmud. "Intelligent traffic monitoring system using VANET infrastructure and ant colony optimization." In 2016 5th International Conference on Informatics, Electronics and Vision (ICIEV), pp. 356–360. IEEE, 2016.
10. Luettel, Thorsten, Michael Himmelsbach, and Hans-Joachim Wuensche. "Autonomous ground vehicles—Concepts and a path to the future." In Proceedings of the IEEE 100, no. Special Centennial Issue, 1831–1839, 2012.
11. Dattathreya, Macam S., and Harpreet Singh. A novel approach for combat vehicle mobility definition and assessment. Army Tank Automotive Research Development and Engineering Center Warren MI, 2011.
12. Osaba, Eneko, Xin-She Yang, and Javier Del Ser. "Is the vehicle routing problem dead? an overview through bioinspired perspective and a prospect of opportunities." Nature-Inspired Computation in Navigation and Routing Problems, pp. 57–84, 2020.
13. Pinedo, Ruben D. Yie. Route Optimization while Improving Safety Using Escort Vehicles. State University of New York at Buffalo, pp. 1–12, 2013.
14. Zhao, Tan, Jincai Huang, Jianmai Shi, and Chao Chen. "Route planning for military ground vehicles in road networks under uncertain battlefield environment." Journal of Advanced Transportation, vol. 2018, pp. 1–10, 2018.

15. Swersey, Arthur J., and Wilson Ballard. "Scheduling school buses." Management Science, vol. 30, no. 7, pp. 844–853, 1984.
16. Yao, Lin, Xu Yuanyuan, Xu Shaoyu, Liu Yurong, and Ji Hongyu. "Path planning obstacle avoidance algorithm based on wheeled robot." In 2020 International Workshop on Electronic Communication and Artificial Intelligence (IWECAI), pp. 61–65. IEEE, 2020.
17. Lumelsky, Vladimir, and Alexander Stepanov. "Dynamic path planning for a mobile automaton with limited information on the environment." IEEE transactions on Automatic control, vol. 31, no. 11, pp. 1058–1063, 1986.
18. Noto, Masato, and Hiroaki Sato. "A method for the shortest path search by extended Dijkstra algorithm." In Smc 2000 Conference Proceedings. 2000 IEEE International Conference on Systems, Man and Cybernetics.'Cybernetics Evolving to Systems, Humans, Organizations, and Their Complex Interactions' (cat. no. 0, vol. 3), pp. 2316–2320. IEEE, 2000.
19. Kalpana, R., and P. Thambidurai. "Optimizing shortest path queries with parallelized arc flags." In 2011 International Conference on Recent Trends in Information Technology (ICRTIT), pp. 601–606. IEEE, 2011.
20. AbuSalim, Samah W. G., Rosziati Ibrahim, Mohd Zainuri Saringat, Sapiee Jamel, and Jahari Abdul Wahab. "Comparative analysis between dijkstra and bellman-ford algorithms in shortest path optimization." In IOP Conference Series: Materials Science and Engineering, vol. 917, no. 1, p. 012077. IOP Publishing, 2020.
21. Kennedy, James, and Russell Eberhart. "Particle swarm optimization." In Proceedings of ICNN'95-International Conference on Neural Networks, vol. 4, pp. 1942–1948. IEEE, 1995.

Chapter 15

Healthcare therapy for treating teenagers with internet addiction using behavioral patterns and neuro-feedback analysis

B. Dhanalakshmi, K. Selvakumar, and L. Sai Ramesh

CONTENTS

15.1 INTRODUCTION

The rapid internet growth has a great impact in the modern era. The digitalized life has given ample benefits; however, exaggerated use of the internet has been a serious threat to the psychological behavior of human. The findings published in the BMC Medicine journal say that internet addiction (IA) has become a public health problem globally [1]. Millions of internet users were officially recognized as having an addiction to using the internet and especially adolescents. Statistics on "Internet usage in India" given by Statista predicted that there will be 600 million internet users by 2021 and approximately 67% of internet users will belong to less than 35 years old age group. The internet users are not aware of the endangerment in the

DOI: 10.1201/9781003269144-15

challenging world. A national study done by Psychological Science during 2009 revealed that the human in the age group from 8 to 18 years will perform poor academic performance. The responsibility to nurture the good behavioral skills among adolescents makes them to expertise in their interpersonal interactions. Every day, we carry a tool with us that give limitless social, artistic and entertaining opportunities. Activities enabled by our smart phones have always been central to the developmental goals of adolescents—as young people turn to their peers as their primary social support system, their phones provide constant connection to their friends as well as access to popular media that often defines and shapes youth culture. Focusing on a single activity, such as computer gaming, does not reflect the range of media usage issues that young people face. Because online functionality is increasingly seamless and pervades all activities on a phone, computer, tablet, gaming system, or television, the term "internet" may not be particularly clear or consistent in definition.

Cognitive behavioral therapy treatment helps improve students' awareness and mental health who are addicted to the internet. As a result, an intervention may be utilized as a helpful therapy to lessen the symptoms of online addiction and improve the condition of persons suffering from behavioral addictions such as internet dependence. The purpose of this study was to look at the efficacy of cognitive behavioral therapy for IA symptoms, quality of life and mental health in students who were addicted to the internet.

15.2 RELATED WORK

Zhang, Ying-Ying et al. [2] analyzed the psychological effects of Cognitive Behavioral Therapy (CBT) on IA in adolescents. Two experts conducted data selection, extraction and quality assessment. In case of any disagreements between two authors then a third author solves the problem through discussion. This work aggregates current evidence of CBT on addiction towards the internet for adolescents and may guide both intervention and future researchers. In this model, analyzing the psychological effects is recommended for the treatment of adolescents with IA. The quality of the system is evaluated using the Cochrane risk of bias tool which is designed to assess randomized control trials. This system investigated the psychological effects of CBT in adolescents having addiction towards the internet.

Bador, K., Kerekes, N [3] evaluated an integrated intensive cognitive behavioral therapy for an individual with the substance-related syndrome. The impulsivity of the patients was assessed and integrated treatment programs for patients with substance-related syndrome proved that all outcome measures of mental health had been improved in patients and positive effects were entailed. A total of 50 patients in a cognitive behavioral treatment clinic in western Sweden were given treatment for one year during the study period. The improvements in patients' cognitive behaviors were monitored every week. The cognitive behavioral therapy treatment has reduced risk factors psychologically for addiction control.

Yuan-Wei Yao, Lu Liu et al. [4] disentangled the individuals with behavioral addictions were examined and the neural features of addiction from the direct exposure to substance effects. The neural responses of the individuals having behavioral addiction and internet gaming disorder have been recorded and analyzed. The adolescents with internet gaming disorder were identified with reward processing using Monetary Incentive Delay (MID) task. The neural responses were compared to monetary gains and losses between individuals having internet gaming disorders.

Wei Peng, Xinlei Zhang and Xin Li [5] aimed to develop an intelligent system for monitoring students' internet consumption information on the campus. The addiction levels of students towards internet were analyzed quantitatively. The behavioral data patterns of the students on the campus were identified and the online activities of the students were predicted. Instead of using research methods such as questionnaires and statistical analysis in analyzing students, neural network IA model, linear IA model and clustering-based IA model were used to calculate students' IA level. The similarity among students' behavior from the real-world dataset from Chinese college was taken for conducting experiments and the results were consistent with earlier psychological findings.

Baturay, M.H., Toker, S [6] monitored the impact of IA among college students for identifying the causes and effects of excessive usage of internet. The study participants are undergraduate students and are analyzed to diagnose IA level and aware of physiological consequences.

Van Rooij, A.J., Zinn, M.F., Schoenmakers, T.M. et al. [7] identified the individuals with IA and were evaluated with the pilot treatment program. Twelve patients were identified and focused to control internet usage, improve their behavioral patterns and expanding social activities.

Miller et al. [8] identified the IAs in central Greece through a questionnaire-based approach among 2,200 internet users and found online gaming as the dominant factor. Kim et al. [9] found this IA leads to suicide based on a questionnaire survey among 1,573 Korean adolescents who are all high school students. Johansson et al. [10] also conducted a similar IA questionnaire survey among Norwegian youth with an age range of 12–18 years.

Bong, Su Hyun et al. [11] added music therapy (MT) to cognitive behavioral treatment (CBT) affected symptoms of smart phone/IA and mental comorbidities. Adolescents benefitted from a combination of MT and CBT for symptoms of smart phone/IA, anxiety and impulsivity. As a result, this combination might be an effective treatment for smart phone or IA, as well as behavioral problems, including anxiety and impulsivity.

Hirota, T, et al. [12] analyzed the network architecture of IA symptoms and identified central/influential symptoms in 108 teenagers with autism spectrum disorder (ASD) and used network analysis, which conceptualized

IA as a complex network of mutually influencing symptoms. In this cohort, defensive and secretive behaviors, as well as the concealment of internet use, were identified as important symptoms, implying that addressing these symptoms could help avoid the onset and/or maintenance of IA in adolescents with ASD. Psychoeducation on the function of core symptoms above in IA for teenagers and their carers can be a useful tool.

Lo CKM, et al. [13] suggested family-focused strategy as an IA treatment modality for teenagers, little research has been done from the clinician's perspective on family engagement in the treatment process. This study used a qualitative approach to investigate practitioners' perspectives on the roles and challenges of family involvement in IA intervention. Ten practitioners worked with adolescents with IA were interviewed in total. The transcribed interviews were analyzed using thematic analysis. Three overarching themes emerged: the importance of family participation in IA intervention, changing the focus from the adolescent to the relationship and providing tailored services and intervention to address the heterogeneity of situations. The data demonstrated that involving family members in IA treatment improves favorable outcomes. Individual counselling and psychoeducation were used to meet the requirements of adolescents with IA and their families.

Conjoint therapy sessions helped people communicate more effectively, improve family connections and functioning and rebuild relationships. When deciding whether or not family involvement was appropriate, however, care must be taken to examine family dynamics. When working with family members, practitioners must form therapeutic partnerships and be flexible in terms of the degree and pattern of engagement. When deciding whether or not family involvement was appropriate, however, care must be taken to examine family dynamics. When working with family members, practitioners must form therapeutic partnerships and be flexible in terms of the degree and pattern of engagement.

Bickham et al. [14] have inspired a lot of research to prove that the diagnostic methodologies for the addition of internet gaming disorder in the DSM-5 and ICD-11 are accurate. However, there was a push for a larger definition of the condition that includes a wider spectrum of media-use habits than only gaming. To standardize terminology and clinical techniques, efforts to reconcile these approaches were required. Clinical trials of treatments, particularly in the United States, and longitudinal studies of the disorder's origin should be the focus of future research.

Sonia Khodabakhsh et al. [15] investigated the COVID-19, a new version of the COVID where people's mental health was damaged by the pandemic. Individuals preferred to gather information on the virus, disease, symptoms, statistics, therapies and any other aspect of the pandemic from the internet. The goal of this study was to investigate the impact of internet use on health anxiety among Malaysia's young population at three different levels of users (internet addicts, over-users and average-users). The online survey, which included a demographic questionnaire, a short-form Health Anxiety Inventory and an IA Test, was completed by 438 young adults in Malaysia.

Ambika et al. [16] decision supports system for diagnosing the hypertesnion. In this chapter, they discussed the multiple features which create hypertension among the peoples. In that, IA or continuous usage of gadgets or mobile devices really increase the possibility of hypertension. Even though, it happens through gene or any other family disorder, the most common feature or the feature which increases the factor in less age is only because of IA. Ambika et al. [17] also suggest the method to prevent hypertension using some intelligent techniques. In that, reducing the usage of computer-related applications is one among them. They do not suggest that the usage of gadgets will increase the possibility but the possibility will be more if we use it for less time.

Saranya et al. [18] suggested the machine-learning approach for medical data storage and retrieval. This system suggested the formal guidelines to store the records which reduce the manual searching of information in large data warehouse which also reduce time spent in any kind of application for simple searching. Sairamesh et al. [19] suggested the system which really tracks the IoT devices connected through wireless access points. This methodology helps to acquire the users access points and the information they are try to access from the points. This mechanism helps to create the restrictions from accessing the unwanted content from the internet service providers based on the packet filtering or any other firewall mechanisms.

Based on this literature survey, the changes in social-cognitive abilities are observed and driven by neural circuits. Recently, we can hear about the various impacts of IA in adolescent life. The adaptive adolescents begin to engage with increasingly complex peer networks. Adolescence has also been suggested as a period of impulsive learning. In the modern world, due to advancement in communication technologies, ever trending social networks and abuse in internet usage makes adolescents behave more responsive to emotions.

15.3 PROPOSED WORK

The entire proposed work is organized into various modules with the necessary algorithms and techniques to be used in experiments. The overall proposed methodology is shown in Figure 15.1.

Adolescents with IA are analyzed for identifying the cause of IA using behavioral pattern analysis and neuro-feedback. The social network profiles of adolescents with IA were analyzed using Neural Network algorithm to predict their personality traits. The neuro-feedback of the addictive internet using adolescents are observed using the Emotiv Epoc headset.

The EEG signals are recorded stating the brain wave activity. The recorded EEG signals of the excessive internet using adolescents are compared with

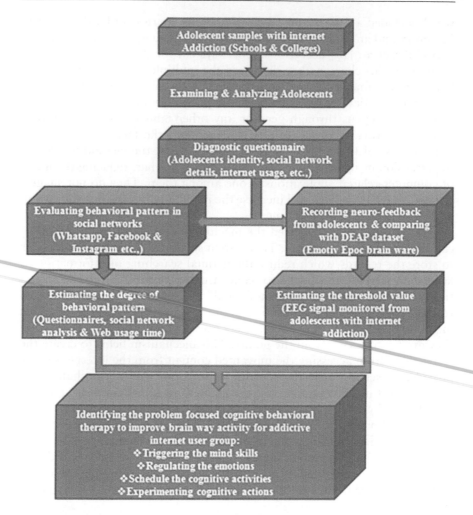

Figure 15.1 Flow chart of the proposed methodology.

Dataset for Emotional Analysis using Physiological signals (DEAP dataset) to determine the cause of IA. Problem-focused cognitive behavioral therapy is suggested to improve brain wave activity.

15.3.1 Study setting and criteria for choosing the adolescents with internet addiction and identifying the cause of internet addiction

The adolescents having IA from Tier-1 Chennai City schools and colleges having age group from 13 to 18 years are analyzed to determine the cause of IA. Some 200 adolescent samples are monitored during the study period. IA may be due to mental health disorder, information addicts having thirst for knowledge, social disorders, excessive online gaming and shopping.

The cause of IA can be determined using a behavioral pattern and neurofeedback analysis. The students from various schools and colleges willing to participate in the study are chosen using a simple random sampling technique. The study participants can enroll for the diagnostic process to monitor their behavioral pattern in social network and their web usage time. The students who are unwilling to participate can be excluded from the study. Ethical Clearance certificate can be produced for conducting an experimental study of students in schools and colleges. A consent letter will be taken from the students and their parents before the experimental study. Initially, a questionnaire will be given to students to know their identity, social network participation and involvement, personal-social status, economic status, internet usage patterns to analyze and examine IA symptoms.

15.3.2 Evaluating the behavioral pattern of adolescents by analyzing their social networks and web usage time

The social network profiles (WhatsApp, Facebook and Instagram) of adolescents with online addiction are identified. The behavioral patterns of the adolescents are examined and classified using a neural network algorithm. The social network behavior of the study participants will be examined to predict the association of social accounts like WhatsApp, Facebook and Instagram with IA. The correlation between web usage time and IA is also studied to infer the addictive behavior of internet usage. The personality traits such as emotional stability, neuroticism, impulsivity, relationship status and sexual orientation are predicted by analyzing the behavioral patterns of addictive internet users using neural network algorithm.

15.3.3 Recording behavioral pattern of adolescents by analyzing their social networks and web usage time

The neuro-feedback of adolescents with excessive online usage syndrome are observed and the brain wave activities of them are recorded using Emotiv Epoc headset. EEG signals are observed and compared with recorded signals of non-addictive internet user group available in DEAP dataset. The cause for IA is determined and appropriate treatment is suggested.

Neural network technique is used to estimate the degree of each behavioral pattern data collected through students in the form of a questionnaire, social network behavior analysis and web usage time. This experimental study gives the threshold value at which the loss of control in using internet based on which cognitive therapy is suggested.

15.3.4 Suggestion of cognitive behavioral therapy in improving the brain activity of non-addictive internet users

The causes for the addictive internet users, determined using behavioral pattern analysis, are focused on further therapy. Based on the focused cause, the mindfulness skills are triggered to restructure cognitive behavior. The emotions are regulated and the cognitive activities are scheduled. A team of health professionals and psychologist team can be involved for consultation and recommendation of appropriate therapy. The cognitive behavior and responses experiment again and thus cognitive health care is provided for the addictive internet user group.

15.4 RESULT AND DISCUSSION

The experimental study deals with adolescents in the age group 13–18 years having IA and hence this experiment is not location specific and it can be implemented in any location where IA is found among adolescents.

For the experimenting purpose, we considered training samples consisting of data of adolescents with specific age group who have excessive addiction towards the internet. In this proposed study, adolescents from tier-1 City College and school in Chennai are considered testing samples. The symptoms of IA observed in hundred internet addict samples are shown in Figure 15.2. It shows the percentage of the people affected due to IA. In this, online gaming acquires the highest percentage with 27 and next is taken by mental health disorder. The other major things are information addicts, online shopping and disorders due to social behavior. These symptoms show that the person has the possibility of different disorders.

The impact of applications for the tested samples from the hundred internet addict samples is given in Figure 15.3. In that chart, social media acquires the maximum percentage where the time spent by the person. The good thing is that E-learning acquires more than 50% in IA. In addition to

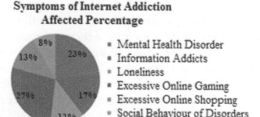

Figure 15.2 Symptoms of internet addiction (IA) found from a hundred internet addict samples; presented in percentage affected.

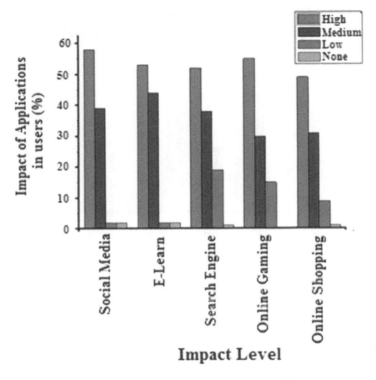

Figure 15.3 Impact of applications in internet addict.

this, online gaming and shopping takes the next place in IA. The associations of IA with the school-going and college-going students in Chennai city of hundred samples of internet addicts and hundred samples of controlled internet users are shown in Figure 15.4 and their behavioral patterns are analyzed for suggesting problem-focused cognitive health care.

In that, some of the social media applications have restricted access to the user for reduce the misbehavioral approaches. Telegram and YouTube are placed at top in controlled internet access. And the lowest controlled access or restriction for users is given by Instagram. The restrictions in social media will reduce the IA because that the user cannot upload or view the content which is really not under their topics or age groups.

15.5 CONCLUSIONS

The risks of addictive internet usage among the adolescent population demand the systematic investigation and detection of addictive symptoms in adolescents. There is no conventional diagnostic standard in classifying the mental illness and disorder due to excessive usage of the internet. The adolescent

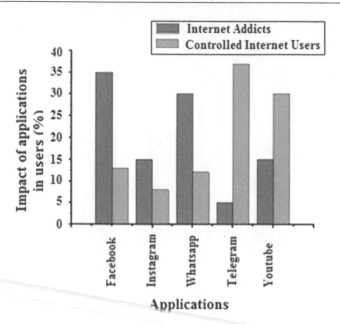

Figure 15.4 Symptoms of internet addiction affected by internet addicts and controlled internet users.

samples in the age group 13–18 years with addictive internet usage are randomly chosen and recorded from tier-1 city, schools and colleges. Earlier research works related to IA focus on detecting causes of IA, calculating IA levels and statistical analysis which required domain knowledge from experts. In this proposed work, adolescents' IA levels can be estimated using behavioral pattern analysis and neuro-feedback analysis. The daily behavior of adolescents in social networks and web usage records can be analyzed using a neural network algorithm along with neuro-feedback analysis are used to estimate the IA level. The appropriate cognitive behavioral therapy is suggested based on the analysis report.

REFERENCES

[1] Dimitri A. Christakis. Internet Addiction: A 21st Century Epidemic?, BMC Medicine, 2010; 8:61.
[2] Ying-Ying Zhang MM, Jian-ji Chen MM, Hai Ye MM, & Lupe Volantin MB. Psychological Effects of Cognitive Behavioural Therapy on Internet Addiction in Adolescents: A Systematic Review Protocol. Medicine 2020; 99(4): doi: 10.1097/MD.0000000000018456
[3] Bador K., Kerekes N. Evaluation of an Integrated Intensive Cognitive Behavioural Therapy Treatment within Addiction Care. Journal of Behavioural Health Services & Research 2020; 47(1): 102–112. https://doi.org/10.1007/s11414-019-09657-5

[4] Yao Y.-W., Liu L., Worhunsky P., Lichenstein S., Ma S.-S., Zhu L., Shi X.-H., Yang S., Zhang J. & Yip S. Is Monetary Reward Processing Altered in Drug-Naïve Youth with a Behavioural Addiction? Findings from Internet Gaming Disorder. NeuroImage: Clinical 2020; 26: 102202. 10.1016/j.nicl.2020.10220

[5] Peng W., Zhang X. & Li X. Intelligent Behaviour Data Analysis for Internet Addiction. Big Data Management and Analytics in Scientific Programming 2019. https://doi.org/10.1155/2019/2753152

[6] Baturay M. H. & Toker S. Internet Addiction among College Students: Some Causes and Effect. Education and Information Technologies 2019; 24: 2863–2885. 10.1007/s10639-019-09894-3

[7] Van Rooij A. J., Zinn M. F., Schoenmakers T. M., & van de Mheen D. Treating Internet Addiction with Cognitive-Behavioural Therapy: A Thematic Analysis of the Experiences of Therapists. International Journal of Mental Health and Addiction 2012; 10(1): 69–82. https://doi.org/10.1007/s11469-010-9295-s

[8] Miller S., Konstantinos, Dafouli E., Braimiotis D., Mouzas O. & Angelopoulos N. Internet Addiction among Greek Adolescent Students. Cyberpsychology & Behaviour: The Impact of the Internet, Multimedia and Virtual Reality on Behaviour and Society 2008; 11: 653–657. 10.1089/cpb.2008.0088

[9] Kim K., Ryu E., & Chon MY. Internet Addiction in Korean Adolescents and Its Relation to Depression and Suicidal Ideation: A Questionnaire Survey. International Journal of Nursing Studies 2006; 43(2): 185–192. doi: 10.1016/j.ijnurstu.2005.02.005

[10] Johansson A., Götestam KG. Internet Addiction: Characteristics of a Questionnaire and Prevalence in Norwegian Youth (12–18 years). Scandinavian Journal of Psychology. 2004; 45(3):223–229. doi: 10.1111/j.1467-9450.2004.00398.

[11] Bong S. H. et al. Effects of Cognitive-Behavioral Therapy Based Music Therapy in Korean Adolescents with Smartphone and Internet Addiction. Psychiatry Investigation 2021; 18(2): 110–117. doi:10.30773/pi.2020.0155.

[12] Hirota T., McElroy E. & So R. Network Analysis of Internet Addiction Symptoms Among a Clinical Sample of Japanese Adolescents with Autism Spectrum Disorder. Journal of Autism and Developmental Disorders 2021; 51: 2764–2772. https://doi.org/10.1007/s10803-020-04714-x.

[13] Lo C.K.M., Yu L., Cho Y.W., Chan K.L. A Qualitative Study of Practitioners' Views on Family Involvement in Treatment Process of Adolescent Internet Addiction. International Journal of Environmental Research and Public Health 2021; 18(1): 86. https://doi.org/10.3390/ijerph18010086.

[14] Bickham D.S. Current Research and Viewpoints on Internet Addiction in Adolescents. Current Pediatrics Reports 2021; 9: 1–10. https://doi.org/10.1007/s40124-020-00236-3

[15] Khodabakhsh S., Ramasamy S., Teng T. Y. & Leng C. S. (2021). Impact of Internet Addiction on Health Anxiety in Malaysian Youth during COVID-19 Pandemic. Malaysian Journal of Medical Research (MJMR) 5(2): 12–18. https://doi.org/10.31674/mjmr.2021.v05i02.003

[16] Ambika M., Raghuraman G., SaiRamesh L., & Ayyasamy A. "Intelligence-Based Decision Support System for Diagnosing the Incidence of Hypertensive Type." Journal of Intelligent & Fuzzy Systems 2020;38(2): 1811–1825.

[17] Ambika M., Raghuraman G., & SaiRamesh L. "Enhanced Decision Support System to Predict and Prevent Hypertension Using Computational Intelligence Techniques." Soft Computing (2020): 1–12.

[18] Saranya M. S., Selvi M., Ganapathy S., Muthurajkumar S., Sai Ramesh L., and Kannan A. "Intelligent medical data storage system using machine learning approach." In 2016 Eighth International Conference on Advanced Computing (ICoAC), pp. 191–195. IEEE, 2017.

[19] Sai Ramesh L., Shyam Sundar S., Selvakumar K., & Sabena S. "Tracking of Wearable IoT Devices through WAP Using Intelligent Rule-Based Location Aware Approach." Journal of Information & Knowledge Management 2021; 20(supp01): 2140005.

Chapter 16

Containerization in cloud computing for OS-level virtualization

Manoj Kumar Patra, Bibhudatta Sahoo, and Ashok Kumar Turuk

CONTENTS

16.1 INTRODUCTION TO CLOUD COMPUTING

Cloud computing recently emerged as one of the most promising technologies in the field of IT. The main idea of cloud computing is to make different types of computing resources available to the end-user through the internet. It allows users to access a large pool of computing resources such as CPU and memory on a pay-as-you-go basis. The user will pay for the number of resources they have used, and the user need not worry about the maintenance

DOI: 10.1201/9781003269144-16

of the physical infrastructure. The actual physical infrastructure is managed by the cloud service provider (CSP). The servers in cloud computing are often placed in a different location in a distributed manner, and each location can be termed a data center. There are different types of cloud models, such as private, public, and hybrid cloud. The private cloud is especially meant for personal use, i.e., this type of cloud infrastructure is mainly operated by only one organization. Only a few selected users will get access to the cloud services. The public cloud is designed for public use, i.e., anyone with an internet connection can access the cloud resources. In a public cloud, services may be offered free of charge or with a paid subscription. The hybrid cloud model is a combination of both public and private clouds.

In cloud computing, different service models are there, such as infrastructure as a service (IaaS), platform as a service (PaaS), and software as a service (SaaS). In IaaS, the cloud service offers the required IaaS to the end-users over the internet. The essential hardware for infrastructure in the cloud is storage, computing, virtual machines (VMs), load balancers, and networking resources. IaaS provides the flexibility to scale up and down your resources on demand. In PaaS, the cloud offers a complete development environment where developers can develop, manage, and test their applications. Here, the cloud provider provides a computing environment to the developer. The software developer does not require buying and managing the underlying software and hardware infrastructure; instead, they access them over the internet on a pay-as-you-go basis. In SaaS, the CSP offers a complete software solution that allows users to access different cloud-based applications over the internet. The service provider is responsible for managing hardware, software, and data and application security. One of the typical examples of SaaS is email services.

Virtualization in cloud computing plays an essential role in the overall performance of cloud systems. The process of creating a virtual representation of cloud resources such as storage, server, virtual application, or networks is called virtualization in cloud computing. The virtualization technology allows users to execute multiple OSs and their applications simultaneously on the same physical machine. There are several benefits of virtualization, including:

- **Reduce IT expenses:** The application consolidation in a virtualized environment certainly reduces a cloud system's overall costs. Due to virtualization, several VMs are created from a single physical machine. Hence, the number of servers reduces, and the number of hardware also reduces. The VMs in a server can have different OS and can run different applications.
- **Easier IT management:** The virtualization technology drastically reduces the effort required for management, provisioning work, and maintenance that actual physical machines require.

- **Better scalability:** The virtualization technique can allocate and de-allocate the computing resources based on the users' requirements. It reduces the operating cost and increases the reliability of the systems. Whenever there is a need for extra resources, we can scale up the resources instead of buying additional components. Similarly, if extra resources are being allocated, we can deallocate the extra resources.
- **Faster deployment and recovery:** If there is any physical server crush, redeployment is relatively faster and simpler in a virtualized data center. There are several tools for virtual backup such as Veeam that speed up the backup process and the recovery process in virtualized environment is very simple.
- **VM migration:** A VM can be migrated from one physical machine to another and redeployed very quickly.

There are mainly two types of virtualization techniques in cloud computing. The first one is hardware virtualization, and another one is software virtualization. In hardware virtualization, an abstraction layer is created over the physical hardware using the software. By doing so, it creates a virtual representation of a computing system known as a VM. Multiple VMs can now be run on a single physical machine. A VM is a virtual representation of an actual physical machine. The number of VMs that can be created from a single physical machine depends upon the available resources. The different VMs on a single system can have different operating systems. A software layer called hypervisor is responsible for creating the VM. A hypervisor assigns the required hardware such as storage, memory, and computing power to each VMs and prevents any interaction among them. All VMs interact with the physical machine upon which they are running through a hypervisor. The second approach for virtualization is software virtualization or containerization.

16.1.1 Containerization

Containerization is the way to OS-level virtualization where applications run in isolated user spaces, called containers. A container encapsulates everything required to run an application, such as libraries, dependencies, and configuration files. All containers share the same operating system and are portable, i.e., a containerized application can run in different infrastructures such as on bare metal, within a VM, or in any cloud environment. A container does not have a separate guest OS, so the startup time is much less than a VM. A container engine is responsible for creating and managing containers. The container engine pulls and creates a package of libraries and binaries required to run an application. A container can either be deployed in a physical machine or on a VM. All containers share the same operating system, so they are not entirely isolated from each other, and there is a chance of threat to data security.

16.1.2 Need for containerization

Although the VM-based virtualization addresses security concerns through isolation, several limitations exist. Each VM requires binaries and libraries to run the application along with a complete guest operating system [1]. The full guest OS creates concerns related to the space, i.e., it requires larger size RAM and disk storage. The startup time increases because the full guest OS needs to be booted, and booting time is generally in minutes. The VM with a full-fledged OS is heavily weighted may be in GBs, but lightweight containers may only be in MBs. So, all the above concerns can be addressed by a container. The containers are lightweight and more portable than VMs. The cost of migrating a container from one machine to another is much less than that of a VM. Another benefit of a container is that a single physical machine can host more containers than VMs because the size of the containers is much less than a VM. The small-size containers are suitable for greater modularity. Rather than running an entire application in a single container, the application can be split into several modules. Hence, containerization is one of the most efficient ways of resource virtualization in cloud systems. It allows users to make the best use of cloud resources and improve the system's overall performance.

16.2 CONTAINERIZATION OVER HYPERVISOR-BASED VIRTUALIZATION

The traditional hypervisor-based virtualization technique provides strong isolation and creates a virtual system. In hypervisor-based virtualization, the host OS is present on a physical server. A hypervisor is a software placed on top of the host OS responsible for creating several VMs from the same physical machine. The hypervisor enables sharing hardware resources with multiple VMs and runs multiple OS on VMs. Each VM communicates with the physical server through the hypervisor. Each VM will have its own guest operating system, and they are completely isolated from each other. Since each VM has its own guest operating system, they require more memory and take more time to start. Hence, the hypervisor-based VMs are heavily weighted [2].

On the other hand, in containerization, the host OS is present on top of the physical server and container engine, which is the alternative to the hypervisor present on top of the host OS. The container engine is responsible for creating container images, and all communication between the container and the physical server takes place through the container engine. The container engine creates a package of the required libraries and binaries

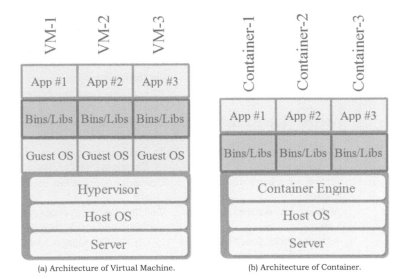

(a) Architecture of Virtual Machine.   (b) Architecture of Container.

Figure 16.1 architectural difference between a virtual machine and a container. (a) Architecture of a Virtual Machine. (b) Architecture of a Container.

files to run an application. Each container shares the same host operating system, and they do not have a separate OS, unlike a VM. Hence, containers are lightweight and provide faster resource provisioning. Since all containers share the same operating system, they are less isolated than VMs, and there is a chance of security issues and interference between containers. The architecture of the VM and container is presented in Figure 16.1 [3].

In short, the container and VM differ from each other in many ways. Still, the main difference is that virtualization comes up with a mechanism to virtualize the hardware, and multiple OS instances are run on the same hardware. In containerization, an OS is virtualized, and multiple applications can run on a single OS.

16.2.1 Difference between virtual machine and container

The main difference between a VM and a container are listed in Table 16.1.

16.2.2 The benefits of using containers

There are several benefits of using containers over VMs:

- **Lightweight:** Containers are lightweight because they do not have separate OS for each container, but they share the same operating system and are isolated from the OS layer, so the memory requirement is less, and hence they are lightweight.

Table 16.1 Difference between virtual machine and container

Feature	Virtual machine	Container
Virtualization	VM provides hardware-level virtualization	Container provides OS-level virtualization
Operating system	Each VM runs in a separate OS	All containers execute in the same host OS
Isolation	VM provides better isolation	Containers are less isolated because they share the same OS
Startup time	The startup time of a VM is in minutes	The startup time of a container is in milliseconds
Memory size	VM requires more memory space	Container requires less memory space
Security	VMs are fully isolated and more secure	Container provides process-level isolation and less secure
Providers	VMware, VirtualBox, Hyper-V are some VM providers	LXC, LXD, CGManager, and Docker

- **Portability:** Since containers create a package of all dependencies and libraries required to run an application, you can move it between different environments once you have created it. The VMs are heavily weighted, so moving them from one system to another is difficult and costlier.
- **Scalability:** Containers are small in size, so you can START/STOP them when required, and based on the dynamic resource requirement, you can scale UP/DOWN the container resources.
- **Cost-effective:** Containers require fewer resources, support better scalability, and provide a resilient solution. The hardware requirement is less and cost-effective.
- **Less infrastructure management:** The requirement of infrastructure management is very negligible in a container. The container engine only pulls the required libs and bins to run the application and is less concerned about the infrastructure.
- **Accelerate development:** Containerization gives a stable environment for development, and the prediction of required resources such as CPU/memory is optimized. Containers provide better modularity than VMs.
- **Modern architecture:** Using containerization, an application can be split into microservices that accelerate development and deployment. Once the microservices are deployed, they can be scaled up/down individually.
- **Security:** The container provides isolation to the application, prevents malicious interference of other containers, limits the interaction of needless resources, and blocks unnecessary components. This makes the container secure and improves cohesiveness.

16.3 SOFTWARE RESOURCES FOR CONTAINERIZATION

Several software resources are available to implement containerization or OS-level virtualization; the most popular ones are the Docker engine and Google Kubernetes. Several other container tools are there, such as AWS Fargate, Amazon ECS, Container Linux by CoreOS, Microsoft Azure, Portainer, and Apache Mesos. This section describes the two most popular container tools, Docker and Kubernetes.

- **Docker:** One of the most popular and widely used container engines is the Docker engine. It is an open-source software based on runC. Docker containers support OS-level software virtualization, interoperability, and an efficient environment to execute applications, build and test applications, etc. Docker container divides the application into different modules and allows these modules to run, deploy, test, and scale independently. The core architecture of a Docker consists of four different components: images, containers, registers, and Docker engine.
- **Images:** A Docker image is just like a template containing a set of instructions used to create a container. The instructions in the image define what should run inside a container. The docker image defines the list of processes that should run during the application lunch. A docker image binds all the required dependencies, libraries, binaries, and application code and creates a package to run an application.
- **Containers:** A container is nothing but a live instance of a container image. It is a virtualized runtime platform where an application runs. We can create multiple containers from a single container image. From an object-oriented programming point of view, a container image is a class, and a container is an instance of that class. This improves operational efficiency by initiating multiple instances from the same container image. A runnable image should exist in the system to run a container because a live instance of the container depends on the image and is used to create a runtime environment.
- **Registries:** A repository of container images is called a docker registry. A default registry called Docker Hub stores all official and public images used for different platforms and languages. The docker registry is a highly scalable open source and allows everyone to distribute Docker images. A few basic commands for the registry are:

Start your registry: docker run -d -p 5000:5000-name registry
     registry:2
Pull (or build) some images from the hub: docker pull ubuntu
Tag the image so that it points to your registry:

docker image tag ubuntu localhost:5000/myfirstimage
Push it: docker push localhost:5000/myfirstimage
Pull it back: docker pull localhost:5000/myfirstimage
Now stop your registry and remove all data: docker container stop
    registry && docker container rm -v registry

- **Docker engine:** One of the core components of the Docker architecture is the docker engine. All applications run on the docker engine. The docker engine is an application responsible for managing containers and images. The docker engine follows a client-server architecture and is composed of three sub-components. Docker Daemon is responsible for building docker images and managing those images, while Docker client is responsible for sending the instruction to the daemon and connecting with daemon remotely through REST API that is responsible for establishing communication between daemon and the client.

- **Kubernetes:** Kubernetes is a container orchestration tool initially developed by Google and given to CNFS for further maintenance enhancement. It is extensible, portable, and an open-source platform that helps manage containerized applications and services in different environments such as physical machines, VMs, or even cloud environments. The Kubernetes supports both automation and configuration. This allows you to run distributed system with scaling and resilience. Some of the features of Kubernetes are high availability, scalability, and disaster recovery. The high availability ensures that the application has no downtime and is always accessible by the users. The scalability ensures better utilization of resources. The application can be scaled up when it has more load, and more users are trying to access it. Similarly, we can scale it down when the load goes down. The disaster recovery ensures the safety of data. If there is any issue in infrastructure or the server is damaged, the container application can run from the latest recovery [4].

16.4 DOCKER ARCHITECTURE

The docker architecture consists of three main components that are Docker client, Docker host, and Docker registry. It follows client-server model as demonstrated in Figure 16.2 [5, 6].

- **Docker client:** The docker user can interact with Docker through the docker client. The client sends any command to the Docker Daemon that carries them out when any command runs. There can be more than one Docker Daemon, and one client can interact with more than one daemon.

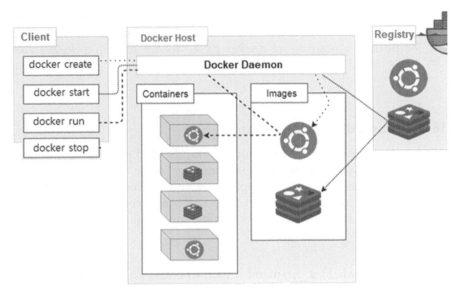

Figure 16,2 Architectui e of docker coiitainer.

- **Docker host:** The docker host provides the complete platform to create, build and run an application. It consists of docker daemon, containers, images, networks, and storage. The docker daemon is responsible for all container-related actions and receives the command through the command-line interface or the REST API. It can also communicate with other daemons to manage its services. The docker daemon fetches and generates container images based on the client's request. It uses a set of instructions known as the build file to create a working model for the container once it pulls a desired image. Instructions for the daemon to preload other components before launching the container or instructions to be sent to the local command line after the container is built can also be included in the build file. There are various docker objects, such as images, containers, networking, and storage. Images and containers are described in detail in Section 16.3. The third object, docker networking, is a package through which all the isolated containers communicate. Docker supports three network drivers: bridge, overlay, and macvlan. The bridge driver is the default network driver for the docker container. The overlay driver enables containers to communicate with others. The macvlan driver assigns MAC addresses to the containers that make them look like physical devices. The storage object of the container allows storing data within the writable layer of a container. For this, it requires a storage driver.
- **Docker registry:** The docker registries are the services from where you can store and pull images. The docker registry contains repositories that host one or more docker images. Docker hub and Docker cloud

are examples of public registries; however, private registries can also be stored and used. A few common commands used in order to work with docker registry are *docker push*, *docker pull*, and *docker run* [7].

16.4.1 Basic docker commands

As already discussed in the previous section, the docker image and docker container are two different things. A container image is built with a set of instructions required to run an application and written in a docker file. A container is the live instance of an image and can execute different tasks. Below is the list of a few basic docker commands required to operate with containerization [8]:

- **docker build.** This command is used to create an image from Docker file.
- **docker create:** This command can be used to create a new image and a writeable container layer over the specified image.
- **docker start:** This command can be used to start a created container. As soon as this command is executed, the container will go to running state.
- **docker run:** This command is used to deploy a container image and then run and manage that container with different other commands. This command creates as well as starts the container. This command takes one parameter, i.e., the name of the docker image.
- **docker pull:** This command is used to pull a container image from the repository. A simple example of using this command is *docker pull ubuntu:latest*. This command will pull the most recently updated image by default, but it will not instantiate the container. Suppose you want to pull the ubuntu version 20.05, then the command to do that would be like *docker pull ubuntu: 20.05*.
- **docker stop:** This command is used to STOP a running container instance without deleting it. We need to pass container ID as the parameter. If you want to stop a container with container ID: 2143, the command would be like *docker stop 2143*.
- **docker pause:** This command is used to pause the running container.
- **docker rm:** This command will delete the container from docker host memory.
- **docker ps:** To see the currently running container instance and their status, *docker ps* command is used. By default, it shows only currently running containers. To see all containers, we can use *-a* or *-all* as *docker ps -a* or *docker ps -all*. There are many other parameters that can be applied to filter the result.

- **docker tag:** This command is used to control the container versions. When an image is built successfully, it becomes the most recent one. So, when *docker pull* command is run, it will pull the most recently updated image.
- **sudo:** The *sudo* command is used to provide user access to the docker container. The command *sudo usermod -G docker username* will give the access to the user *username*.

16.5 LIFECYCLE OF DOCKER CONTAINER

When a container is being created, it goes through different stages in its lifecycle. So the question arises how does the container lifecycle work? The detailed lifecycle of a docker container is presented diagrammatically in Figure 16.3. The container lifecycle starts when it is just being created. As we have already discussed the *docker create* command in the previous section, this command will create a new container from the container image. Once the container is created, it will go to the created state. In the created state, the container is just being created, i.e., it is existing but not in the running state. When we start the docker container using *docker start* command, it will go to the running state. As soon as we start the container, it will start executing. Instead of going for a two-step process of creating and then running, we can use a single command *docker run* to create and start the container. If you want to stop a running container, then you can run *docker stop* command with container ID or container name. Then the container will go to the stopped state. Stopping the container means the container is not running but still exists in the docker host memory. It can come back from a stopped state to a running state again by starting it again. Furthermore, we can remove the container from docker host memory by running the command *docker rm* command. Once you run this command, the container will be deleted permanently from the system. We can even pause the running container by *docker pause* command. The difference between stop and pause is

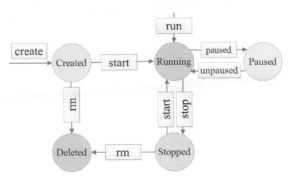

Figure 16.3 Lifecycle of docker container.

that when you stop a container, the container processes are completely killed, and the container moves to the exit state. However, when you pause the container, processes are still there in the memory, but they are not executing or utilizing any resources. They are just on hold. The paused container can be started again and go to a running state by using *docker unpause* command [9, 10].

16.6 KUBERNETES ARCHITECTURE

The Kubernetes automates container deployment, scaling and descaling, and container load balancing. It groups containers that make up a logical unit for easy management. The Kubernetes facilitates various features such as load balancing, storage orchestration, configuration management, horizontal scaling, and automatic rollback. It also restarts the containers that fail and replace.

The master node, worker node, and distributed key-value store, etcd, are the three fundamental components of the Kubernetes architecture. The detailed architecture of Kubernetes is depicted in Figure 16.4 [11, 12]

- **Master node:** The master node is responsible for managing the Kubernetes cluster. The master node acts as a single point of entry for all administrative tasks. The user will be able to communicate with

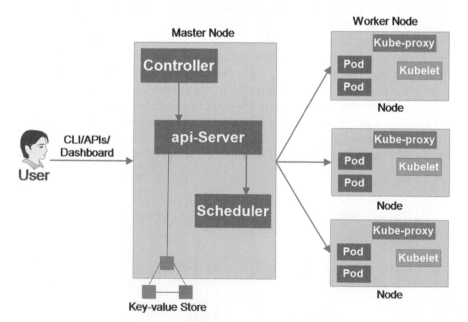

Figure 16.4 Architecture of Kubernetes.

the master node through CLI (command line interface), API (application programming interface), or graphical user interfaces (GUIs). In a cluster, there may be multiple master nodes to handle fault tolerance in a better way. If there is multiple master node, only one will be the leader node performing all the tasks, and the leader node will be followed by remaining master nodes. The master node has four main components: API server, scheduler, controller, and etcd. The API server in the master node takes care of all the administrative tasks. The user issues the command, which is subsequently validated and processed by the API server. After completing the request, the cluster's final state is saved in a distributed key-value store. The scheduler is responsible for assigning the work to different worker nodes. The scheduler holds the resource usage information of each worker node. As the name implies, controller manager manages different non-terminating control loops that regulate the Kubernetes cluster's state. The cluster state is stored in the etcd, which is a distributed key-value store.

- **Worker node:** A worker node is a machine or any physical server controlled by a master node that runs the applications using pods. The worker nodes, on which pods are scheduled, have the required competencies to run and link the pods. So a pod is basically a scheduling unit in Kubernetes. A pod is a logical collection of one or more containers that are always scheduled together. So, to access the application from the external world, one has to connect to the worker node. The worker node has three components: kube-proxy, kubelet, and container run-time. The job of container run-time is to run and manage the container lifecycle on the worker node. The kubelet runs on each worker node and act like an agent to establish communication with master node. The kube-proxy is a network proxy that runs on each worker node and listens for the creation or deletion of service points on the API server. As a result, kube-proxy creates a route for each service point so that it may contact it.
- **etcd-Key-value store:** An etcd is an open-source key-value store database based on raft consensus algorithm. It stores the state and configuration information of the cluster.

16.7 KUBERNETES VS DOCKER SWARM

The Kubernetes and Docker Swarm are currently the two most popular container orchestration tools. This section presents the main features and important differences between them to choose the appropriate one according to the requirement. Their similarities and differences are discussed from a different point of view as mentioned below.

16.7.1 Installation

Before installing any one of them, one is advised to have basic require-ments and a basic understanding of cloud computing. The Kubernetes can be installed by downloading **kubectl**; it is the command-line interface for Kubernetes. Kubernetes can be installed on Windows, Linux, or MacOS. On Windows, it can be installed using curl, Powershell, or Scoop command-line installer. On Linux, it can be installed using curl or as a snap applica-tion. On MacOS, it can be installed using curl or MacPorts. The installation of Docker is relatively easier than Kubernetes. The deployment of a docker container is easy once the docker engine is installed in a system. One has to assign the IP address to the host and open protocols among them before initializing the swarm.

16.7.2 Graphical user interface (GUI)

Kubernetes supports a user friendly web user interface or dashboard. The Web UI facilitates easy deployment of container application, easier man-agement of cluster resources, and easier troubleshooting; it shows the error log. On the other hand, Docker does not support Web UI; however, it comes with GUI.

16.7.3 Availability

Kubernetes allows more than one master node to run for maintaining high availability. For this, it has to manage the etcd cluster node either in the control plane or externally. On the other hand, docker uses service replica-tion to maintain high availability.

16.7.4 Scalability

Kubernetes supports both horizontal scaling and cluster auto-scaling. Horizontal scaling involves increasing or decreasing the number of pods. In Docker, containers are deployed very faster and support on-demand scaling. Docker replicates the number of connections to the application to handle a high workload.

16.7.5 Networking

Here, the main disadvantage of docker is its dynamic IP address. Because of the dynamic IP, the IP address changes on the restart. Dockers are con-fined to the host and do not support communication between two different docker containers in two different machines. But Kubernetes support inter-host communication.

16.7.6 Monitoring

In Kubernetes, one can monitor the services deployed in a cluster. The different ways it can be done are inspecting containers and pods. The monitoring can also be done by observing the cluster behavior from time to time. On the other hand, the docker does not support monitoring facilities. One has to rely on third-party software to monitor docker entirely [13].

16.8 RESEARCH CHALLENGES AND FUTURE DIRECTIONS

Despite the rapid development of containerized clouds, several issues need to be addressed. One of them is security; since all containers share the same OS and are not completely isolated, there is a chance of interference. The container is best suited for small applications because it supports small storage, so memory is another issue in the container. Extensive applications are not suitable for containers. Dynamic container resource allocation and container migration are still significant challenges for researchers. While migrating a container from one host to another, selecting a destination host is also a critical problem. The best suitable destination host must be selected for migration. In a cloud-edge environment, efficient container application deployment is a challenge, and still much research is going on [14].

REFERENCES

[1] C. Pahl. (2015). Containerization and the PaaS Cloud. *IEEE Cloud Computing*, vol. 2, no. 3, pp. 24–31, May–June 2015, doi: 10.1109/MCC.2015.51.
[2] M. K. Patra, D. Patel, B. Sahoo and A. K. Turuk. "A Randomized Algorithm for Load Balancing in Containerized Cloud," 2020 10th International Conference on Cloud Computing, Data Science & Engineering (Confluence), 2020, pp. 410–414, doi: 10.1109/Confluence47617.2020.9058147.
[3] M. K. Patra, D. Patel, B. Sahoo and A. K. Turuk, "Game Theoretic Task Allocation to Reduce Energy Consumption in Containerized Cloud," 2020 10th International Conference on Cloud Computing, Data Science & Engineering (Confluence), 2020, pp. 427–432, doi: 10.1109/Confluence47617.2020.9058041.
[4] E. Casalicchio. (2019). Container Orchestration: A Survey. *Systems Modeling: Methodologies and Tools*, vol. 2019, pp. 221–235.
[5] S. Chamoli. (2021). Docker Security: Architecture, Threat Model, and Best Practices. *Soft Computing: Theories and Applications*, pp. 253–263. Springer, Singapore, 2021.
[6] Cloud Native wiki. (2020). Docker Architecture. *Cloud Native Wiki*, https://www.aquasec.com/cloud-native-academy/docker-container/docker-architecture/.
[7] D. Jaramillo, D. V. Nguyen and R. Smart. (2016). Leveraging Microservices Architecture by Using Docker Technology. *SoutheastCon*, vol. 2016, pp. 1–5, doi: 10.1109/SECON.2016.7506647.

[8] A. Mouat. (2015). Using Docker: Developing and Deploying Software with Containers. *O'Reilly Media, Inc.*

[9] D. Chakraborty. (2021). Docker Commands for Managing Container Lifecycle (Definitive Guide). *LINUX HANDBOOK*, https://linuxhandbook.com/container-lifecycle-docker-commands.

[10] C. De la Torre. (2016). Containerized Docker Application Lifecycle with Microsoft Platform and Tools. www.download.microsoft.com.

[11] J. Shah and D. Dubaria, "Building Modern Clouds: Using Docker, Kubernetes & Google Cloud Platform," 2019 IEEE 9th Annual Computing and Communication Workshop and Conference (CCWC), 2019, pp. 0184–0189, doi: 10.1109/CCWC.2019.8666479.

[12] V. Chemitiganti. (2021). Kubernetes Concepts and Architecture. *PLATFORM9*, https://platform9.com/blog/kubernetes-enterprise-chapter-2-kubernetes-architecture-concepts.

[13] S. Sengupta. (2020). Kubernetes vs Docker Swarm: Comparing Container Orchestration Tools. *bmc blog*, https://www.bmc.com/blogs/kubernetes-vs-docker-swarm/.

[14] P.-J. Maenhaut, B. Volckaert, V. Ongenae and F. De Turck. (2020). Resource Management in a Containerized Cloud: Status and Challenges. *Journal of Network and Systems Management*, vol. 28, no. 2, pp. 197–246.

Chapter 17

An adaptive deep learning approach for stock price forecasting

Reshma MO, Jitendra Kumar, and Abhishek Verma

CONTENTS

17.1 INTRODUCTION

"Stock market" has now become the synonym for wealth generation among the millennials and other younger generations with the advancement of digital platforms. Unpredictable price movement is a part and parcel of the stock market. "Efficient market hypothesis" (EMH) developed by Paul A. Samuelson and Eugene F. Fama means that market is not forecastable as it reflects all the available information [1]. However, investors have been endeavoring to predict future values. The investors like Warren Buffet, Radhakishan Damani, and others have successfully beaten the markets' unpredictable behavior, which is contrary to the EMH. Due to the advent progress of the social economy, the organizations that are getting listed in the market are also increasing [2]. As a result, investing in the market has become one of the democratized ways of making money. This in turn affects the economy of the nation as well. Consequently, stock market prediction has become an interesting topic among the research community.

Accurate prediction of the price movement could lead to huge profit. The volatility and non-linear behavior make the prediction process very chaotic [3]. The investor must churn out a lot of information manually. To have an organized methodology in prediction, machine learning is a competent approach. There is plenty of research happening in this regard as machine learning has the efficiency to throw accurate results. Usage of

DOI: 10.1201/9781003269144-17

neural networks in the field of prediction has become in demand because of their ability to learn non-linear behavior and adaptive self-learning.

With the advent of deep learning, we get hope to develop a prediction model so that the investors can arrive at an informed decision while investing in stocks to maximize their profit. The LSTMs have displayed capable results that support forecasting of financial time series (FTS) [4]. However, the LSTM-based models need to tune its hyper-parameters for effective results. This research presents a hybrid forecasting model "GAL" based on LSTMs which has capability of learning its hyper-parameters for improved forecasting.

This chapter is organized as follows: Section 17.2 briefs about the major research that discussed stock forecasting using machine learning algorithms. The proposed model used to forecast is explained in Section 17.3. Section 17.4 discusses the experimental results. Finally, this chapter is wrapped up with conclusive remarks in Section 17.5.

17.2 RELATED WORK

In the field of security, sports, finance, cloud computing, healthcare, and so on, the prediction has become the most happening area of interest. Various prediction models [5–11] have been developed in the above-mentioned fields for the advancement of the domain.

Many researchers have experimented with stock forecasting using the autoregressive integrated moving average (ARIMA) model and artificial neural network (ANN) [12, 13]. The Indian stock market was analyzed and a linear regressive model using ARIMA was developed to forecast time series data [13]. Similarly, the performance of two predictive models based on ARIMA and backpropagation-based neural network was analyzed on Bitcoin price forecast [12]. While comparing the two algorithms, it was evidenced that the BPNN is far more efficient than ARIMA. The researchers have widely explored ANN to forecast the stock price [14, 15]. For instance, a forecasting model based on neural network is developed to predict the intra-day stock movement of the Moroccan stock market [14]. Another study uses hidden Markov model (HMM), for predicting the unknown value in stock market [15].

Deep learning is the most trending technique that is being used contemporarily for prediction. LSTM model in deep learning can indeed give a better performance for predicting FTS, as it has the ability to learn long-term dependencies [16]. In [17], forecasting of the price-earnings ratio (P/E ratio) is done using the LSTM model. Whereas a predictive model based on LSTM was proposed for steel price forecasting model [18]. Apart from deep learning-based predictive models, the researchers have shown a great interest in developing the hybrid models for forecasting [19, 20]. For instance, GA is used with auto regressive moving average (ARMA) to get the optimal weights and parameters for linear and non-linear functions [21]. To simplify the stock trend prediction, combined BPNN and pattern matching algorithms are used in [22].

Experimenting with various evolutionary algorithms (EAs) to improve the machine learning model's performance mostly ended in a good result [23, 24]. In [25], a novel enhanced hybrid model is developed using particle swarm optimization (PSO) and LSTM for forecasting the Australian stock market which optimizes the inertia weight of PSO using a non-linear method. Another popular EA, GA, is used in [26, 27] to pick the important features from all the independent variables to predict the dependent variable. By neglecting unimportant features in the hybrid model, GA-SVM resulted in better performance than the support vector machine (SVM) model alone. Another model used GA for feature selection and developed an optimized LSTM model for the stock forecast [26]. An improved hybrid model was developed to identify the window size and the topology of LSTM model using GA for forecasting the Korean stock market [28].

The above-mentioned analysis indicates that hybrid models perform better than their counterparts. Thus, this chapter proposes a forecasting model built using LSTM and GA. The integration of GA has helped LSTM to learn its hyper-parameters effectively. In turn the forecast accuracy of hybrid model is improved significantly.

17.3 FORECASTING METHODOLOGY

In this section, a detailed description of the proposed approach is presented. The developed model uses LSTM network as an underlying technique and genetic algorithm helps in hyper-parameter tuning of the network. RNN has a problem of short memory, that is, with the increasing number of time steps, the information from the past data exponentially disappears. LSTM is a type of RNN and it has a property called long-term dependencies. The deep RNN structure of LSTM makes sure that it could selectively remember valuable information from past data [29]. Thereby adding new information to the network, it will get modified in such a way that the important information will be remembered, and the rest will be forgotten. Each input has three dependencies: previous hidden state, cell state, and current input time step.

LSTM can remember and forget information using three gates: forget gate, input gate, and output gate as shown in Figure 17.1.

- **Forget gate:** Information that needs to be forgotten is decided by the forget gate. As depicted in Figure 17.1, x_t and previous hidden state (h_{t-1}) are used as inputs. The sigmoid function is applied after multiplying x_t and h_{t-1} with its weight matrices and adding bias to it as in eq. 17.1.
- **Input gate:** In the input gate, the cell state of LSTM is updated using eq. 17.2 and a *tanh* function is applied as shown in eq. 17.3. Later, the

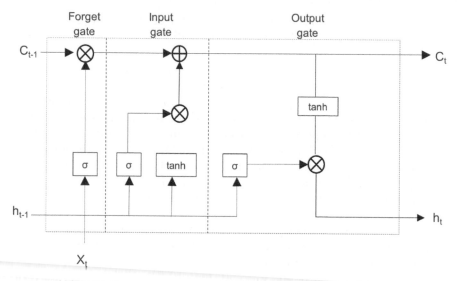

Figure 17.1 Architecture of LSTM layer.

old cell state is getting updated by forget gate as in eq. 17.4 and it will add new information to the current cell state.

- **Output gate:** Finally, the output gate decides what information needs to go out. The output of the gate is calculated using eq. 17.5 and new hidden state is calculated as in eq. 17.6, where x_t, h_t and C_t represent current input, hidden state, and cell state, respectively. W, U, and b represent weight matrices corresponding to each gate and respective biases.

$$t = \sigma(W_f \times x_t + U_f \times h_{t-1} + b_f) \tag{17.1}$$

$$i_t = \sigma(W_i \times x_t + U_i \times h_{t-1} + b_i) \tag{17.2}$$

$$\hat{C}_t = \tanh(W_c \times x_t + U_c \times h_{t-1} + b_c) \tag{17.3}$$

$$C_t = i_t \times \hat{C}_t + f_t \times C_{t-1} \tag{17.4}$$

$$o_t = \sigma(W_o \times x_t + U_o \times h_{t-1} + b_o) \tag{17.5}$$

$$h_t = o_t \times \tanh(C_t) \tag{17.6}$$

However, the performance of an LSTM network is highly sensitive to a wide number of parameters, including the network architecture. In order to leverage from computational power of LSTM networks, these parameters must be optimized which is a very difficult and complex task. This research

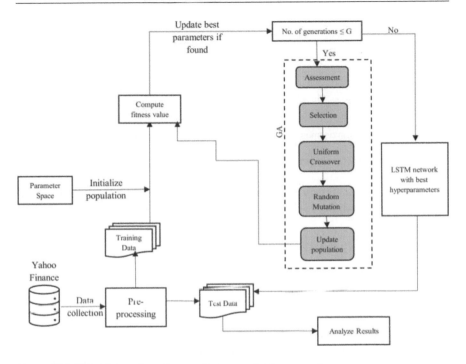

Figure 17.2 Hybrid deep learning predictive model framework.

work uses genetic algorithm to optimally select the network structure. The genetic algorithm is not a new fad in the domain [30] as it has been predominant for more than 40 years. It is one of the most popular EAs that follows the Darwinian theory of natural selection [30]. For obtaining superior solutions in optimization problems, genetic algorithm uses mutation, crossover, and selection operators. An iterative process which involves the generation of new solutions from existing solutions using above-mentioned operators is executed over a number of times or until a desired solution is achieved.

Through the processes of selection, crossover, and mutation, GA could reach the global optimal solution rather than be trapped in a local optimal one. The structure of the GAL model is represented in Figure 17.2. In this chapter, genetic algorithm is used to optimize four hyper-parameters: the number of neurons in the LSTM layer, epochs, batch size, and learning rate (alpha). The model workflow to obtain the global optimal solution is shown in Algorithm 1. The population (pool of randomly generated solutions) is evaluated using mean squared error (MSE), which can be calculated based on eq. 17.7, where y_i and $\hat{y}_i$ are actual and predicted prices. Offspring solutions are generated by implementing uniform crossover [30] as in Figure 17.3, followed by random mutation represented in Figure 17.4. A set of solutions to

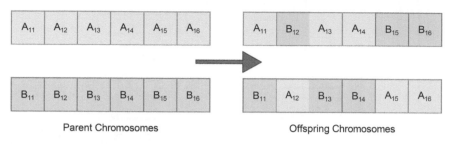

Figure 17.3 Uniform crossover.

participate in next iteration of evolution is selected based on the individual fitness values as a better solution replaces the worst one.

$$MSE = \frac{1}{n}\sum_{i=1}^{n}(y_i - \hat{y}_i)^2 \qquad (17.7)$$

17.4 RESULTS AND DISCUSSION

In this section, forecast results of proposed method are presented and compared with other methods along with a detailed discussion. The experiments are conducted on a machine equipped with Intel(R) Core(TM) i5-8265U processor and memory of 8GB. The proposed model tested with three stocks which are sourced from Yahoo Finance website [31]. Data sets of six different organizations listed on NSE of India are taken for this project; the organizations are Tata Power (NSE name: TATAPOWER), Tata Consumer Products (NSE name: TATACONSUM), Tata Consultancy Services (NSE name: TCS), Tata Chemicals (NSE name: TATACHEM), Tata Motors (NSE name: TATAMOTORS), and Titan (NSE name: TITAN). Data from 14 January 2010 to 14 July 2021, i.e., eleven years and six months of daily data, are considered. The performance of the proposed model is measured using MSE and compared with existing baseline models.

The data comprises six attributes: open price, closing price, high price, low price, adjusted closing price, and volume of shares traded for the day.

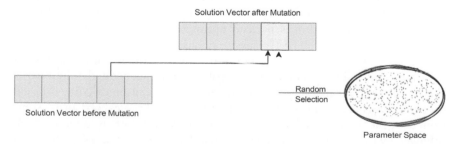

Figure 17.4 Random mutation.

ALGORITHM 1: HYPER-PARAMETER TUNING USING GA

Input: G, N, p
Output: best
1: Initialize population P randomly with all p number of parameters
2: Evaluate fitness value for each population
3: best fitness = max (fitness values)
4: **while** $G \geq 0$ **do**
5:   **for** $i = 1$ to N **do**
6:       selects parents to reproduce
7:       crossover to produce offspring
8:       mutation to offspring
9:   **end for**
10:   **for** $i = 1$ to N **do**
11:       Evaluate fitness value for each population
12:   **end for**
13:   **for** $i = 1$ to N **do**
14:       Update P with the offspring by replacing the weakest individual with it
15:   **end for**
16:   **if** best fitness < max (fitness values) **then**
17:       best fitness = max (fitness values)
18:       best = population corresponding to best fitness
19:   **end if**
20:   $G = G - 1$
21: **end while**
22: Implement LSTM model with best parameters

All the features are standardized, as LSTM is vulnerable to the range of input and output values. Standard scaler is used, where all the elements are standardized using eq. 17.8, where μ is the mean and σ is the standard deviation. Standardization is employed in both the dependent variable and independent variables for analysis. The standardized data is divided into training and test data with a ratio of 8:2.

$$X' = \frac{X - \mu}{\sigma} \qquad (17.8)$$

LSTM has various hyper-parameters that affect the accuracy of the model. To improve the performance of the LSTM model, four hyper-parameters of LSTM are selected for the tuning, which are the number of units, epoch, batch size, and learning rate of the optimizer. The detailed pseudocode of the proposed approach can be seen in Algorithm 1 which iterates over a

Table 17.1 Parameter space

Parameters	Range
Learning rate	[0.001, 0.07]
Epoch	[20, 70]
Batch size	[32, 64, 128]
Number of units	[20, 70]

number of times to find an optimal set of parameters. The algorithm begins with a set of randomly generated solutions in the parameter space defined in Table 17.1. These solutions get evaluated on training data and their performance is recorded. By the means of reproduction system of genetic algorithm, a pool of new solutions is generated in every iteration. The newly observed better individuals replace their counterparts in the parent population to participate in next evolution. Finally, the algorithm returns the best solution (the approximation of optimal network architecture) and this chapter presents the performance of the best network achieved.

The forecast results are shown in Figure 17.5 (a) Figure 17.5 (f), as it is evident that the proposed model generates the forecasts very close to the actual prices. For evaluation purpose, MSE is used due to the fact that it is one of the most widely used measurement tool for any regression problem. The MSE results are shown in Table 17.2 and it can be seen that the proposed approach significantly improves the forecast quality with a notable reduction in MSE. For instance, the proposed method was able to reduce the forecast error at least up to 52.94%, 44.18%, 40.00%, 46.06%, and 11.11% over listed state-of-the-art methods. From the results, it is evident that the proposed approach outperformed the existing models based on linear regression, decision tree, neural network, and LSTM techniques with a significant margin.

17.5 CONCLUSION

This chapter tries to support the huge investing population that is emerging in India and across the globe because of digitalization and transparency, due to the outbreak of the pandemic COVID-19. Due to the chaos existing in the manual analysis of stock market price movements through candlesticks [32] analyst meets, etc., the best possible way of understanding the price movements is through structured statistical analysis. Even though there is a small improvement through GA, it need not be always the case. The model may refine further if a greater number of hyper-parameters like the number of hidden layers, activation function, etc. are tuned. This chapter takes volume traded as a single attribute that constitutes the buying and selling volumes. If these volumes are considered separate attributes, there are possibilities for further refinement.

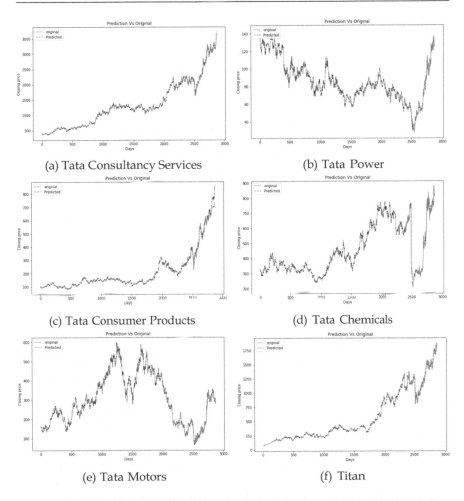

(a) Tata Consultancy Services

(b) Tata Power

(c) Tata Consumer Products

(d) Tata Chemicals

(e) Tata Motors

(f) Titan

Figure 17.5 Forecasting of different stocks using proposed methodology. (a) Tata Consultancy Services, (b) Tata Power, (c) Tata Consumer Products, (d) Tata Chemicals, (e) Tata Motors, and (f) Titan.

Table 17.2 Comparative analysis (MSE) of proposed forecasting method with state-of-the-art methods

Algorithms	TCS	TATAPOWER	TATACONSUM	TATACHEM	TATAMOTORS	TITAN
Univariate linear regression	0.082	0.410	0.102	0.435	0.35	0.086
Multivariate linear regression	0.062	0.333	0.086	0.352	0.354	0.075
Decision tree regressor	0.041	0.065	0.080	0.241	0.49	0.072
Neural network	0.063	0.271	0.089	0.323	0.321	0.069
LSTM	0.006	0.018	0.173	0.035	0.006	0.021
Proposed method	0.005	0.016	0.048	0.026	0.004	0.008

REFERENCES

[1] Eugene F. Fama. Efficient capital markets: A review of theory and empirical work. *The Journal of Finance*, 25:383–417, 1970.

[2] Eugene F. Fama and Kenneth R. French. Common risk factors in the returns on stocks and bonds. *Journal of Financial Economics*, 33(1):3–56, 1993. ISSN 0304-405X.

[3] Sameer Yadav. Stock market volatility – a study of Indian stock market. *Global Journal for Research Analysis*, 6:629–632, 04 2017.

[4] Sima SiamiNamini and Akbar Siami Namin. Forecasting economics and financial time series: ARIMA vs LSTM. *ArXiv*, abs/1803.06386, 2018.

[5] Zhen-Nao Cai, Jianhua Gu, and Huiling Chen. A new hybrid intelligent framework for predicting Parkinson's disease. *IEEE Access*, page 1, 08 2017.

[6] Jitendra Kumar and Ashutosh Kumar Singh. Cloud resource demand prediction using differential evolution based learning. In *2019 7th International Conference on Smart Computing Communications (ICSCC)*, pages 1–5, 2019.

[7] Jitendra Kumar and Ashutosh Kumar Singh. Decomposition based cloud resource demand prediction using extreme learning machines. *Journal of Network and Systems Management*, 28:1775–1793, 2020.

[8] Jitendra Kumar, Ashutosh Kumar Singh, Anand Mohan, and Rajkumar Buyaa. *Machine Learning for Cloud Management*. Chapman and Hall/CRC, 1st edition.

[9] Jitendra Kumar, Ashutosh Kumar Singh, and Anand Mohan. Resource-efficient load-balancing framework for cloud data center networks. *ETRI Journal*, 43(1):53–63, 2021. URL https://onlinelibrary.wiley.com/doi/abs/10.4218/etrij.2019-0294.

[10] R. B. Asha and K. R. Suresh Kumar. Credit card fraud detection using artificial neural network. *Global Transitions Proceedings*, 2(1):35–41, 2021. ISSN 2666-285X. URL https://www.sciencedirect.com/science/article/pii/S2666285X21000066. 1st International Conference on Advances in Information, Computing and Trends in Data Engineering (AICDE - 2020).

[11] Ashutosh Kumar Singh, Deepika Saxena, Jitendra Kumar, and Vrinda Gupta. A quantum approach towards the adaptive prediction of cloud workloads. *IEEE Transactions on Parallel and Distributed Systems*, 32(12):2893–2905, 2021.

[12] Chung-Chieh Chen, Jung-Hsin Chang, Fang Lin, Jui-Cheng Hung, Cheng-Shian Lin, and Yi-Hsien Wang. Comparison of forcasting ability between backpropagation network and ARIMA in the prediction of bitcoin price. pages 1–2, 12 2019.

[13] Sheikh Mohammad Idrees, M. Afshar Alam, and Parul Agarwal. A prediction approach for stock market volatility based on time series data. *IEEE Access*, 7:17287–17298, 2019.

[14] B. Labiad, A. Berrado, and L. Benabbou. Intelligent system for intraday stock market forecasting. In *2019 5th International Conference on Optimization and Applications (ICOA)*, pages 1–6, 2019. doi: 10.1109/ICOA.2019.8727658.

[15] Md. Rafiul Hassan and Baikunth Nath. Stock market forecasting using hidden Markov model: a new approach. In *5th International Conference on Intelligent Systems Design and Applications (ISDA'05)*, pages 192–196, 2005.

[16] Kavitha Rajakumari, M. Kalyan, and M. Bhaskar. Forward forecast of stock price using lstm machine learning algorithm. *International Journal of Computer Theory and Engineering*, 12:74–79, 01 2020.

[17] Ge Li, Ming Xiao, and Ying Guo. Application of deep learning in stock market valuation index forecasting. In *2019 IEEE 10th International Conference on Software Engineering and Service Science (ICSESS)*, pages 551–554, 2019.

[18] Kemal Çetin, Serdar Aksoy, and İsmail İşeri. Steel price forcasting using long short-term memory network model. In *2019 4th International Conference on Computer Science and Engineering (UBMK)*, pages 612–617, 2019.

[19] Paramita Ray, Bhaswati Ganguli, and Amlan Chakrabarti. A hybrid approach of Bayesian structural time series with lstm to identify the influence of news sentiment on short-term forecasting of stock price. *IEEE Transactions on Computational Social Systems*, pages 1–10, 06 2021.

[20] Xianghui Yuan, Jin Yuan, Tianzhao Jiang, and Qurat ul Ain. Integrated long-term stock selection models based on feature selection and machine learning algorithms for China stock market. *IEEE Access*, 8:22672–22685, 2020.

[21] Yasuo Ishii and Kazuhiro Takeyasu. A hybrid method to improve forecasting accuracy utilizing genetic algorithm and its application to stock market price data (j-reit: Residential type). In *2014 Joint 7th International Conference on Soft Computing and Intelligent Systems (SCIS) and 15th International Symposium on Advanced Intelligent Systems (ISIS)*, pages 1280–1283, 2014.

[22] Lin Qian Yu and Feng Shao Rong. Stock market forecasting research based on neural network and pattern matching. In *2010 International Conference on E-Business and E-Government*, pages 1940–1943, 2010.

[23] Jitendra Kumar and Ashutosh Kumar Singh. Performance evaluation of metaheuristics algorithms for workload prediction in cloud environment. *Applied Soft Computing*, 113:107895, 2021. ISSN 1568-4946. URL https://www.sciencedirect.com/science/article/pii/S1568494621008176.

[24] Deepika Saxena, Ashutosh Kumar Singh, and Rajkumar Buyya. OP-MLB: An online VM prediction based multi-objective load balancing framework for resource management at cloud datacenter. *IEEE Transactions on Cloud Computing*, 1, 2021.

[25] Yi Ji, Alan Wee-Chung Liew, and Lixia Yang. A novel improved particle swarm optimization with long-short term memory hybrid model for stock indices forecast. *IEEE Access*, 9:23660–23671, 2021.

[26] Shile Chen and Changjun Zhou. Stock prediction based on genetic algorithm feature selection and long short-term memory neural network. *IEEE Access*, 9:9066–9072, 2021.

[27] Rohit Choudhry and Kumkum Garg. A hybrid machine learning system for stock market forecasting. *World Academy of Science, Engineering and Technology*, 39:315–318, 01 2008.

[28] Hyejung Chung and Kyung-shik Shin. Genetic algorithm-optimized long short-term memory network for stock market prediction. *Sustainability*, 10:3765–3775, 10 2018.

[29] Hasim Sak, Andrew W. Senior, and Françoise Beaufays. Long short-term memory recurrent neural network architectures for large scale acoustic modeling. *INTERSPEECH*, 10:338–342, 2014.

[30] K.F. Man, K.S. Tang, and S. Kwong. Genetic algorithms: concepts and applications [in engineering design]. *IEEE Transactions on Industrial Electronics*, 43(5):519–534, 1996.

[33] Yahoo finance api. https://finance.yahoo.com/. Accessed: 2021-08-30.

[32] Venkatesh Palraj, A. Krishna Sudheer, and Senthilmurugan Paramasivan. A study on technical analysis using candlestick pattern of selected large cap stocks listed in National Stock Exchange (NSE), India with reference to steel sector. *GSI Journals Series B: Advancements in Business and Economics*, 3:62–71, 06 2021.

Index